The Bridge

The Bridge

Revelation and Its Implications

Michael McGowan

◥PICKWICK *Publications* · Eugene, Oregon

THE BRIDGE
Revelation and Its Implications

Copyright © 2015 Michael McGowan. All rights reserved. Except for brief quotations in critical publications or reviews, no part of this book may be reproduced in any manner without prior written permission from the publisher. Write: Permissions. Wipf and Stock Publishers, 199 W. 8th Ave., Suite 3, Eugene, OR 97401.

Pickwick Publications
An Imprint of Wipf and Stock Publishers
199 W. 8th Ave., Suite 3
Eugene, OR 97401

www.wipfandstock.com

ISBN 13: 978-1-62032-700-5

Cataloguing-in-Publication Data

McGowan, Michael

    The bridge : revelation and its implications / Michael McGowan

    xiv + 236 p. ; 23 cm. Includes bibliographical references.

    ISBN 13: 978-1-62032-700-5

    1. Revelation—Christianity. I. Title.

BT127.3 M245 2015

Manufactured in the U.S.A.

To Mike and Bev McGowan
—non modo parentes, sed etiam optimi amicorum estis—

Oh chestnut tree, great rooted blossomer,
Are you the leaf, the blossom, or the bole?
Oh body swayed to music, oh brightening glance,
How can we know the dancer from the dance?
~ Yeats

Contents

Preface | ix
Acknowledgments | xiii

Introduction: The Subject, Questions, and Approach | 1

PART ONE

CHAPTER 1
The Mediated Word: Rome and Revelation | 25

CHAPTER 2
The External Word: The Yale School and Revelation | 54

CHAPTER 3
The Written Word: Evangelicals and Revelation | 80

PART TWO

CHAPTER 4
The Big Picture: Toward an Integrative Model of Revelation | 113

CHAPTER 5
Making Connections: Narrative Symbolism and Traditional Systematic Loci | 177

CHAPTER 6
Leveling the Field: The Implications of Revelation | 205

Conclusion: Old Wine, New Wineskins | 216

Bibliography | 223

Preface

In the past few decades, events of global significance have once again thrust religion onto the world stage. We have seen the extent to which religious conviction contributes to unthinkable death and destruction. But we have also seen religious devotion as the impetus for unmatched altruism, charity, and compassion.

The resurgence of religion in the public consciousness has breathed new life into the study of religion in the academy. Scholars can be found rehashing old debates about what precisely a "religion" is or what being "religious" means, how and whether religious truth claims relate to philosophical and/or scientific ones, and the means by which we should judge between competing claims. The methods scholars use to explore religion vary a great deal. The subject can be studied by focusing on the practices and culture of members of this or that tradition, an endeavor with sociological and anthropological value. Religion can also be examined by looking at the ideas those members hold dear or take to be true, that is, the beliefs they hold, assessing them according to the standards of reason and logic. This has a certain philosophical utility. More recently, we are finding that religious beliefs and practices have a biological impact, an insight with "neurotheological" scientific value. There are also emotional factors involved in religiosity, which yields important insights into the psychology of religion. One can also explore the individual religions and particular expressions of those religions, each with their own unique set of sources, norms, rules, and limitations. This would likely generate theological wisdom. And of course, there are countless other ways to explore the subject of religion.

Some topics cut right across these disciplinary lines. That is, some topics are not only germane to the sociology and anthropology of religion, but also to other areas like philosophy of religion and theology. The concept of revelation is one of them. It can be equally at home in a discussion of the philosophy of religion, psychology of religion, systematic and constructive theology, biblical studies, and religious ethics. In philosophy of religion, for example, revelation is related to the discussion of miracles insofar as both are special acts of a supernatural being—call it "God"—intended to uncover what was previously hidden, authorize messengers, or build a relationship. In the psychology of religion, revelation is that which provides meaning and coherence to life such that its recipient is able to make sense of her world and live well in it. In biblical studies, one can discuss how ancient authors understood revelation, how it functioned authoritatively, and the media through which it came. In theology, revelation is thought to be a direct act of God to and for individuals or a group of people.

Most religionists believe in some sort of God who is involved at some level in the world. Even if God's activity is minimal or if divine intentions can be frustrated by the free use of one's will, these people will likely accept some level of revelation. The idea is that humans need revelation because they are limited spatially, temporally, and morally. Put another way, we simply do not know all that we would like to know with respect to matters of ultimate importance, so God is thought to have bridged the gap.

What is more, most of the great world religions, certainly the Abrahamic faiths, understand this revelation to be related somehow to specific writings. In these contexts, revelation is often imagined in conjunction with a body of sacred texts. Members of these traditions believe that their texts are in a very real sense *the* revelation of and from God.

Herein lies a problem. Because these texts are thought to have their origin in God, they can easily be mistaken for the deity who is thought to issue them. The "dance," as it were, is mistakenly identified with the Dancer. If not outright identification of the two, sacred texts may be seen as sharing some of God's traditionally accepted properties (e.g., perfection). For if God has pulled back the curtain on what is truly real and important, who are humans to frustrate the unveiling?

For members of religious communities in which a strong bond unites revelation and texts, there is often disappointment and discouragement when their understanding and view of those writings is called into question. If a text is perfect as an extension of God's perfection, then it would and should be accurate in anything to which it attests, whether or not the subject is confessional or concerns religious practice. Because text and revelation are held so closely for some religionists, when the accuracy of the texts is questioned, religionists within the tradition for whom the text is authoritative may give up on the idea of revelation itself. In some cases they may go so far as to abandon their belief in a God who reveals. Or they can go in the opposite direction, reacting to challenges by barricading themselves in, reinforcing their positions to themselves and their peers, denying what to outsiders appear to be blatant discrepancies, and retreating into the sectarian haven of their own communities. If one does not hear challenges to one's view, and if one demonizes those who disagree, then one does not deal with the alleged conflict.

This book is a response to this situation. It has two audiences in mind: those who would—in my view, prematurely—abandon the idea of God or revelation, and those who would—in my view, naively—insulate themselves from uncomfortable ideas that conflict with their understanding of reality.

Conversations among the latter were popular within conservative Christian circles three to four decades ago as debates raged concerning the extent to which texts were wholly accurate in minute details. The defensive spirit of these conservative Christians is still with us today. In mid-2014, for example, absolute accuracy of biblical texts in all matters to which they speak was at stake as the evangelical magazine, *Decision*, headlined its May issue warning of "The Danger of Compromise." Taken to its extreme, this group risks "obscurantism."[1]

The former group—those who would abandon the idea of God or revelation as a result of problems in texts—has become popular in the last ten years. Bart Ehrman's journey toward agnosticism began, for instance, with the realization that one of the Gospels may have contained an historical inaccuracy, a journey told in his 2005 *New York Times* bestselling book, *Misquoting Jesus*. While at Princeton Theological Seminary, one of Ehrman's professors impressed upon him the existence of at least one error in the Gospel of Mark. After that, he says, "the floodgates opened." He continues: "My study of the Greek New Testament, and my investigations into the manuscripts that contain it, led to a radical rethinking of my understanding of what the Bible is. This was a seismic change for me. Before this—starting with my born-again experience in high school, through my fundamentalist days at Moody, and on through my evangelical days at Wheaton—my faith had been based completely on a certain view of the Bible as the fully inspired, inerrant word of God."[2] Ehrman and others—the abandoners—have given up on the idea of God and divine revelation as a result of higher criticism.

This is a problem so long as text and revelation are identical concepts. In this book I argue that text and revelation are related yet *distinct* concepts. I attempt to find a balance between the all-or-nothing approaches one finds from both groups above. The endeavor is not new, and the argument will be relevant to some religious cultures more than others, particularly traditions

---

1. Ramm, *After Fundamentalism*, 19.
2. Ehrman, *Misquoting Jesus*, 9–11.

containing internecine conflicts over the nature and authority of sacred writings. Moreover, what is said in the constructive portion of the book has ramifications for interreligious dialogue on this issue. This book argues that the texts can be valuable and life-giving even when and if they err, a position many find incoherent. "How are texts to be trusted in large things if they err in small things?" one hears. By clarifying, reconceiving, and repackaging the relationship between text and revelation, one is given a model for approaching texts in a new way.

Acknowledgments

I would like to thank a number of people for their help as I thought about, configured, and reconfigured my view of divine revelation. First, special thanks go to Ingolf Dalferth, Philip Clayton, and Stephen Davis, all of whom read an early draft and offered several valuable suggestions for improvement. Second, I am thankful for my family: Mike and Bev McGowan and Cameron and Kacey Crawford. Third, I also appreciate my church communities, present and past, including Greg Ganssle, Kathryn Greene-McCreight, and Todd Hunter. Fourth, I wish to thank my friends: Phil McFarland, Chester Surran, Tim Fox, Sanjay Merchant, Daniel Spillman, Brian Vannest, Tucker Russell, Josh Olson, and Pam Schock. Fifth, I would like to thank mentor-type figures: Steve Moroney, Duane Watson, Miroslav Volf, Serene Jones, and Jim Spiegel. Finally, I would like to thank my colleagues at Florida SouthWestern State College. I'm honored to be a part of such a great team. Each contributed in his or her own way to my life and thinking about divine revelation.

Introduction

The Subject, Questions, and Approach

REVELATIONS ABOUND

For most of us, May 21, 2011 came and went just like any other day. The world did not end, and nor did it end five months later after Harold Camping recalculated. Life continued uninterrupted, much to the chagrin of the *Family Radio* listeners who had quit their jobs, given away their life savings, and actively spread the message of worldwide destruction at the hands of a divine judge. When asked if he would return his followers' money, Camping said, "I can't be responsible for anybody's life.... I'm only teaching the Bible."[1]

Shortly thereafter, Trey Parker and Matt Stone won the "Best Musical" Tony Award for a show that makes a powerful statement about the origins of religion. In *The Book of Mormon*, Arnold Cunningham is an out of place, imaginative, awkward young man sent to Uganda on a two-year mission. When faced with the challenge of speaking meaningfully to the situation of Africans suffering in unimaginable ways—extreme poverty, famine, AIDS, cruel warlords—Cunningham improvises narrative portions of sacred scripture. He passes his newly created stories and exhortations off as divinely appointed words. In a particularly interesting song, Arnold's father and figures from the history of the LDS Church (Joseph Smith, Mormon, and Moroni) caution him: "You're making things up again, Arnold. You're stretching the truth.... And you know it.... A lie is a lie.... You're taking the Holy Word and adding fiction.... When you fib, there's a price.... You can't just say what you want, Arnold." His response: "I'm making things up again, kind of. But this time it's helping a dozen people!" By the show's end,

---

1. Hagerty, "Doomsday Redux," *NPR* online.

the characters take Cunningham's bizarre stories as authoritative: they are written down, edited, copied, bound, and distributed to the Ugandan villagers. Rather than accepting the religion and text he initially came to promote, Cunningham becomes the leader of a new movement. The show closes as the village proudly stands under the banner of a new religion with a new sacred text: "The Book of Arnold."[2]

It is beyond dispute that sacred texts can be used in all sorts of ways, some constructive and others destructive, and it is not limited to Christianity. Consider Rafey Habib, a Muslim literary theorist whose collection of poems and Qur'an translations in *Shades of Islam* sharply criticize terrorism. Intending to correct the misperception of uninformed Westerners, Habib invokes Islamic sacred texts as peaceful ammunition *against* violent extremists. In a particularly moving poem he writes "To A Suicide Bomber," which deserves quoting at length:

> You do not speak for me: You who soak yourselves in blood are far from the Prophet's mantle. You who act beyond the Book are far from the Word. . . . You call yourselves holy warriors: But you have never read the Holy Book, never tried to understand, never struggled with yourself. You took the easy way. . . . It is not you who bear the Prophet's sword; the True sword is a word, a thought, touched by light, forged in wisdom and relentless in love. It is not you who wear the Prophet's mantle but those who strive, armed not with bombs but with Patience, with a Book, High in words and deeds. You do not speak for me, or the sweetness of my God. You do not speak for me.[3]

For members of more conservative communities, a text thought to be sacred is often treated as a "point and shoot" answer book to many of life's problems. In conversations with friends and family, conservatives are encouraged to seek the scriptures for the answers to many of their questions. Sociologist Christian Smith says that such an approach can have unhealthy consequences. He worries that it ultimately undermines the purpose for which the approach was adopted in the first place. He cautions against this practice, arguing that in doing so *The Bible* [is] *Made Impossible*.

Among conservative academics, the "sufficiency" of sacred texts can lead one to believe that one need not seriously entertain advances in other disciplines. In its moderate form, whatever one needs to know about distinctively religious ends (e.g., liberation, salvation, faith, etc.) is found in the text's pages. In its extreme form, the text is an authoritative teacher on

---

2. Parker, Stone, and Lopez, *Book of Mormon*, 54–59.
3. Habib, *Shades of Islam*, 77–79.

all matters it addresses, not only religious issues. In this latter category, the perspective in a sacred text may supersede insights generated in science, history, anthropology, geology, sociology, psychology, etc. The absolute deference to sacred texts, even down to the very words the authors use, comes from a religious commitment to view them as the primary or only revelation of God. That is, texts are given this level of authority because they are thought to come from God, and if God issues God's perspective, humanity cannot question it.

Herein lies a paradox: many devoted religionists view their sacred text as authoritative but fail to know its contents. As Dan Brown gained notoriety in the publishing world, Bart Ehrman was known to ask his young University of North Carolina students early in the semester how many of them read *The Da Vinci Code* in its entirety. Most of them raised their hands. He follows this question with another: "How many of you have read the Bible from cover to cover?" Far fewer hands are raised. He follows his second question up with a statement: "If God wrote a book, wouldn't you want to know what he had to say?" Boston University's Stephen Prothero has had similar experiences with his students, who, like the general population, suffer from a lack of *Religious Literacy*. Prothero says nearly two thirds of Americans believe that the Bible holds the answers to all or most of life's basic questions, yet only half of American adults can name even one of the four Gospels and most Americans cannot name the first book of the Bible.

Many people for whom the Bible is important lack rudimentary understanding of the book, which inevitably leads to distortions and misrepresentations of its nature and content. Camping's doomsday miscalculations, *The Book of Mormon* musical, and Habib's moving words of protest show some of the many ways in which texts can be marshaled in support of disparate conclusions. Behind many praiseworthy or strange religious beliefs and actions, one can often find devotion to a sacred text. And behind devotion to a sacred text, one often finds a specific view of divine revelation. Without a view of divine revelation informing one's perspective on the sacred texts, the writings would be interesting literature at best and, as an old Englishman once told me, merely "black ink on white pages" at worst. To make the point explicit, in many of the hotly debated issues of our day with which religion is involved—gay marriage, terrorism, abortion, and capital punishment, to name just a few—the real issue operating behind the scenes is divine revelation. One finds people dedicated to a particular understanding of an ancient text and a corresponding conviction regarding its applicability today.

In life as in art, many people claim that God communicates to humanity. Divine revelation is said to be at work when God lifts the veil of human ignorance and shows something of Godself. Revelation also shows something of one's relationship to ultimate reality. Revelation is thought to take many forms from ancient texts to audible voices, and with God on their side people can advance all sorts of causes or participate in all sorts of activities. Sometimes these causes are violent on a small or large scale, on local, national, and international levels. For example, a specific view of revelation is the guiding force impelling a pro-life advocate to kill an abortion doctor, a gathering of extremists who believes God desires America's downfall, *and* leaders of nations waging war.[4] Revelation is at work at all levels of atrocity. However, revelation is also at work in peaceful causes: as the impetus for Mother Teresa's ministry to the poor of Calcutta[5] and Rev. Dr. Martin Luther King's non-violent civil disobedience.[6] A specific perspective on divine revelation undergirds the anti-intellectual creationist[7] as well as the educated liberal pluralist.[8] Whenever one claims some religious knowledge of ultimate reality, the idea of revelation lurks not far behind it. Recognized or not, the idea of revelation informs us, controls our interpretations, and sets the boundaries on what we can and cannot say about ultimate reality, who God is, and what God requires. These stories, varied though they are, all betray a specific understanding of revelation and its implications. More often than not, however, we find people talking past one another because they concentrate on the implications without realizing that the divisive issue is revelation itself.

Behind the scenes, the *use* of revelation is everywhere, but philosophical and theological inquiry into the subject is rather scant these days. The issue of revelation does not seem to be soliciting the type of attention it once did. In our contemporary context, this is very strange. It is common knowledge that religious beliefs are among the deepest and most firmly held, and when those views are aligned with causes that promote human flourishing, religious belief has great potential to impact societies for the good. However, the converse is also true, as occasionally religious beliefs drive adherents toward acts of atrocity that are wholly incompatible with peace. For all the trouble he caused philosophers of religion, David Hume was certainly correct about this much: religion is a powerful force with great

---

4. MacAskill, "George Bush."
5. Teresa, *Come Be My Light*, 44.
6. King, Jr., "Revelation"
7. Balmer, *Thy Kingdom Come*, 109–42.
8. Hick, *God Has Many Names*, 26–28, 48, 51–52, 66–67, 74–75 in Hodgson and King, eds., *Readings*, 397–402.

potential to motivate enthusiastic action, much greater than philosophy done dispassionately.[9]

Religious beliefs often drive public actions, and one's views on divine revelation are often central to one's theological views. So if one were to examine and modify one's view of revelation, it would naturally have implications for the way in which one viewed God and, therefore, it would affect the behaviors stemming from those beliefs. In other words, the concept of revelation is not merely a methodological concern in the philosophy of religion; nor is it only a theological issue within specific traditions. It is also—perhaps more urgently—a matter of profound ethical and geopolitical importance.

God gets blamed for an awful lot these days. Certainly no one is so relativistic as to suggest that every putative revelation is legitimate, for not all of the revelations can be harmonized into one "super-revelation" since some revelations conflict with others. Such absolute relativism only results in nonsense. As C. S. Lewis reminds us, "It is no more possible for God than for the weakest of His creatures to carry out both of two mutually exclusive alternatives; not because His power meets an obstacle, but because nonsense remains nonsense even when we talk it about God."[10]

But neither is the opposite true. Members of religious communities cannot claim that none of the putative revelations are legitimate, for surely their faith rests at least in part on some interaction between God and the world in which God has bridged the divine/human divide to unveil something of ultimate reality to the extent that human creatures can comprehend it. So there must be some standard against which claims to revelation can be measured or good reasons to accept that a revelation can be self-authenticating. These are some of the issues this book explores in an attempt to construct a satisfying philosophical and theological view of revelation.

REVELATION IN PHILOSOPHY OF RELIGION AND THEOLOGY

A temptation when dealing with the concept of revelation is to think one can explore it on its own, without concrete examples weighing one down. However, revelation is not the sort of thing that can be explored in the abstract. Before one is able to ask the "what is revelation?" question, other questions rear their heads, e.g., who does the revealing and to whom does revelation come? Some reification is necessary to get a handle on an abstract

9. Hume, *Treatise*, I/IV, VII.
10. Lewis, *Problem of Pain*, 25.

and potentially limitless discussion. While there are many fruitful avenues for inquiry on the subject, this book has been limited in some important ways. Three are most important, listed here from general to specific.

First, this book is limited in its academic scope. As mentioned above, revelation can be explored using a number of methods, all of which are avenues for fruitful academic inquiry. However, for this study the primary lenses will be philosophy of religion and theology. For in these fields the relationship between text and revelation and between reason and revelation becomes most pronounced and this relationship is what this book seeks to explore. To be sure, the methodological lines between these two fields and other areas (e.g., comparative religion) are not always easy to discern. No doubt many of us will keep trying to advancing the conversation about revelation using these and other valuable primary lenses worthy of serious scholarly attention. But insofar as the being "God" is thought to reveal and insofar as the authority of texts is at play, philosophy of religion and theology are the most fruitful lenses for that sort of inquiry. Rather than attempt to approach revelation from the so-called "view from nowhere," void of methodological presuppositions and biases, this book will be asking philosophical and theological questions. This corresponds to an interesting development of the past five years, namely, analytic philosophers of religion turning their attention to distinctively theological questions. To my knowledge, the "analytic theology" movement, spearheaded by philosophers at the University of Notre Dame, has yet to explore revelation as a locus in and of itself. Another way in which this book is limited in its academic scope concerns the language used to discuss revelation. In short, efforts have been made to avoid overly technical language whenever possible.

Second, this project is limited in its religious scope. One must start from somewhere; one views the world from a specific location. Therefore, to explore the issue of revelation Part One of this book will look at people who operated within the largest religion in the world (numerically), Christianity. Part Two brings other voices into the discussion and makes the argument that the model is useful as a comparative device in interreligious dialogue. However, insofar as the book is not exhaustive, it is limited to Christianity.

Third and finally, one must limit one's scope with respect to the voices to be heard. The decision to limit the project to philosophy of religion and theology impacts the type of figures one chooses. While the book will encounter the work of prominent figures in less philosophically or theologically oriented fields, this book, for reasons that become clear in due course, is limited in Part One to views of revelation originating from great thinkers who straddle the methodological borderline between philosophy of religion and theology. For these purposes, one finds helpful interlocutors with allegiance to Rome (Catholic thinkers), the Yale School (postliberal thinkers), and conservative traditions (evangelical thinkers). Future works of this author and others will explore the ways in which liberation, feminist, postcolonial, and other voices impact the idea of revelation.

REVELATION IN HISTORY

The idea of revelation as a specific locus of philosophical and theological reflection, that is, as a technical concept in systematic treatments of Christian understandings of God and the world, emerged late on the scene. Unlike some matters that achieved unanimity a millennium ago or more, revelation was not treated systematically until unified Protestants and Catholics resisted the extreme rationalism of the Deists, who argued that reason alone could ascertain truth.[11] However, while revelation was not treated technically before this period, a tacit understanding of divine communication is found in earlier thinkers. Here it is sufficient to note four periods in the history of revelation thought to set the stage for subsequent chapters: (a) the era in which the Christianity's sacred texts were written, (b) revelation from the time from the biblical period until the dawn of the Enlightenment, (c) revelation after the Enlightenment, and (d) revelation in the twentieth century.[12]

First, one finds the idea of revelation in Christianity's sacred texts. In the Hebrew Bible revelation took the shape of a covenant between the god of the ancient Israelites—Yahweh—and Yahweh's chosen people. The "Word of God" was often addressed to Israelites through chosen prophets and messengers. In the New Testament the "covenant" revelation is extended and fulfilled in the person early Christians took to be the ultimate manifestation of God (Jesus of Nazareth), the incarnate Word, who symbolizes and enacts a new covenant between God and *all* people.

From biblical times through the dawn of the Enlightenment, the concept of revelation changes. In the patristic era, revelation was seen as the force by which God illuminates the inward parts of the human soul. Medieval Scholasticism saw revelation as a body of sacred truth, a deposit of information that answers life's most pressing questions where philosophical inquiry fell short. Christianity's sacred texts were thought to contain this information imparted to humans by prophetic voices and apostles; therefore, these "scriptures" became a primary source for reflection on ultimate

---

11. Dulles, *Models of Revelation*, 20.
12. See Dulles, *Revelation Theology*, esp. ch. 6.

reality.[13] Following Luther and other Protestants, revelation came to be seen as a response to humanity's anxious search for an ultimately gracious God. In the Reformation, revelation was imagined as the good news of God's salvation through Christ's efforts, and certain portions of the Bible are vitally important for this message (e.g., the New Testament in general and the Pauline corpus specifically). Catholics of the Counter Reformation doubled down; they went back to and insisted on the idea of revelation as "doctrine," and emphasized the Church as the authoritative teacher. Revelation, according to this understanding, is the objective content of Church doctrine while tradition and sacred texts were its sources.

As mentioned above, early in the Enlightenment the idea of revelation became systematized in an attempt to rebut the rationalism of the Deists. For members of nineteenth-century Evolutionary Idealism, revelation was the Absolute Spirit's emergence in history. "Theologically concerned Idealists tend to look upon the appearance of Jesus Christ, the God-man, as the crucial moment of this emergence."[14] As sentimentalism and individualism gained momentum in morality, and as scientific approaches gained momentum in the search for objective truth, the liberal/modernist suggested that revelation was a matter of religious experience. Revelation essentially came to be seen as an interior sense of God's loving fatherhood and a commitment to the sisterhood/brotherhood of humanity.

Finally, in the early twentieth century, existentialism impacted the notion of revelation. Life seemed absurd in the middle of two World Wars, and the despair impacted the understanding of what role revelation needed to play. Revelation, therefore, gave meaning or value to life in light of these confusing "boundary situations." In several twentieth-century thinkers, revelation was the "manifestation of that which concerns man ultimately."[15]

Recently the conversation has taken another interesting turn, particularly as it relates to the relationship between text and revelation. A number of contemporary scholars have resurrected the "theological interpretation of Scripture."[16] Their work moves in all directions: historians study classical biblical interpretations,[17] scholars of the Bible are found writing theological commentaries on books of the Bible,[18] and systematic theologians write

---

13. As noted by Kelsey in *Proving Doctrine*, to term a group of texts "scripture" is to have already made a judgment about their nature and authority.

14. Dulles, *Revelation Theology*, 174.

15. Ibid.

16. Cf. Treier, *Introducing Theological Interpretation of Scripture*.

17. For example, the Ancient Christian Commentary on Scripture series (IVP).

18. For example, the Two Horizons Old Testament Commentary series (Eerdmans), edited by Gordon McConville and Craig Bartholomew, and the Two Horizons

commentaries on biblical books.[19] Yale University theologian, Miroslav Volf, boldly suggests that "the return of biblical scholars to the theological reading of the Scriptures, and the return of systematic theologians to sustained engagement with scriptural texts—in a phrase, the return of both to theological readings of the Bible—is *the most significant theological development in the last two decades.*"[20]

From this brief history, one can see that revelation and text are often viewed together. New Testament authors viewed the Hebrew Bible authoritatively; Catholics of medieval scholasticism and the Counter Reformation saw sacred texts as a vital source of theological reflection; and the theological interpretation of scripture is currently generating much scholarly attention.

However, reading sacred texts for the purpose of understanding ultimate reality—that is, philosophically and theologically—only makes sense *if they are revelatory* in some sense. And if they are revelatory in some sense, they concern humanity ultimately. Revelation as that which concerns humanity ultimately is an idea that was fleshed out in the twentieth century using a metaphor with which this book sympathizes: a *bridge*.

THE BRIDGE: BARTH AND VON BALTHASAR

A bridge does a number of things. It provides access to inaccessible areas, connects two entities over a space that is otherwise unable to be traversed, lets one get from the proverbial "here" to "there," and vice versa. A bridge also provides a common location of coming and going for each party involved, a space or point of contact in which these parties can establish a relationship. Some bridges are informative; their length, for instance, reveals just how far one is from the other side, an insight that may also be confirmed once one begins the trek from one side to the other. Some bridges serve an aesthetic and teleological function. Looking upon them shows something of their makers, their makers' order and design, and their makers' purposes for the bridge. One can even say that bridges provide work or purpose. Bridges need people to design them, construct them, maintain them, and destroy them when they have served their purpose and become more dangerous than helpful if left standing.

The similarities notwithstanding, bridges also vary a great deal in size, strength, and appearance. Different terrains call for different designs, as do

New Testament Commentary series, edited by Joel Green and Max Turner (Eerdmans).

19. For example, the Brazos Theological Commentary on the Bible series, as mentioned in Volf, *Captive*, 12–15.

20. Volf, *Captive*, 14.

varying levels of resources. It is not as straightforward as one might think to define the "essence" of a bridge given the various examples and types one finds throughout the world.

So what makes a bridge? How does one separate the idea of a "bridge" from other ways to get from here to there? Does one identify bridges by the intention of the designer or the success with which they serve their purpose? Should one judge a bridge by what it attempts to do rather than what it accomplishes? Or is it more a matter of how well it does it?

The revelational parallels to the "bridge" metaphor are quite obvious. Divine revelation is thought to provide access to that which is otherwise inaccessible. It connects God and humankind over the "infinite qualitative distinction" that is otherwise unable to be traversed. Revelation lets one get from "here" to "there," where "here" is ignorant and/or alone and "there" is informed and/or in relationship. Revelation provides a common location of coming and going for God and people. Revelation also shows just how far the distance is between God and humankind, for God is often revealed as concealed and incomprehensible.[21] Revelation is said to establish a relationship between God and people.[22] Some revelations of God serve an aesthetic and teleological function; some are pleasing to the eyes or heart or mind, and experiencing them is to experience the Reality behind them. And some revelations provide sustenance to humans when nothing of this world has the potential to speak life into difficult situations. Revelation is the creation and design of God, but it has been interpreted by humans, maintained by the church, and destroyed by prophetic voices who call for renewal and revival when old patterns no longer work.

This book suggests that revelations, like bridges, vary in size, strength, and appearance. Different situations call for different types of revelations, and one's unique situation will impact the sort of revelation one will experience. Moreover, one needs criteria against which claims to revelation can be judged, for not all revelations are equal or equally valid.

The bridge metaphor is not new. Examples abound to show it in practice. For example, consider two twentieth-century thinkers who used "bridge" language to describe revelation: Karl Barth in *Der Römerbrief*[23] and Hans Urs von Balthasar in *Das Herz der Welt*.[24] Barth and von Balthasar use

21. Dalferth, *Philosophy and Theology*, 158–59; 197.

22. Davis "Revelation and Inspiration," 32.

23. This work is Barth's response to both liberal theology and the context of the First World War, as noted in Adam, "Die Theologie der Krisis," 271–86. What follows is how Barth conceives of revelation in chapters 1–4.

24. The purpose for using this work consists in the fact that it can be seen as "containing in outline the themes of his mature theology." Cf. sections pertaining to Barth

the metaphor in different ways and in the process they emphasize different understandings of the way revelation works. This is not surprising since they wrote for different reasons and different audiences. Barth wrote *Der Römerbrief* in response to two injustices he noticed within early twentieth-century Europe, one specific and one general: (a) specific—the class struggles and economic oppression faced by the parishioners of the church he was leading in Safenwil; (b) general—World War I and his former teachers' adherence to the war policy of Kaiser Wilhelm.[25] Both scenarios contributed to Barth's re-evaluation of the dominant liberal agenda in which he was schooled, both theologically and politically. Regarding the situation for which Barth wrote, he notes in the Preface to its sixth edition that, "a great deal of the scaffolding of the book was due to my own particular situation at the time [Safenwil] and also to the general situation [World War I]."[26] By all accounts, this work "fell like a bombshell on the playground of the theologians."[27]

In the first four chapters, Barth develops several themes that situate his views on revelation: (a) God as ultimately inscrutable; (b) humanity as unmistakably fallen; (c) the incarnate Word as tangential; and (d) history as collapsed. On the incomprehensibility of God, Barth interprets the Pauline letter as purposefully conveying God's wholly-otherness: "the essential theme of his mission is not within him but above him—unapproachably distant and unutterably strange."[28] Moreover, Barth is quite clear that humanity is that which is both ungodly and incapable of its own restoration; for Barth, this condition consists both in evil actions and the existential situation under which humanity finds itself. According to Barth, "Everything which emerges in men and which owes its form and expansion to them is always and everywhere, and as such, ungodly and unclean."[29] Into this scenario of depravity, the incarnate Word acts as a bridge from God to humanity, or otherwise expressed, a hinge to the door of the divine, entering as a tangent from the unknown realm into ours: "The name Jesus defines an historical occurrence and marks the point where the unknown world cuts the known world."[30] The resurrection, therefore, is that which collapses history—drawing on Kierkegaard's notion of the infinite and finite meeting

in Cross, ed., *Oxford Dictionary*.

25. See Jones, ed., *Blackwell Companion to Modern Theology* and sections pertaining to Barth in Grenz and Olson, *20th Century Theology*.

26. Barth, *Romans*, 25.

27. Grenz and Olson, *20th Century Theology*, 67.

28. Barth, *Romans*, 27.

29. Ibid., 56.

30. Ibid., 29

in the person of Jesus—and provides the context for understanding Barth's doctrine of revelation: "The new Day which has dawned for men in the resurrection, the Day of Jesus Christ, this . . . is the day that ushers in the transformation of all time into eternity."[31]

Utilizing this framework, Barth imagines revelation as God's timeless act of breaking through the barriers of human fallenness, thereby revealing Godself by suspending and holding the sinner in the place of unknowing: "In His utter strangeness God wills to make Himself known and can make Himself known. . . . Beyond human good and evil the arm of God is extended in power."[32] In response to this divine self-revelation, humans "have encountered the grace of God; have met the incomprehensibility of God."[33] Despite the inability of humans to rescue themselves, or even to recognize that they are in need of rescuing, God breaks through, and this provides the context for Barth's views on revelation: "Grace is the gift of Christ, who exposes the gulf which separates God and man, and, by exposing it, *bridges* it."[34] In this passage, the gulf itself is the setting of revelation. In the exposition of the gulf, God "bridges it." In this way, divine revelation is both the gulf and the bridge; they are one and the same for the early Karl Barth.

To be sure, the picture of divine revelation given by the younger Barth may be seen as intrusive, as it interrupts and reforms our preconceived notions of who God is and what God is about. Revelation's "good news" is not optional. It "*demands* participation, comprehension, co-operation; for it is a communication which presumes faith in the living God, and which creates that which it presumes."[35] The mature Barth, however, mitigated the force of this claim, as he assumes agency of the creature (the second partner) at some level simultaneously with God (the first partner). Barth says, "No self-determination of the second partner can influence the first, whereas the self-determination of the first, *while not cancelling the self-determination of the second*, is the sovereign predetermination which precedes it absolutely."[36] The relationship between human agency and the reception of revelation is an issue more fully addressed in Part Two of this book. For now, the salient feature of Barth's view of revelation is this: God exposes and bridges the difference between God and humans, and both the exposition and bridging are the work of God. They are both revelation.

31. Ibid., 69
32. Ibid., 70
33. Ibid., 59.
34. Ibid., 31 (emphasis added).
35. Ibid., 28.
36. Barth, *CD*, 2/1, 312 (emphasis added).

In *Das Herz der Welt,* Hans Urs von Balthasar takes a different view. Just as Barth wrote in response to two stimuli, one general and one specific, the impetus for von Balthasar's little book also follows a similar pattern: (a) specific—his observance of the mystical and traumatic experiences of Adrienne von Speyr; (b) general—the experience of World War II. Regarding von Speyr, Andrew Louth claims that this book was "written out of the initial impact of his friendship with that remarkable woman, whose influence on his own thought Balthasar readily admits."[37] Moreover, Erasmo Leiva, who translated the work into English, notes in his introduction that this book was "steeled in the furnace of the Second World War."[38] And just as Barth's *Römerbrief* adumbrated a view of revelation made more explicit in his mature work, von Balthasar's work contains "in outline the themes of his mature theology"[39] that one finds in his theological triptych.

Das Herz der Welt is a useful tool for exploring the idea of revelation not only because it shows another angle on the "bridge" metaphor, but also because it devotes attention to a common reason why revelation goes unrecognized or ignored. Philosophers of religion have long dealt with this major objection to belief in an omnipotent and omnibenevolent God: human pain and suffering. To address the issue, von Balthasar discusses the Christian notion of "Holy Saturday," the space between Good Friday's crucifixion and Easter Sunday's resurrection, the time during which Jesus descends into hell. This space is valuable for von Balthasar because it represents the greatest separation of the Father and Son, the "second death" following Jesus' first death on the cross. Envisioned as a deeply trinitarian event, von Balthasar asserts that what was once the triune God has been divided, now missing that which was constitutive of its identity (three-in-oneness). God is, therefore, no longer living. On Holy Saturday, the view from above indicates, "there is nothing more but nothingness itself. The world is dead. Love is dead. God is dead."[40]

While the view from above is bleak, a perspective with which many people who resist the idea of revelation and God today would concur, there is, nonetheless, a revelation to be found in the view from below. Far from being a tragedy, von Balthasar mentions a spark that proceeds from the point of separation: "What is this light glimmer that wavers and begins to take form in the endless void? . . . A nameless thing, more solitary than God,

---

37. Riches, *Analogy of Beauty,* 147.
38. Leiva, "Introduction," 10.
39. Cf. Cross, ed., *Oxford Dictionary,* 148.
40. Balthasar, *Heart,* 150. See also Pitstick, *Light in Darkness.*

it emerges out of pure emptiness."[41] As to the identity of this "viscous flow," von Balthasar here speaks of the Holy Spirit. In his sermons, von Balthasar imagines the Spirit as the builder of a "bridge" over the abyss of hell: "It is a lightly built bridge, and yet it suffices to carry us. . . . So we have no alternative but to trust in him, knowing, as we walk across the bridge, that he built it. Because of his grace we have been spared the absolute abyss."[42] Functionally, the Spirit "maintains the infinite difference between them, seals it and, since he is the one Spirit of them both, *bridges* it."[43] Whereas Barth viewed Christ as the vehicle of God's revelation, von Balthasar uses the Spirit. Whereas Barth's "abyss" is both exposed and traversed by God, von Balthasar's abyss is known prior to revelation.

In the early writings of both thinkers, revelation is understood as a bridge. But so powerful was the metaphor that it persisted into their mature writings. In his magnum opus, Barth declares that

> the love of God always throws a bridge over a crevasse. It is always the light shining out of darkness. In His revelation it seeks and creates fellowship where there is no fellowship and no capacity for it. . . . [W]hat He sees when He loves is that which is altogether distinct from Himself, and as such is lost in itself, and without Him abandoned to death. That He throws a bridge out from Himself to this abandoned one, that He is light in the darkness, is the miracle of the almighty love of God.[44]

The bridge is also present in von Balthasar's *Theological Aesthetics*. Revelation is at work bridging the distance between the primary revelation in Jesus Christ and our own era. The Holy Spirit's self-disclosures fall

> down from heaven vertically . . . [and] immediately blend into the landscape of tradition, there to lend new life to the Biblical message, to bridge over the supposed distances between the time of revelation and the present time, to act as a sign for the actuality and the loving proximity of the true World to this our visionless existence.[45]

God speaking, bridging the gap, holding and suspending humans and offering grace . . . these are matters of *ultimate concern*. This book uses the bridge metaphor throughout because it is a helpful anchor, an organizing

---

41. Balthasar, *Heart*, 151.
42. Balthasar, *You Crown the Year*, 91.
43. Balthasar, *The Action*, 324 (emphasis added).
44. Barth, *CD* II/1, 278.
45. Balthasar, *Seeing the Form*, 416.

motif that grounds the discussion. If it is true that God has communicated truths and God's very self to humanity, it would be a subject not only of ultimate concern, but the subject of *greatest* concern. On this much, conservatives who hold the their sacred texts in high esteem are correct. This shows the seriousness with which they approach the matter of revelation. One of the hallmarks of the evangelical tradition throughout its history has been biblicism.[46] One might go so far as to call it the *sine qua non* of the conservative tradition. Although philosophers and theologians whose identities do not necessarily rest on a particular understanding of or commitment to God or a particular sacred text may be able to simply stop discussing the issue of revelation, as many have, most conservatives cannot.

Discussing the matter is problematic, especially when revelation is equated with sacred texts, for the types of biblicism that worked for conservatives fifty years ago or more is said to be untenable these days among academic philosophers and theologians, even those in evangelical circles.[47] For these reasons and others, the idea of divine revelation itself faces many challenges.

CHALLENGES TO REVELATION

Since Barth and von Balthasar, interest in revelation theology has dwindled (with a few exceptions). Some philosophers of religion have had valuable things to say about the matter,[48] but mainline theologians today are simply not discussing revelation much. For the *Modern Theology* journal, Kathryn Tanner surveyed the field from 1985–2010, and not once was a substantive comment made about advances in the theology of revelation. This is due in no small part to the challenges one faces when attempting to explore revelation today.[49] As mentioned above, there is no "view from nowhere," so these challenges are specific to the communities for whom text and revelation are

---

46. Bebbington, "Evangelicalism in Its Settings," 367. I mention that biblicism "has been" an evangelical distinctive because many younger evangelicals are questioning this commitment. See Christian Smith's analysis in *The Bible Made Impossible* for the idea that "Biblicism is not a truly evangelical reading of scripture."

47. See, for instance, Smith, *Bible Made Impossible* and Olson, *Reformed*, ch. 5.

48. See, for example, Swinburne, *Revelation* and Dalferth and Rodgers, eds., *Revelation*.

49. Cf. Dulles, *Models of Revelation*, 6–8. Included on Dulles's list of problems for the idea of revelation are some of the same features I describe here, but given only where they are still problems for the idea of divine revelation. His list includes philosophical agnosticism, linguistic analysis, modern epistemology, empirical psychology, biblical criticism, the history of Christian doctrine, comparative religion, and critical sociology.

identical or nearly identical. Six challenges are worth mentioning: (a) the philosophical charge of question begging, (b) increased awareness of advances in higher criticism, (c) cultural, ethical, and religious relativism, (d) the resurgence of naturalism, (e) the nature of God, and (f) the complicated nature of the revelation question. In the process of laying out the challenges to exploring revelation today, one begins to get a clearer view of some of the questions a relevant and contemporary view of revelation must answer.

First, inquiries into divine revelation must contend with the challenge of question begging. The charge goes something like this: any defense of revelation—certainly when revelation is discussed in conjunction with sacred texts—will inevitably assume that which it attempts to prove. Revelation's critics are not far off on this point, as evidenced by conservative thinker, Wayne Grudem. In his *Systematic Theology*, Grudem defends the sufficiency of his sacred text by pointing to the text itself: "Significant scriptural support and explanation of this doctrine [of the sufficiency of scripture] is found in Paul's words to Timothy . . . [and] other passages indicate that the Bible is sufficient to equip us for living the Christian life."[50] Grudem is using the Bible to defend the Bible. At best, this type of reasoning results in an antinomy, and at worst it is simply fallacious. Even in instances where a specific view of revelation is not already in place, a specific view of God may be operative in the background, and the view of God is largely based on what has been revealed, which brings with it a pre-existing—if unrecognized—view of revelation and its implications. So the first set of questions any contemporary view of revelation must answer are these: How does one discuss the idea of revelation without relying on the very model one is attempting to defend? Is circularity inevitable? Are there degrees of circularity? Are there satisfying defenses of revelation as "self-authenticating," and if so, would they effectively respond to this challenge? And if some measure of circularity is inevitable, which view of revelation withstands criticism due to its positive influence in religious and nonreligious contexts?

Second, the idea of revelation is challenged today by an increased public awareness of higher criticism. As revelation became incorporated into systematic theologies after the Enlightenment, many conservatives took to equating revelation with sacred texts. In Christian circles, the "Word of God" became commonly associated with the Bible. Yet emerging methods of interpreting these texts—chiefly historical and text criticism—called the legitimacy of these views into question. Recently a number of scholars have popularized higher criticism, and what once only bothered conservatives who learn new methods of biblical interpretation has now reached the

---

50. Grudem, *Systematic Theology*, 127.

masses. The younger generation of conservative scholars were told the Bible is one thing—free of all error whatsoever—and they are taught later that it is something quite different. So a second set of questions this book answers are these: how can one imagine revelation in such a way that it does not contradict advances in other disciplines, including and especially biblical higher criticism? Should the idea of revelation itself be reconfigured to account for changes in the texts? And if so, in what ways can one maintain the uniqueness of Christianity's sacred texts qua divine revelation?

Third, revelation is challenged by the "locatedness" of its alleged receivers. Critics may assert that the idea of revelation is not feasible because different cultures claim to experience or receive the divine in different ways. Ultimately, then, there is said to be no universal revelation or universal model into which we can place specific revelations. Each culture, each philosophy, and each religion has its own view of God's communication and none is superior to the others. Relativism makes claims to any universally binding revelation seem impossible. John Caputo nicely summarizes the problem: "The truth is that there is no truth."[51] This is the perspective of noted philosopher of religion, John Hick, who argues not for a standard or objective revelation but rather a revelation that mirrors the various religious traditions: a "plural revelation." So a third set of questions this book seeks to answer include these: How can one determine if a putative revelation is from God or if it originated elsewhere? Are there criteria to judge specific revelations that would be widely appealing? And how would using these criteria relate to the universal/particular problem in divine revelation?

Fourth (and fifth), perhaps the greatest challenge to the idea of specifically *divine* revelation today is the resurgence of naturalism in which any claims to the *super*natural or miraculous are held in suspicion. Postmodernism, one might say, has given way to naturalism as a great threat to a theistic view of the world (again). So pervasive is naturalism that one can even find proponents of *religious* naturalism. Consider Charlene Spretnak's *States of Grace*, in which the entire world is interconnected such that there is a "grand unity, the ground of the sacred."[52] Her religious naturalism has no room for the supernatural; indeed, it is more akin to *extra*ordinary, which she perceives to be *ultra*natural. Naturalism takes two forms, only one of which challenges divine revelation.[53] Methodological naturalists, who act, explore, and research *as if* the universe were all there is do not concern this project. Metaphysical naturalists, believing that the material universe is all

---

51. Caputo, *Radical Hermeneutics*, 156.
52. Spretnak, *States of Grace*, 20, in Stone, *Religious Naturalism Today*, 223.
53. Spiegel and Cowan, *Love of Wisdom*, 132–35.

there is, pose a challenge to divine revelation insofar as they rule out one of divine revelation's central premises, namely, a *divinity or divine agent* who reveals. So, the fourth and fifth set of questions this book answers concern naturalism and the nature of God respectively: What does revelation look like in conversation *with* advances in other disciplines—particularly in science, anthropology, communication studies, psychology, and as mentioned before, higher criticism—instead of against them? Is burying one's head in the sand inevitable when it comes to science? Do religion and science simply occupy non-overlapping magisteria when it comes to the revelation question? What do advances in these areas mean for the concept of revelation? How does the naturalism/supernaturalism debate impact the idea of revelation? If, indeed, there is a divine presence who does the revealing, what is the nature of this God? What is this God's relationship to the world? Does God's power overwhelm the recipient of revelation in the moment of revelation? What is God's relationship to time and how does it impact the notion of revelation? In short, what is the relationship between the nature of God and revelation?

Sixth and finally, the issue of revelation seems far too complicated to make any progress. While it is true that religionists accept that their world includes a measure of divine revelation and live according to what they believe God communicates, elucidating what "revelation" means or how it works is problematic for the average person and the philosopher of religion alike. It is a similar problem as those faced by those who try to find satisfactory philosophical grounds for concern for others, that is, for human dignity:

> Let's imagine that a person has collapsed in an airport terminal. Others quickly rush to his or her aid. We may admire these individuals, even call them heroes for saving the day, but we do not ordinarily consider their behavior to stand in need of justification. Rather, it is the person who strides past without stopping to help from whom we demand (or would like to demand) some explanation. . . . The point here is that our sense of human dignity is closely related to how we actually respond to other human beings.[54]

Could it be that our sense of divine revelation is closely related to how we actually respond to God? Why bother offering a philosophical or theological explanation for it? What does that add to the difficult work of living in obedience to God? Even if we admit that we need a theory of revelation, the best minds today think it an unwise use of time. For example, eminent

---

54. Amesbury and Newlands, *Faith and Human Rights*, 45–46.

theologian David Kelsey shows some of the problems one faces in his magnum opus, *Eccentric Existence*, a work self-consciously void of revelation talk. Kelsey worries that the move in modern theology to view revelation as "the person of Jesus Christ," God's absolute self-communication which is not the same as information about God, forces "irreducibly different notions onto a procrustean bed, with the result that on close inspection it exhibits internal inconsistencies and antinomies that require endless adjustments and revisions." One faces endless difficulties trying to discuss revelation these days. Kelsey continues:

> Not only has the history of proposals of doctrines of revelation in dogmatic theology been a story of conceptual tangles, the history of its relationship to philosophical theories of our knowledge of God has been profoundly tangled. The effort to disentangle the intellectual snarls that have developed over a couple of centuries of debate about this topic have been so frustrating that they have, notoriously, set theologians snarling at one another. . . . This interminable effort to clarify *the* Christian doctrine of revelation appears to be a case in which a great deal of theological smoke, contrary to folk wisdom, signals not the slightest theological fire, must less light. It is dubious whether the confusions apparently endemic in systematically christocentric doctrines of revelation *can* in principle be sorted out. . . . Best not to go there.[55]

The sixth set of questions this book seeks to answer, therefore, are these: how can one conceive of revelation in a way that avoids unnecessary complexity and instead illuminates ways in which people relate to God? If past approaches to revelation so popular among twentieth century thinkers drum up little wisdom, what else can "center" the notion of revelation?

To summarize, any view of revelation advanced today in the philosophy of religion and theology must attempt to answer some important questions concerning the charge of begging the question, incorporating higher criticism, overcoming relativism, prevailing against naturalism, the nature of God, and offering *good* news rather than conceptual tangles to its receivers. Most theologians these days refuse to undertake the construction of this kind of view. Indeed, Kelsey wonders if it is even possible. But that is the task of this book, to construct a view of revelation that overcomes these challenges. Rather than scrap the idea of revelation altogether or, worse, scrap the idea of a divinity who reveals; rather than blindly accept this or that sacred text as revelatory; rather than build a philosophical and/or theological

---

55. Kelsey, *Eccentric Existence*, 911.

system or ethic based solely on personal opinion and/or social utility; rather than all these approaches, one should reconsider whether revelation can be understood in such a way that it is capable of overcoming these challenges.

THE APPROACH: THINKERS AND TOPICS

To construct an account of revelation that answers these questions, this book considers several perspectives on divine revelation. Comparative approaches in philosophy and theology are not new. Roughly a century ago Ernst Troeltsch use a typological approach in *The Social Teachings of the Christian Churches* and H. Richard Niebuhr used it in his influential classic, *Christ and Culture*. Avery Dulles, who used a typological approach in his *Models of Revelation*, notes that the value of a models-based approach is that it permits various positions to be presented in their "pure" form, unalloyed by a particular presentation in any one specific thinker. However, the presentation of these issues by individual thinkers is at times useful for engaging the complexities that pure presentations cannot. Niebuhr himself acknowledged this difficulty:

> A type is always something of a construct, even when it has not been constructed prior to long study of many historic individuals and movements. When one returns from the hypothetical scheme to the rich complexity of individual events, it is evident at once that no person or group ever conforms completely to a type. Each historical figure will show characteristics that are more reminiscent of some other family than the one by whose name he has been called, or traits will appear that seem wholly unique and individual. The method of typology, however, though historically inadequate, has the advantage of calling to attention the continuity and significance of the great *motifs* that appear and reappear in the long wrestling of Christians with their enduring problem.[56]

Projects that present a typology are both useful and limiting. They are useful insofar as they initiate a discussion but limiting in their inability to ever be presented purely in specific thinkers.

Ideally, one would adopt a hybrid approach. One would select thinkers who represent their own traditions while also adding their own "spin," as it were, to the material. This book attempts such an approach. Dulles, for

---

56. Niebuhr, *Christ and Culture*, 43–44 discussing Jung's *Psychological Types* of 1924. He says it "is suggestive and illuminating as an example of typological method" (44).

instance, is fully orthodox Catholic while also being open to new ways to imagine revelation in conversation with twentieth-century philosophy. This book balances the typology/model with the individual expressing it, using both to discuss revelation today.

The first three chapters of this book comprise Part One, in which revelation is discussed from the perspective of a prominent thinker in three branches of Christianity. Each of these chapters presents (a) the difficulty in defining the branch of which each thinker is a part, (b) the broader "context" in which the perspective arose, (c) the view of revelation under consideration and its relation to sacred texts, and (d) the view as interpreted and criticized by others in philosophy of religion and theology. The three branches discussed are from Rome, Yale, and conservatives; that is, revelation is explored through Roman Catholicism, postliberalism, and evangelicalism. James Buckley identifies these three branches of Christianity as "radical traditions." Taken in reverse order, evangelicalism is "radical" in the sense that it "is a radical movement within a larger tradition"[57] centered on three Reformation "solas": *Christus*, *fides*, and *scriptura*. Postliberalism is a radical tradition in the sense that it moved beyond the dominant liberal agenda of mainline academics. Finally, Buckley considers today's Catholicism as radical in the sense that after Vatican II it is more open to those with whom it disagreed in the past.[58]

Chapter 1 presents a Catholic view of revelation as presented by Avery Dulles, Laurence J. McGinley Professor of Religion and Society at Fordham University. Dulles is useful for the book not only because he advances his own "symbolic mediation" approach to revelation but also because he systematically lays out other models as well. These will serve as a map on which to locate the other views we will encounter and the view that this book advances. Chapter 2 presents a postliberal perspective on divine revelation as presented by George A. Lindbeck, professor of religious studies for years at Yale University and Protestant representative at Vatican II. Lindbeck discusses the dynamic between the internal and external word of God, and his approach raises the question of how one relates divine revelation to truth claims and religious pluralism, an area still hotly debated among some

---

57. Buckley, "Introduction," viii. Buckley describes Lindbeck's evangelical Lutheranism in this passage, but under the heading of "evangelical" as a radical tradition. It is worth mentioning that Buckley distinguishes Lindbeck's evangelical spirit from North American evangelicals. Lindbeck says of North American evangelicals that they are "the antiecclessial, the anti-or low-sacramental and the anti- or noncreedal" with which evangelical Lutheranism, his own tradition, disagrees. Cf. Lindbeck, "A Panel Discussion," 246.

58. Buckley, "Introduction," x–xi.

philosophers of religion. Chapter 3 presents a conservative approach as advocated by Bernard L. Ramm, who worked within the evangelical tradition. Ramm is helpful for this study because he shows the ways in which an evangelical perspective on revelation can "open up" to advances in mainline philosophy of religion and theology. These three chapters are primarily exegetical. Each chapter mines their writings for a theology of revelation that can be distilled for comparative use. Of particular use in chapters 1–3 is the emergence of three central revelational themes.

Part Two includes three constructive chapters that build on the previous three. These chapters systematically lay out the contents of an integrative model of revelation in conversation with the three thinkers whose work serves as a launching off point. However, these chapters also advance this view of revelation in concert with advances in other academic disciplines. In chapter 4 I organize the central revelational themes by assessing which deserves thematic primacy, elaborate the resulting model of revelation, and discuss its relationship to the uniqueness of sacred texts. Chapter 5 relates this model of divine revelation to some standard religious/theological loci: anthropology, hamartiology, and soteriology. Chapter 5 also presents some criteria for adjudicating between competing putative revelations and describes how the revelation/self-revelation distinction helps in the adjudication process. Chapter 6 shows some of the ways in which the model goes beyond self-consciously "Christian" and "theological" parameters that have, up until this point, constrained it. Chapter 6 also outlines some of the implications of this view. The Conclusion, finally, proposes some areas that may prove fruitful for further inquiry.

The reader is encouraged to view this volume as an invitation to dialogue, not only with one's close associates but also the unfamiliar "other." I hope this model encourages a mindset of hospitality rather than security, open storytelling rather than close-mindedness, listening rather than litigation, and peacemaking rather than violence.

PART ONE

CHAPTER 1

The Mediated Word
Rome and Revelation

"EMINENZA, EMINENZA!"

In his 2008 apostolic journey to the United States, Pope Benedict XVI went out of his way to visit one of his Cardinals—Avery Dulles—whose health prevented Dulles from joining in the events that other Cardinals attended. Anne Marie Kirmse describes the situation: "The pope literally bounded into the room with a big smile on his face. He went directly to where Cardinal Dulles was sitting, saying, 'Eminenza, Eminenza.' . . . Cardinal Dulles kissed the papal ring and smiled back at the pope."

At one point during the meeting, the pope was given a copy of Cardinal Dulles' latest book, *Church and Society*, a compilation of his public lectures delivered at Fordham University over two decades. The pontiff was intrigued by Dulles' book, even going so far as to interrupt Dulles' remarks to repeatedly ask about it. Benedict "eagerly paged through it, and was touched by Cardinal Dulles' inscription to him. The pope seemed disappointed when an aide took the book from him." Kirmse thinks "if the pope had his way, he would have sat down and started reading it immediately. Before leaving, he blessed Cardinal Dulles, assuring him of his prayers for him, and encouraged him in his sufferings."[1]

---

1. Kirmse and Canaris, *Legacy*, 115–16.

Dulles died less than one year later leaving a legacy as one of the great twentieth- and twenty-first-century thinkers in the Catholic tradition. With respect to revelation, Dulles literally "wrote the book," which explains in part the pope's excitement to see him and receive a compilation of his public addresses.

Pope Benedict XVI is not without his own theological prowess. On November 18, 1965, toward the end of the Second Vatican Council, Pope Paul VI promulgated the bishops' "Dogmatic Constitution on Divine Revelation" in a document simply titled, *Dei Verbum*, the "word of God."[2] Using this document as one of its chief sources, Joseph Ratzinger (i.e., Benedict XVI) chaired a committee to write the *Catechism of the Catholic Church*, which Pope John Paul II proclaimed to be "a statement of the Church's faith and of catholic doctrine, attested to or illumined by Sacred Scripture, the Apostolic Tradition, and the Church's Magisterium. [It is] a sure norm for teaching the faith and thus a valid and legitimate instrument for ecclesial communion."[3] In these documents, prominent Catholic leaders outline what they perceive to be Catholic teachings about revelation. Of course, there are scholars who consider themselves "Catholic" whose views bear little to no resemblance to the views outlined in these documents. It appears, therefore, that the term "Catholic" is not understood univocally, especially on the issue of revelation.

This chapter explores the concept of revelation in contemporary Catholic philosophy of religion and theology as expressed Dulles' work. Additionally, it compares Dulles' views of revelation with those of two other prominent Catholic thinkers: Karl Rahner and the aforementioned Joseph Ratzinger. After first discussing the difficulty of defining who is and is not a "Catholic" thinker, the chapter describes the context of Dulles' own view by outlining the five "models" of revelation on which he maps his own view. Third, the bulk of the chapter is intended to explore Dulles' contribution to the idea of revelation in his own "symbolic mediation" approach. Fourth, Rahner and Ratzinger serve as interlocutors for Dulles; the former sought to bridge two positions he found unacceptable and the latter includes a dialectic of revelation and concealment. Fifth, the three thinkers are evaluated in terms of their similarities and tensions as well as the potential of their approaches for reimagining revelation today.

---

2. Abbott, *Documents of Vatican II*, 107–32.
3. John Paul II, "Apostolic Constitution," 5–6.

DEFINING CATHOLICISM

Before explicating the how Dulles, Rahner and Ratzinger understand revelation, a few preliminary remarks are in order to show some of the difficulties involved in treating "Catholicism" in such broad strokes, most significantly with respect to who "qualifies" as a suitable "Catholic" thinker. "Catholic" is itself a widely varying identification, as there are philosophers and theologians who self-identify as such with very little in common. Its lower case-c meaning, "universal," does not represent the diversity within its branch of Christianity today. Although any division risks gross oversimplification of an extremely complex taxonomy, for the purposes of this chapter Catholic theologians will be divided into two camps: orthodox and progressive. The key difference is the epistemological "center" of their work, that which they view as the *sine qua non* of their tradition.

One can conceive of "orthodox" Catholicism as that brand of Catholic teaching in which tradition is given great and measurable weight in philosophical and theological adjudication as opposed to experience.[4] Catholicism conceived this way means that the Magisterium is given a powerful voice in the views parishioners are encouraged to accept or reject. Obviously included on the list of "orthodox" Catholic theologians are Popes and Cardinals (e.g., Ratzinger and Dulles). As Richard McBrien notes, in "the strictest sense of all . . . the term magisterium has been applied exclusively to the teaching authority of the pope and the bishops."[5] Dulles is also an orthodox thinker insofar as he supports the "teaching authority of the church." In his *Models of the Church*, Dulles discusses the Catholic Church in relation to the "institutional" model, in which "the Church is . . . a unique type of school—one in which the teachers have the power to impose their doctrine with juridical and spiritual sanctions. Thus teaching is juridicized and institutionalized."[6] Dulles also makes clear his view on the teaching authority of the Church, as he refers to the magisterium as the "teacher and guardian of the faith."[7] In short, "orthodox" Catholic philosophers and theologians hierarchically prioritize tradition above experience.

If "orthodox" Catholicism gives primacy to tradition over experience, a "progressive" approach prioritizes experience above tradition. Progressive

---

4. Richard McBrien identifies, among some other things, the Eucharist and Petrine ministry office (the papacy) as distinguishing features of Catholicism, both of which are amenable to the "orthodox" perspective I am defining. McBrien, *Catholicism*, 68.

5. Ibid.

6. Dulles, *Models of the Church*, 30.

7. Dulles, *Magisterium*. See esp. Dulles' discussion of the "infallibility" issue in which he draws a strong correlation between infallibility and our concept, revelation.

Catholics might suggest that there is no one "progressive" Catholic approach at all. Experience varies widely. For example, consider three "locations" of experience: gender, religion, and race.[8] With respect to gender, Rosemary Ruether models how the experience of women trumps the tradition of the Church in her *Sexism and God-Talk*, in which she argues that women have been oppressed by the Church. In another book, she argues that "Catholic does not equal the Vatican."[9] On religious experience, Raimon Panikkar maintains a view of religious pluralism in which all religious experiences are rooted in God. In *The Experience of God*, Panikkar emphasizes the namelessness of God, which is undeniably a more progressive stance than that of the orthodox thinkers who claim the superiority of the Christian tradition.[10] Last, with respect to race, Elizabeth Johnson praises James Cone for supporting the concept of a "God who breaks chains."[11] Central to the view of God she praises is the "blackness of God," which is a version of liberation theology.[12]

Orthodox Catholic thinkers were less than enthusiastic about these progressive contextual theologies. They largely dismissed liberation approaches for imagining Christianity's founder as more as a political figure than a spiritual or theological figure.[13] Of course, many more issues could

---

8. Obviously, these are not the only "locations" one could mention. For example, Joseph Bracken's *One and the Many* discusses a dialectic between traditional and progressive insofar as he begins with Trinity and embraces *creatio ex nihilo* (both of which are traditional), but adopts a process metaphysic instead of a classical one. Or consider Metz's *Passion for God*, in which he makes a systematic case about the inability of systems to capture reality (see, esp., chs. 7, 8, and 10).

9. See Ruether, *Catholic Does Not Equal the Vatican*.

10. Here "superiority" is not meant pejoratively but rather as a specific approach to an important theological issue, namely, soteriology. The issue of pluralism is taken up in chapter 2. Spatial constraints do not allow a fuller treatment of the ways in which Panikkar's views do not align with an "orthodox" Catholic perspective; suffice it to say that Ratzinger (and others, Dulles included) do not endorse deep pluralism as a viable Christian option.

11. Johnson, *Quest for the Living God*, ch. 6.

12. See Cone, *Black Theology of Liberation*.

13. Both John Paul II and Joseph Ratzinger condemned liberation theology, even to the point of silencing some of its proponents. For example, in 1984, Ratzinger wrote "Liberation Theology" in which he argued that the Marxist underpinnings to the theology are wrongheaded. Although Ratzinger's specific targets were economic liberation proponents, his criticism applies to the racial liberation theologies as well. In 1999, John Paul II suggested that Liberation Theology exploits the disenfranchised for political goals: "No more exploitation of the weak, racial discrimination or ghettos of poverty! Never Again! Those are intolerable evils which cry out to heaven and call Christians to a different way of living, to a social commitment more in keeping with their faith." John Paul II passages were taken from the BBC online website, which are found at: www.

be added to the list of progressive Catholic foci, perhaps chief among them socioeconomic issues (a la Gustavo Gutierrez). An exhaustive explication of various strains of liberation theology is unnecessary, however, to make the general point that in the philosophical and theological adjudication of thinkers who qualify as orthodox tradition is prioritized over experience and in thinkers who qualify as progressive experience is prioritized over tradition.

Absent from the list of either "orthodox" or "progressive" Catholic thinkers is Karl Rahner, because his approach was in interesting ways both orthodox and progressive. In continuity with the tradition, Rahner held the Christian narrative in high esteem and did so by appreciating traditional sources and methods. However, Rahner also endorsed or initiated some progressive ideas that have found resonance among some philosophers of religion and theologians, e.g., the notion of "anonymous Christians" in which those of other religious persuasions could, in fact, actually be Christians. Even a progressive idea like this has roots in a deeply Christian understanding of God; it shows the lengths to which God's grace reaches. This example demonstrates the difficulty of a hybrid typological approach: while one would like neat categories into which to imagine each person, there is not always a clear delineation of the categories "orthodox" and "progressive." Rather, there are some "family resemblances" about which one can speak. Using Rahner for this study is due in part to his pioneering work in the philosophy and theology of revelation in the twentieth century, work that remains influential today.

For several reasons, orthodox Catholic thinkers make better participants in a study of revelation. First, since there is greater diversity in the

---

bbc.co.uk/religion/religions/christianity/beliefs/liberationtheology.shtml. The Church *is* called to serve the oppressed and poor, said the Pope, "but it should not do it by partisan politics, or by revolutionary violence. The Church's business was bringing about the Kingdom of God, not about creating a Marxist utopia." The real problem is *sin*, in John Paul's view, and in a sermon in Mexico in 1990 he cautioned Christians to "Be careful ... not to accept nor allow a Vision of human life as conflict or ideologies which propose class hatred and violence to be instilled in you; this includes those which try to hide under theological writings ... Jesus makes it a condition for our participating in his salvation to give food to the hungry, give drink to the thirsty, clothe the naked, console the sorrowing, because 'when you do this to one of my least brothers or sisters you do it to me (Mt. 25:30)." Ratzinger lead the "Congregation for the Doctrine of the Faith," which reacted to Liberation Theologies in the same way. Ratzinger emphasizes that *orthodoxy* precedes *orthopraxis*; right thinking precedes right action. This stands in stark contradiction to the emphases of all three versions of Liberation Theology above, which contend that a theology which does not alleviate the suffering of oppressed peoples is no theology at all. For liberation theologians, *orthodoxy* follows from and is measured by *orthopraxis*. See also "Liberation Theology" in Cross, ed., *Oxford Dictionary*, 983.

"progressive" Catholics, if they were put into conversation with one another on the issue of revelation, it is likely that they would be talking past one another. There is little commonality on which to generate a discussion between disparate, varied progressive Catholics. Second, I think Dulles is correct in his assessment of the relationship between "orthodox" and "revelation." According to Dulles,

> it is clear that from the beginning the Church meant by orthodoxy holding to the truth of revelation. The importance of orthodoxy in this sense is self-evident: Everyone by nature wants to know; the human mind craves truth. Particularly desirable is the truth of revelation, which comes from God and leads to saving union with him. Religious beliefs are right or wrong to the extent that they agree or disagree with the word of God. . . . The value of orthodoxy in [a] second sense—conformity with Church teaching—should also be clear . . . we cannot imagine that God would bestow a revelation without making provision for its preservation.[14]

Restated, the second (and third) reasons for using the "orthodox" Catholic perspective in this book are that (a) orthodox Catholicism takes more seriously than progressives that God reveals "truths" through revelation—however revelation is conceived and wherever it is found—and (b) the "orthodox" perspective provides a structure within which authentic revelation is safeguarded and/or demarcated from inauthentic revelation.

THE CONTEXT: MODELS OF REVELATION

Avery Cardinal Dulles' work on revelation addresses both its historical development[15] and its various configurations in contemporary philosophy of religion and theology.[16] In his view, "the acceptance of revelation . . . is of fundamental importance to the Christian faith."[17] He describes five "models" of revelation that have taken root in contemporary theology.[18] Dulles uses a model-based approach after seeing its utility in other theologians mentioned in the introduction (e.g., the "typological approach" in Ernst

---

14. Dulles, "The Orthodox Imperative," 31.
15. See, Dulles, *Revelation Theology*.
16. See, Dulles, *Models of Revelation*.
17. Dulles, *Models of Revelation*, 13.
18. For an excellent summary of Dulles' five models, see Ormerod, *Introducing Contemporary Theologies*, 43–46. Or, see Dulles' own summary in *Models of Revelation*, 27–28.

Troeltsch and H. Richard Niebuhr[19]). He himself had used it in his *Models of the Church*. There are five prominent models of revelation to which he devotes attention: (a) revelation as doctrine, (b) revelation as history, (c) revelation as inner experience, (d) revelation as dialectical presence, and finally (e) revelation as new awareness. To each model he poses four questions: What is the form of revelation? What is its content? What relationship does it have to salvation? And, what is the required response?

First, when revelation is conceived as *doctrine*, God is the authoritative teacher who issues "clear propositional statements,"[20] most of which come from an allegedly "inerrant" Bible for Protestants or "the official teaching of the Church"[21] for Catholics. The Protestant version of this view is often associated with conservative philosophers of religion and theologians, many of whom were influenced by the old "Princeton School" (e.g., Benjamin B. Warfield). However, it can also be found in Catholic Neo-Scholasticism from about 1850–1950.[22] Both present-day Protestant conservatives and the Neo-Scholastics agree that revelation is two-fold: on the one hand it there is natural revelation and on the other hand there is supernatural revelation; the former "is given by deeds (*per facta*)"[23] and the latter by words. Conservatives know these categories as "general" and "special" revelation. Divine revelation is a propositional matter for these thinkers: words are given that clearly contain propositional content, and this content is needed for the religious end of salvation. Among those who endorse the "revela-

---

19. Dulles' use of "a typological approach" is due in part his appreciation for Niebuhr's *Christ and Culture*. In *Models of the Church*, he notes: "The basic idea of a typological approach to theological problems came to be some years ago when pondering the problem of faith and reason with the help of H. R. Niebuhr's classic, *Christ and Culture*. I found Niebuhr's five typical visions of the relationship between Christ and human culture exceptionally stimulating and helpful. Later, when preparing a paper on ecumenism, I was struck by the realization that the various points of view on the relationship between the Church and the churches are determined, to a great extent, by the models of the Church that one is presupposing" (3). A similar approach is found in his *Models of Revelation*, wherein Dulles cites Troeltsch as a progenitor of the style and Niebuhr as its master: "Typology has been extensively used in theological literature since the epoch-making work of Ernst Troeltsch, *The Social Teachings of the Christian Churches*. The method is brought to high perfection in H. Richard Niebuhr's classic, *Christ and Culture*. . . . The method of types, as pursued by Troeltsch and Niebuhr, is extremely valuable for pointing out the issues and choices to be made and the theoretical implications of pure positions" (25). The method is not without its flaws, however, as Dulles sympathizes with Niebuhr's recognition that it risks pigeonholing individual positions. See Dulles, *Models of Revelation*, 25–26 and Niebuhr, *Christ and Culture*, 43–44.

20. Dulles, *Models of Revelation*, 27.

21. Ibid.

22. Ibid., 41.

23. Pesch, *Praelectiones dogmaticae*, 116, no. 115.

tion as doctrine" model, Christianity's sacred texts are seen as a collection of propositional statements, or at least as statements that can be propositionalized. Conservatives and Neo-Scholastics also agree on the Bible *as* revelation (interpreted as doctrine), but Neo-Scholastics add another source—tradition—which is intended to supplement or interpret the sacred texts.[24]

Second, when revelation is understood as *history*, God "reveals himself primarily in his great deeds,"[25] e.g., those found in sacred texts and Church teaching, both of which act not as revelation *per se*, but as "witnesses to revelation."[26] Two figures are given significant attention as Dulles describes this view: Oscar Cullmann and Wolfhart Pannenberg. Cullmann described a threefold process in which (a) a naked event is seen by non-believer and believer alike, (b) God discloses a divine plan through the event to a "prophet," and (c) the prophet sees the revelatory event in conjunction with other, prior revelations in the history of salvation.[27] The "prophet" is required because, in Cullmann's view, revelation is not self-interpreting. Another proponent of revelation as history—Pannenberg—disagrees with him on this point. Pannenberg goes so far as to suggest that the totality of history is divine revelation, and it moves toward an appointed consummation. The revelatory events are self-interpreting, as they carry in them the explanation of their own meaning. According to Pannenberg, when the events "are taken seriously for what they are, and in the historical context to which they belong, then they speak their own language, the language of facts."[28] For philosophers and theologians who view revelation as history, the response on behalf of the receiver should be one of faith in God's acts in history.[29]

Third, revelation is imagined by some thinkers as an *inner experience* of the divine, a "privileged interior experience of grace or communion with God"[30] that is either immediate or mediated. A number of great minds are found under this umbrella, many of whom can trace their intellectual lineage to Schleiermacher in one way or another. Dulles notes some similarities in their views. They affirm that God is at once transcendent and immanent, tend to reject the dichotomy that sometimes exists between "revealed" and "natural" religion and, similarly, they do not generally like

---

24. Dulles, *Models of Revelation*, 45.
25. Ibid., 27.
26. Ibid (emphasis removed).
27. Ibid., 56. Ideas taken from Cullmann, *Salvation in History*, 90, and summarized in Boys, *Biblical Interpretation in Religious Education*, 34–49.
28. Pannenberg, *Revelation as History*, 137. See also Pannenberg, *Faith and Reality*, 61–63. Cf. Dulles, *Models of Revelation*, 59, 294.
29. Dulles, *Models of Revelation*, 60.
30. Ibid., 27.

the sharp distinction that is often made between "special" and "general" revelation.[31] If revelation is an inner experience, A. Sabatier notes, "it will be interior because God, not having phenomenal existence, can only reveal Himself to spirit."[32] The object of divine revelation according to this model is not knowledge about God—as the "revelation as doctrine" proponents think—nor is it simply historical information—as the "revelation as history" proponents think—but rather the content is *God's own self*. Consider Sabatier again: "Let us boldly conclude, against all traditional orthodoxies, that the object of the revelation of God could only be God himself, that is to say the sense of His presence in us, awakening our soul to the life of righteousness and love."[33] Often revelation as inner experience comes unmediated, according to some of these thinkers, but occasionally it is mediated. The response of faith is "a kind of mediated immediacy."[34]

A fourth model finds the first two overly objective and the third overly subjective, and views revelation as a *dialectical presence* in which an utterly transcendent "God encounters the human subject" to simultaneously reveal and conceal the deity.[35] The proponents of this model can at times disagree quite strongly with one another, but there are some areas of commonality we can mention: (a) they tend to view God as an absolute mystery and God's revelation as mysterious; (b) therefore, revelation's content is the incarnate Word who is at once judgmental and forgiving; and (c), if divine revelation is primarily christological, it is not natural. Brunner, for instance, believed "revelation for the Christian occurs only in Christ, beside whom no other name is given,"[36] a sentiment that finds resonance in Barth[37] and Bultmann.[38] Revelation is also salvific, identified with grace, and cannot be apprehended by reason, only faith. Its form is Christ; its content is Christ; its salvific value is Christ, and the only appropriate response is first faith in Christ and then assent to propositional knowledge later (which is less important).[39]

---

31. Ibid., 71.

32. Sabatier, *Outlines of a Philosophy of Religion*, 54, in Dulles, *Models of Revelation*, 71.

33. Sabatier, *Outlines*, 47, in Dulles, *Models of Revelation*, 72.

34. Dulles, *Models of Revelation*, 77.

35. Ibid., 28.

36. Dulles, *Models of Revelation*, 87. Idea taken from Brunner, "Die Offengarung als Grund und Gegenstand der Theologie," 311–12.

37. Barth, *CD* II/1, 168. For more on this point, see von Balthasar, *Theology of Karl Barth*, 140–42.

38. Bultmann and Weiser, *Faith*, 86.

39. Dulles, *Models of Revelation*, 92–93.

Finally, revelation has been understood by some to be a *new awareness of God qua mystery*. In this model, God "is not a direct object of experience but is mysteriously present as the transcendent dimension of human engagement in creative tasks."[40] This model is also called the "consciousness" model because it changes the perception of the receiver. The form of revelation here is one of elevation: the "self" breaks through earlier stages of consciousness to more advanced ones illumined by God's presence. It is an ongoing process without a fixed content: "Past events and doctrines are revelation only insofar as they have illuminative power for the present. They are also subject to continual reinterpretation in the perspectives of contemporary awareness."[41] Proponents of this model may also, on the basis of their views of revelation as awareness instead of propositional content or historical fact, be open to the idea of salvation in other religions. Rahner, for instance, believes "the Catholic Tradition holds that grace is universally offered to mankind—before Moses and Christ, beneath explicit faith. *If grace is universal, so is revelation.*"[42]

Dulles' typology is helpful as a map on which we can place a web of philosophical and theological commitments related to revelation. Obviously, insofar as they are only models they are neither inflexible nor monolithic. Dulles says, "the typology here proposed does not rest on the assumption that [everyone] can be neatly pigeonholed within one and only one of the five types. Some of the greatest modern [thinkers] . . . have developed highly personal positions that are difficult to classify. Others combine elements from two or more different types."[43] Dulles will have something to say about each one. They all offer something valuable, even while they all fail to adequately discuss revelation for other reasons. Their merits and shortcomings are best illustrated in conjunction with his own view, to which we now turn.

DULLES ON REVELATION: SYMBOLIC MEDIATION

Dulles sets up his own view by comparing, contrasting, and evaluating the models he has presented. Although each model has much to commend it, each one is also not without its faults. He praises the propositional model for having foundations in both Christianity's sacred texts and tradition, being internally coherent, contributing to the Church's "unity and growth,"

---

40. Ibid., 28.

41. Ibid., 109.

42. This is Rahner as summarized by O'Meara, "Toward a Subjective Theology," 418 as found in Dulles, *Models of Revelation*, 107.

43. Ibid., 29.

and fostering "a lively sense of mission."[44] However, Dulles also notes that it may not be *most* faithful to the texts or tradition, for "the Bible does not seem to claim such propositional infallibility for itself."[45] Further, it cannot adequately appropriate higher criticism or experience and it may hinder dialogue with others outside the conservative fold.[46] This is the same challenged mentioned in the introduction, namely, that any constructive view of revelation today should be conversant with (or at least not hostile to) advances in other disciplines, including higher criticism.

Dulles lauds the historical model over against the propositional model for recognizing the great power of deeds, bringing to the fore underemphasized themes, organically linking historical phases in the Christian story, and being less authoritarian.[47] However, he says the historical model is based on a modern historical consciousness to which the majority of Christianity's adherents throughout two millennia had no access. It also fails when it wrongly subordinates the "word" element in Christianity's sacred texts.[48] Moreover, the historical model, says Dulles, limits "ecumenical and interreligious dialogue"[49] with those for whom history is not a central category and it risks implausibility and incoherence. For Dulles, this model has little basis on which to claim a historical resurrection (specifically in Pannenberg's version) and it assumes that divine acts are self-interpreting.[50]

Dulles commends the experiential model for reducing the need to justify all of Christianity's concepts and beliefs. He says it promotes devotion and fosters more positive attitudes to other "religions than had been customary for Christians."[51] Yet experiential orientation risks selectively using one's sacred texts to one's own ends and is prone to foster experiential elitism rather than election.[52] Dulles also criticizes it for standing in tension with Christianity's traditional teachings and offering no real wisdom or meaning to seekers. Dulles worries that the experiential model is not fully differentiated

---

44. Merits of this model are found in Dulles, *Models of Revelation*, 46–48.

45. Ibid., 48.

46. Ibid., 48–52. Ormerod amplifies this criticism by suggesting that it "fails to come to grips with the question of meaning" (*Introducing Contemporary Theologies*, 43–44). If "propositions are fixed," there is no way to encounter the changing natures of cultures. In an environment of change, "the meaning given to propositions will vary" (43) and, therefore, "one would have to say that it is hermeneutically naïve" (44).

47. Dulles, *Models of Revelation*, 61–62.

48. This criticism also found in Ormerod, *Introducing Contemporary Theologies*, 44.

49. Dulles, *Models of Revelation*, 64.

50. Ibid., 62–67.

51. Ibid., 77–78.

52. This criticism also found in Ormerod, *Introducing Contemporary Theologies*, 45.

from mere human psychology and is rather narrow in its understanding of "experience."[53]

Dulles appreciates the dialectical model for having at least some basis in Christianity's sacred texts and enabling Christian proclamation after liberalism and positivism. He also says that the dialectical model removes the "implausibility" objections from Christianity's message and recognizes that God is an absolute mystery.[54] However, both progressive and conservative orthodox thinkers alike criticized this model. Conservatives noted its circumvention of key scriptural passages or church pronouncements, and liberals contrarily faulted it for attempting to "rehabilitate the authority of Scripture and the themes of traditional dogmatics."[55] The dialectical model is further criticized for incoherence: philosophers and theologians have to speak about the ultimately ineffable God, which raises further questions about the efficacy and utility of religious language. Some Christian critics claim it does not sufficiently relate the Jesus of history with the Christ of faith, and others say it is "unfavorable to interreligious dialogue."[56]

Lastly, Dulles praises the "new awareness" or "consciousness" model for being amenable with a modern scientific and evolutionist mind and resurrecting the "life" of ancient sources today. Moreover, it sufficiently includes the human in the revelatory process and is the best of all the models at encouraging interreligious dialogue.[57] While it has much going for it philosophically, Dulles thinks "new awareness" faces theological difficulties. It strains the reliance of theology on its traditional sources (scripture and tradition),[58] is christologically and noetically reductionistic,[59] and often has

53. Dulles, *Models of Revelation*, 78–83.
54. Ibid., 93–94.
55. Ibid., 94. A related, yet distinct criticism is found in Ormerod: "As an extreme stance, its end result is fideism, i.e., faith without any ground other than the divine authority, without any reference to human reason" (*Introducing Contemporary Theologies*, 45–46).
56. Dulles, *Models of Revelation*, 94–97.
57. Praise for this model is found in Dulles, *Models of Revelation*, 110–11.
58. Ormerod restates this criticism as follows: "However, this model also underplays the 'objective' side of revelation since it denies that there is any revealed 'object.' While this may be appealing to some, it does come up against traditional concerns about the centrality of Jesus, of scripture, of Church dogmas" (*Introducing Contemporary Theologies*, 46). I would mitigate Ormerod's claim, however, by pointing out, as I do later in this chapter, that Rahner, who blends this approach with some of the other models, did not deny an "object" of revelation at all but rather recast revelation in a way so as to make it amenable with transcendental *and* subjective idealism. For Dulles' perspective on this point, see *Models of Revelation*, 99.
59. Christologically, this model risks reducing Christ "into a mere cipher for an epochal advance in human consciousness" (ibid., 112) and noetically, it seems to imply

ambivalence toward ecclesiastical authorities. This makes "it difficult to give a fully coherent account" of the position,[60] Dulles says, and it is prone to be inadequate to experience and theoretical fruitfulness.[61]

Notwithstanding their differences, which are substantial,[62] Dulles finds some common themes in the various models of revelation. Most thinkers who support one model or another would most likely agree that revelation is a free action of God to and for creatures. Revelation is also often seen as a gift beyond that of the initial creation, and (in some sense) revelation perfects creation. Revelation is the means by which God communicates not only truth concerning God but also truth about humanity's relationship to God. Humanity cannot apprehend the types of truth it gets in revelation by its own "natural" powers. Reason only goes so far, Dulles suggests. Moreover, Dulles finds that the truth in revelation is important on a "spiritual" level.

What is more, all the models agree that revelation is related in fundamental ways to the Christian religious end of salvation, even while there are revelations that have no salvific components. Of course, salvation is itself understood differently among proponents of the various models. Most of the Christian thinkers Dulles uses to present each model would likely agree that Jesus is the final, decisive, incarnate Word of God who *is* revelation. They also agree that after the preeminent revelation in Christ one needs sacred texts to access revelation (bracketing out, of course, differences in opinion on the best way to read and interpret them). Finally, most agree that revelation invites a response on behalf of its receivers, which "is usually designated by the term 'faith.'"[63] Dulles builds a definition of revelation based on what these models have in common: "Revelation is God's free action whereby he communicates saving truth to created minds, especially

---

that the "revelation given in biblical times" is insufficient; taken to its logical extreme, this model risks saying that the authors of scripture and earlier members of the tradition were too uneducated or unsophisticated to fully grasp God's revelation.

60. Ibid., 113.

61. The aforementioned criticisms of this approach are found in Dulles, *Models of Revelation*, 111–14.

62. There are significant differences in the four main areas to which Dulles posed questions: the form of revelation, the content of revelation, the ways in which it relates to salvation, and how the response of faith is imagined. These "divergences" are described in Dulles, *Models of Revelation*, 118–20, and what he perceives to be outright "contradictions" are discussed on pp. 120–22. Since this book is more interested in developing a "meta-model" that incorporates the strengths and similarities of the other models than in choosing a "side," as it were, I concentrate less on their differences and more on their similarities.

63. Ibid., 117.

through Jesus Christ as accepted by the apostolic Church and attested by the Bible and by the continuing community of believers."[64]

In consideration of the merits and pitfalls of the five models, Dulles offers his own constructive "symbolic mediation" approach.[65] According to this model, revelation "is always mediated . . . through an externally perceived sign that works mysteriously on the human consciousness so as to suggest more than it can clearly describe or define."[66] To elaborate Dulles' model, I will clarify what Dulles means by "symbol," where he finds symbolism in scripture, areas of overlap between symbolism and revelation, and examples of it.

What is a "symbol" and how does it work? Dulles differentiates "symbol" from both "indicator" and "conventional cipher" by noting that signs are pregnant "with a plenitude of meaning which is evoked rather than explicitly stated."[67] Appropriating Michael Polanyi's understanding of symbolic communication, Dulles speaks of a three step process: first, one encounters a symbol and is drawn to it; second, one surrenders to its power; third, it "carries us away, enabling us to integrate a wider range of impressions, memories, and affections than merely indicative signs could enable us to integrate."[68] There is not a clear line between the symbolic and the non-symbolic, and the sort of experience here described is participatory, not isolated or removed: "we must give ourselves" up to it.[69] A symbol can also take a variety of forms: natural (e.g., the sun), historical (e.g., David), artistic (e.g., icons), etc.[70] Dulles further distinguishes a symbol from an "analogy, myth, metaphor, allegory, parable, and ritual."[71] Analogies are often self-interpreting while symbols often require interpretation; metaphors depend on previous association with the concepts/ideas discussed; myths are wider-ranging than symbols; allegories may be "postsymbolic," and ritual is simply "symbolic or mythic narration in action."[72]

The "symbolic mediation" approach to revelation, according to Dulles, is consistent with the events in biblical history, e.g., the exodus or theophany at Sinai for the Hebrew Bible. In the New Testament, there is also extensive

---

64. Ibid.
65. Ibid., ch. IX.
66. Ibid., 131.
67. Ibid., 132.
68. Ibid..
69. Ibid., 133.
70. Ibid.
71. Ibid., 133–34.
72. Ibid.

symbolic imagery: the Spirit descending as a dove, the transfiguration, and ultimately the crucifixion itself.[73] Dulles finds that at each major "turning point," as it were, of Christian history, there is a symbolic event. He views history as a series of these "disclosure situations."[74] He also views this perspective on revelation as consistent with the pedagogical themes in the ministries of Christianity's most important people: Jesus, the prophets, and the apostles.[75] For example, the "kingdom of God" is a wide-ranging symbol that had a host of meanings for Jesus and for his followers today.[76] Dulles says that is how a symbol works: it is always doing more work than initially meets the eye, and it always suggests more than it clearly states.[77] In this process, not only was the "kingdom of God" symbol revelatory for its first hearers, but it is also revelatory for readers of Christianity's sacred texts today.

There are strong correlations between symbolic communication and revelation, notes Dulles. Four deserve mention. First, the type of knowledge gained by symbols is not distanced but rather participatory and "of a self-involving type" in which one is lured into a universe of value and meaning;[78] similarly, revelation gives the same sort of "participatory awareness."[79] Second, symbols and revelation both have transformative effects in the knower. Dulles illustrates this point using psychotherapy; there is a healing capacity when it "arouses not only thought, but delight, fear, awe, horror, and the rest."[80] Revelation similarly opens up the spiritual world.[81] Third, symbols and revelation both powerfully influence a person's behavior and commitments. Symbolism "arouses the will to consistent and committed action," which is why political and social movements usually gather under some sort of banner, flag, or anthem.[82] This is also the case with revelation, which

---

73. Ibid., 135.

74. Richardson, *History Sacred and Profane*, 223–27, in Dulles, *Models of Revelation*, 135.

75. Dulles, *Models of Revelation*, 135.

76. Ibid. Cf. Perrin, *Jesus and the Language of the Kingdom*, 33.

77. Dulles, *Models of Revelation*, 136.

78. Ibid. Cf. Mitchell, "Symbols Are Actions," 1–2: "A symbol is not an object to be manipulated through mime and memory, but an environment to be inhabited. Symbols are places to live, breathing spaces that help us discover the possibilities that life offers. . . . To put the matter succinctly, every symbol deals with a new discovery and every symbol is an open-ended action, not a closed-off object. By engaging in symbols, by inhabiting their environment, people discover new horizons for life, new values and motivation."

79. Dulles, *Models of Revelation*, 138.

80. White, *God and the Unconscious*, 233–34 in Dulles, *Models of Revelation*, 137.

81. Dulles, *Models of Revelation*, 138.

82. Ibid., 137.

fosters commitment and obedience to the divine will. Fourth, a symbol is powerful in its ability to introduce us to "realms of awareness not normally accessible to discursive thought."[83] In basic agreement with Tillich on this point, Dulles says it is a mysterious process in which a symbol "opens up levels of reality which otherwise are closed to us . . . and also unlocks dimensions and elements of our soul which correspond to the dimensions and elements of reality."[84]

Dulles gives three examples of revelation as symbolic mediation: light, the cross, and sacramental worship.[85] With respect to light, one finds the metaphor used in texts (e.g., the Word as the "light of the world" in the opening chapter of the Gospel of John). So pervasive and ubiquitous is the symbol of light in religious experience that it is recognized in other religious traditions.[86] Another example is the cross, which indicates not only the crucifixion but also the intersection of "encounter, crisis, and choice," as found in the term "crossroads."[87] It can also indicate unfavorable treatment (e.g., "being crossed"). In Christian symbolism, the cross symbolizes both evil (condemnation, suffering and death) and goodness (personal and difficult submission to God's will).[88] One also sees symbolic mediation in sacramental worship, which illustrates—as John Macquarrie points out—the whole "gamut of religious moods and emotions."[89]

In sum, each of the five models offers Dulles something valuable, and his own "symbolic mediation" approach seeks to overcome their failures while building on their strengths. The extent to which he succeeds in this endeavor will be explored below.

CATHOLICS IN CONVERSATION: RAHNER AND RATZINGER

Dulles' symbolic mediation approach can be further appreciated and elaborated when put into conversation with other Catholic thinkers. The conversation underscores the fact that there is no single "Catholic" approach to revelation but rather family resemblances among the orthodox Catholics.

83. Ibid.
84. Tillich, *Dynamics of Faith*, 42.
85. Dulles, *Models of Revelation*, 139–41.
86. Ibid., 139.
87. Ibid.
88. Dulles, *Models of Revelation*, 140.
89. Macquarrie, *Paths in Spirituality*, 73, in Dulles, *Models of Revelation*, 140.

Why explore Rahner's work on revelation? In short, Karl Rahner is often heralded as one of the greatest thinkers of the twentieth century, philosophically sophisticated and theologically faithful to his tradition. Rahner's synthesis resulted in work that was both traditional and innovative. He "has come to symbolize the Catholic Church's entry into modernity"[90] through such monumental events as the second Vatican Council. Of central importance to Rahner's work is the notion that the human creature is a starting point for philosophical and theological reflection, and using this method Rahner all but reversed Feuerbach's critique of religion, which had suggested that people project the best of themselves onto the deity. Instead, Rahner suggested that attending to the question of what it means to be human reveals an opening out toward the ultimate mysterious horizon of God, which pulls humanity ever closer into its mystery.

For Rahner, the nature of God impacts the concept of revelation. God is the being who "is immanent in the world yet precisely as such is absolutely superior to the world."[91] Any proposal of revelation must, according to Rahner, seek to synthesize these two insights. Inquiring into the nature of revelation, Rahner asserts, "is thus equivalent to asking what is the highest and most radical case of that general relationship in which the actual coming to be of the higher from the self-transcending lower is only one aspect of the one wonder of becoming and history, the other being its perpetual creation from above. Both aspects," for Rahner, "are equally true and real."[92] However, not all perspectives on God and revelation adequately maintain the balance between these two poles, and Rahner points to two unacceptable options: immanentism and extrinsicism.

Rahner was critical of views of revelation in which God's (self-)communication with humanity could be reduced to a fulfillment of human religious needs and/or based on human experience, otherwise known as *immanentism*. He criticizes modernity for this move: "For Modernism, at least in the systematized summary presented in the Church's condemnation, revelation is merely the inevitable development (immanent in history) of man's religious needs."[93] On this account, revelation is merely the expression of human needs. Reminiscent of the Feuerbachian critique of Christianity mentioned above, this view of revelation views humanity as searching for God when, in fact, there is "no one up there." This modernist tendency at first levels the religious field, as "those needs find expression in

---

90. Marmion and Hines, eds., *Cambridge Companion to Karl Rahner*, 1.
91. Rahner, "Revelation," 1460.
92. Ibid.
93. Rahner, "Revelation," 1461.

an endless variety of forms in the history of religions, and gradually to grow to greater purity and comprehensiveness until they find their expression in Judaism and Christianity."[94] This notion of revelation is problematic for Rahner because it cannot be seen as an act of God or God's grace, even if it "fits" with a modern worldview. In one of his more personal pastoral writings, Rahner spells out the implications of this understanding of revelation as he asks, "Why does God have to appoint particular bringers of revelation in addition to what is achieved by his will to save? . . . Why only one way and not many?"[95]

Rahner also avoided what some might call a "Barthian" move in revelation, namely, to suggest a measure of *extrinsicism*. In the extrinsicist view, revelation is God's act of breaking through from transcendence in concrete ways authorized by none other than God. Rahner describes this unacceptable option as follows: "This regards revelation as a divine intervention coming purely from outside, speaking to men and conveying to them through prophets truths in the form of propositions which would otherwise be inaccessible to them, and giving moral and other commands which men have to obey."[96] While this concept of extrinsic revelation is beneficial for preserving the notion of God's real communication, it is problematic for two reasons: (a) it is less amenable to a modern worldview, and more significantly (b) this type of revelation does not at first glance concern human beings. For Rahner, something about revelation has to resonate with humanity, and the extrinsicist notion of revelation fails to do that when that which is revealed is propositional information instead of God's very self.

According to Rahner, a proper perspective on the nature of God can fix this. Seeing God in the right way helps bridge this gap between these two unacceptable options; one must recognize that God is a fully immanent *and* transcendent being. Says Rahner: "These considerations make it possible to overcome in principle the barren antithesis between the immanentism of Modernism and a merely extrinsic concept of revelation."[97] A mediation between these two poles is found throughout his writings. In *Our Christian Faith*, for example, Rahner tries to "show that, in the attempt to understand the history of salvation and revelation it is ultimately possible, with all due caution and modesty, to do without a particularist model of external intervention by God in his world at particular points of space and time, without

---

94. Ibid.
95. Rahner, *Our Christian Faith*, 73.
96. Rahner, "Revelation," 1461.
97. Ibid., 1460–61.

having to interpret Christianity 'naturalistically,' in what used to be called a 'modernistic' way."[98]

Rahner believes that by differentiating two types of revelation he can successfully overcome the limitations inherent in both views. Since he imagines his work bridging the seemingly incompatible immanentist and extrinsicist views on revelation, Rahner defines revelation in a variety of ways; his goal is to show how revelation can be at once present everywhere and at all times while also being a free act of God. Concordantly, at times Rahner emphasizes the action of the transcendent God in a manner curiously not unlike Barth, who suggested that "primarily and originally the Word of God is . . . the Word that is spoken to men in revelation, Scripture, and preaching."[99] At other times, however, Rahner develops a markedly Catholic approach to revelation by emphasizing a human capacity for revelation and God's "pulling" humans, as it were, toward Godself.

The types of definitions Rahner gives to revelation fall into two categories—transcendental and categorical—both of which are necessarily joined in God's self-disclosure. The capacity to receive revelation is constitutive of what it means to be human and the transcendental revelation is "basic." However, revelation is also a reality in the categorical realm. Both of these deserve elaboration.

Rahner conceives one mode of revelation as transcendental. With respect to the human capacity for revelation, Rahner is clear that openness to God is constitutive of what it means to be human. Since transcendental inquiry looks for the "conditions for the possibility" of an issue/event, Rahner's *Hearer of the Word* is of paramount importance in explicating this aspect of revelation. In this work Rahner says unambiguously that a "condition supposed for the possibility of revelation is that human nature must possess an openness for the utterance of ultimate being in the luminous word. This openness is an *a priori* presupposition for the possibility of hearing such a word."[100] In Rahner's view, to be human is to be open to ultimate being, or God. He explicitly declares as much: "To be human is to be an absolute openness for being, or to say it in one word, the human person is spirit. . . . This is the first principle of our metaphysical anthropology."[101] In both his concise *Sacramendum Mundi* and in *Revelation and Tradition*, co-authored with Ratzinger, Rahner comments on humanity's receptivity to God's "active" revelation: humanity has a "supernaturally elevated tran-

---

98. Rahner, *Our Christian Faith*, 84.
99. Barth, *CD*, I.1, 191.
100. Rahner, *Hearer of the Word*, 41.
101. Ibid.

scendence as his permanent though grace-given existential" in which case revelation is "always and everywhere operative, present even when refused. It is the transcendental experience of the absolute and merciful closeness of God, even if this cannot be conceptually expressed at will by everyone."[102] What is more, the "thing" that is given in transcendental revelation is not propositional truths *about* God, but rather God's very self. Put plainly, "God is revealed as *communicating himself* in absolute and meaningful presence as God, that is, as absolute mystery."[103] Finally, in his *Foundations of Christian Faith* Rahner suggests that God's act of creating finite creatures functions as a "general revelation" of sorts, as it "already implies a certain disclosure of God as the infinite mystery."[104] The "transcendental experience" is such that the subject possesses "openness to the unlimited expanse of all possible reality."[105] Being human means openness to the revelation of God.

This is not to suggest, however, that divine revelation is limited to the transcendental realm or that the God revealed is perceived correctly and similarly at all times in all places. Human finitude necessitates a categorical revelation. Rahner's categorical revelation comes in history and is expressible in human speech. For Rahner the transcendental is always mediated and as such gives depth to the categorical revelation, but humans know God only in the categorical realm as the one who is infinite mystery. He says, "God's gift of himself, the gratuitously elevated determination of man, the transcendental revelation is itself always mediated categorically in the world, because all of man's transcendentality has a history."[106] On the "event" character of revelation, in his *Sacramendum Mundi* Rahner suggests that revelation is an event (compare with Barth's configuration of a three tiered revelation): "For revelation is the miracle of God's grace in an event at a particular time and place, occurring once and for all in the flesh of Christ, in the voice of the prophet as he speaks, and in the letter of Scripture."[107] Elsewhere Rahner similarly defines revelation as "an historical dialogue

---

102. Rahner, "Revelation," 1461. See also Rahner and Ratzinger, *Revelation and Tradition*, 14.

103. Rahner, "Revelation," 1461 (emphasis added).

104. Rahner, *Foundations*, 170: "If God creates something other than himself and thereby creates it as something finite, if God creates spirit which recognizes this other as finite through its transcendence and hence in view of its ground, and if therefore at the same time it differentiates this ground as qualitatively and wholly other from what is merely finite, and as the ineffable and holy mystery, this already implies a certain disclosure of God as the infinite mystery."

105. Rahner, *Foundations*, 20.

106. Ibid., 172–73.

107. Rahner, "Revelation," 1460.

between God and humanity in which something *happens*, and in which the communication is related to the continuous 'happening' and enterprise of God.... Revelation is a saving Happening, and only then, in relation to this, a communication of 'truths.'"[108] According to Rahner, this form of revelation addresses the issue of God's free decision to reveal and the ways in which this revelation concerns humanity, because "this kind of revelation not only has the character of event and is historical insofar as it is a free decision of God, and insofar as it calls for a free, historical response on the part of every person ... it [also] has a special history within universal history and within the universal history of religion."[109]

In Rahner's view, both the transcendental and categorical aspects of revelation are most fully expressed in the incarnate Word, who represents both "poles" of the revelation of God, not only the mystery revealed as such but also the reception of that revelation in the human. As the Logos became incarnate, "the history of revelation has its absolute climax when God's self-communication reaches its unsurpassable high point through the hypostatic union and in the incarnation of God in the created, spiritual reality of Jesus for his own sake, and hence for the sake of all of us."[110] Otherwise expressed, a fully human and fully divine being can represent the revealed God as mystery and the reception of that revelation. In such a being, Rahner says, "God's communication to man in grace and at the same time its categorical self-interpretation in the corporeal, tangible and social dimension have reached their climax, have become revelation in an absolute sense."[111] It is the ultimate manifestation of God, the fullest divine self-communication possible.

In Joseph Ratzinger's view of revelation, similar themes are found. In their co-authored *Revelation and Tradition* he defines it in this way: "revelation means God's whole speech and action with man."[112] The goal for which it exists is to foster union between God and humankind and between humans themselves. As such, revelation is not solely the communication *about* God, but rather *with* God, whose "purpose is not fulfilled when the greatest possible sum of knowledge has been communicated, but when through the Word love becomes visible." It's an event in which "the Word 'You' and 'You' make contact. Its meaning does not lie in a third thing, in some kind of

---

108. Rahner, *Theological Investigations I*, 48.
109. Rahner, *Foundations*, 174.
110. Ibid.
111. Rahner, *Foundations*, 174–75.
112. Ratzinger, *Revelation and Tradition*, 35.

factual knowledge, but in the partners themselves. It is called 'union.'"[113] In revelation, humanity is shown what or who humanity is and God is shown as well. By claiming union as the chief goal Ratzinger is promoting the idea that the boundaries between the human and the divine are not absolutely fixed, at least in the primary mode of revelation (more on this below).

The types of revelation vary, according to Ratzinger. Although he does not write much about a "general revelation," the concept is active in his work. For example, in his *Introduction to Christianity* he says, "however much we may rebel against proofs of the existence of God and whatever objections philosophical reflection may justifiably make to individual steps in the arguments, the fact remains that the *radiance* of the original creative idea and of its power to build does shimmer through the world and its spiritual structure."[114] This is not unlike the claim made in von Balthasar's *Glory of the Lord*, which shows revelation as "radiance from within"[115] the Godhead toward all that is not God. However, there are other distinctions that can be made in the idea of revelation as expressed in Ratzinger's theology, chief among them the "primordial" and "new" revelations of God. Ratzinger says primordial revelation means "that there occurred in the formation of subjects who would be bearers of tradition primordial realities that were beyond the native understanding of any individual."[116] These "subjects," however, are also open to "new" revelations that are "experienced in obedience by the great patriarchs, by those great ones who kept themselves open to transcendence and assured its acceptance."[117]

Like Rahner, Ratzinger is clear about one form of revelation that surpasses all others, indeed, eclipses the significance of all other revelations entirely. According to Ratzinger, "the actual reality which occurs in Christian revelation is nothing and no other than Christ himself. He is revelation in the proper sense."[118] The incarnate Word acts as a bridge between God and humanity. It bridges "the gulf between eternal and temporal, between visible and invisible, by making us meet God as a man, the eternal as the temporal, as one of us."[119] As the bridge, this form of revelation "knows itself as revelation. Its claim to be revelation is indeed based on the fact that it has, so to

---

113. Ratzinger, *Introduction to Christianity*, 198.
114. Ibid., 193 (emphasis added).
115. Von Balthasar, *GL, 1: Seeing the Form*, 20.
116. Ratzinger, *Principles of Catholic Theology*, 89.
117. Ibid., 89.
118. Ratzinger, *Revelation and Tradition*, 40.
119. Ratzinger, *Introduction to Christianity*, 27.

speak, introduced the eternal into our world."[120] The Trinity's second member reveals the First, whom no one has seen, and without this humanity would have no access to, experience of, or knowledge about the triune God. In the Hebrew Bible, for example, "there is certainly no kind of revelation of the Trinity," only "latent" indicators.[121] Christianity needed its founder to reveal God in God's tri-unity and humankind's existential situation. Jesus *qua* the preeminent revelation of God has not only philosophical significance but also an anthropological significance. God's revelation shows who and what we are. In Christ the "divine existence and human existence touch and unite," which "means at the same time that the goal attained is not a rigid boundary but an open space."[122] This concept of revelation pushes a "propositional" view of revelation to secondary status. He is explicit about this point: "In this process, the reception of individual propositions is secondary; they are only meaningful at all as ways of rendering explicit the one mystery of Christ."[123] Not only is the incarnate Word revelatory of God and humanity, but the symbol of his death is as well. The cross, in Ratzinger's view, is "truly the center of revelation, a revelation that . . . reveals us to ourselves, by revealing us before God and God in our midst."[124]

If revelation is understood primarily in christological terms, how does Ratzinger understand the revelatory function of Christian sacred texts? Interestingly Ratzinger echoes Barth, as he suggests that the Bible is a *witness to* revelation, not revelation itself. Taking only Christ as "materially sufficient,"[125] he notes that the content of the "Christ-reality . . . can be stated with greater or less explicitness, but that is ultimately not decisive, and for that reason it is quite possible for that content to be given further

---

120. Ibid., 27.

121. Ratzinger, *Introduction to Christianity*, 84. The Hebrew Bible obviously has a concept of "God" but not of God's triune nature. In Ratzinger, *Introduction to Christianity*, 79, he notes that the fathers of the Church thought Plato borrowed from the Hebrew Bible (even though it is more likely that the translators of the Bible borrowed from Platonic philosophy in Ratzinger's view). For the Fathers, it was inconceivable that one could even reach any idea of "God" if unaided by revelation; philosophy itself was insufficient to enable that leap. Ratzinger notes, however, that Israel did have a great achievement in the doctrine of God insofar as they creatively transformed the conterminous models of God's presence; Instead of a "local" deity who dwelled in a holy place (e.g., a temple or tent), Israel appropriated a "personal" deity who dwelled with a group of people. Ratzinger notes that this "sort of decision embraces gift, reception and, to that extent, revelation" (83n12).

122. Ratzinger, *Introduction to Christianity*, 199.

123. Ratzinger, *Revelation and Tradition*, 40.

124. Ratzinger, *Introduction to Christianity*, 223.

125. Ratzinger, *Revelation and Tradition*, 40: "It is only the Christ-*reality* which is 'sufficient.'"

explicit formulation *subsequent* to scripture."[126] For Ratzinger the Bible is integrally related to faith (i.e., the "reception of revelation") and Church (the community of the receivers of revelation), but it is not itself identical with revelation. Scripture "bears witness" to the "abiding reality of Christ," but not more.[127] For Ratzinger, the concept of revelation "goes beyond scripture in two respects, in relation to God and in relation to its human recipient."[128] Again, sacred texts and revelation, while related, are not identical.[129] "There can be scripture without revelation"[130] because revelation necessarily entails a response, or the reception of the revelation;[131] hence, in contradistinction to the views of many Protestant thinkers, "there can never really, properly speaking, be a *sola scriptura* in regard to Christianity."[132]

For Ratzinger, revelation is a gracious act, "superfluous" even. God was not required to get involved in the human predicament; God does so as an act of free generosity "in an incredible outpouring of himself . . . to lead man, a speck of dust, to salvation."[133] As such, revelation itself "is the superfluous and for that very reason the necessary, the divine, the love in which the meaning of the universe is fulfilled."[134]

Although revelation is central, its content, form, and structure is not easily perceivable or understood completely. Ratzinger echoes Barth on this point when he claims that part of the structure of revelation is concealment. He uses Moses as a paradigmatic example. God did not give Godself a name to differentiate Godself from the ancient gods (all of whom had names), but

126. Ibid.
127. Ibid., 41.
128. Ibid.
129. Similar themes are found in Ratzinger, *God's Word*, 51: "Scripture is the material principle of revelation . . . but is not that revelation itself. . . . This statement is not intended to mean that Scripture is merely an account, without any substance, of facts that remain entirely outside of it. Rather, . . . the view that the reality of revelation is a reality of the word—that in the word, the proclamation of the reality of revelation comes to me—should remain fully valid. It nonetheless remains true that the mere word before us, available to us, is not yet itself the reality of revelation, which is never just 'available' to us. What is said here is simply intended to point to the difference between the word and the reality that occurs within it, a difference not abolished by the nature of revelation as word."
130. Ratzinger, *Revelation and Tradition*, 36.
131. Ibid: "Revelation is in fact fully present only when, in addition to the material statements which testify to it, its own inner reality is itself operative in the form of faith. Consequently revelation to some degree includes its recipient, without whom it does not exist."
132. Ibid.
133. Ratzinger, *Introduction to Christianity*, 197.
134. Ibid., 198.

rather to do two things at once: (a) to identify Godself as the *true* and *only* God, while also (b) concealing Godself in mystery. The event of revelation "cancels out the significance of the name as a name. . . . It dissolves the name into the mystery, so that the familiarity and unfamiliarity of God, concealment and revelation, are indicated simultaneously."[135] One could also point to the Trinity's second member as modeling the revelation and concealment dynamic insofar as "the very thing which at first seems to bring God quite close to us [i.e., the incarnation of the Word] . . . also became in a very profound sense the precondition for the 'death of God.' . . . God has come so near to us that we can kill him and that he thereby, so it seems, ceases to be God for us."[136] In the incarnation, the revelation of God also involves the concealment of God. Finally, part of that concealment, which is a part of revelation, is the silence of God.[137] As Ratzinger explains the meaning of Christ's descent into hell, he says the Creed "reminds us that not only God's speech but also his silence is part of the Christian revelation. God is not only the comprehensible word that comes to us; he is also the silent, inaccessible, uncomprehended and incomprehensible ground that eludes us."[138]

CONVERGENCE, DIVERGENCE, AND TRADITION

Let us now evaluate how three perspectives given thus far—Dulles' symbolic mediation, Rahner's "transcendental and categorical" revelation, and Ratzinger's "revelation and concealment" dynamic—relate to one another. First, I will map the three views of revelation onto Dulles' taxonomy; second, I describe some similarities in the approaches; and third, I will present some tensions between the three and between Catholics and non-Catholics (particularly with respect to the utility of tradition in the revelation question).

First, each can be explored in relation to Dulles' typology. Dulles claims symbolic mediation is not necessarily a sixth model but rather a way of utilizing the best of the other five: "By recourse to symbol as a dialectical tool it [is] possible, I believe, to enrich and correct the existing models and to achieve a fruitful cross-fertilization."[139] In Rahner's case, the "inner ex-

---

135. Ratzinger, *Introduction to Christianity*, 87.

136. Ibid., 28.

137. Otherwise expressed, silence is part of concealment and concealment is part of revelation; therefore, silence is part of revelation.

138. Ratzinger, *Introduction to Christianity*, 225.

139. Dulles, *Models of Revelation*, 128. Elsewhere, Dulles contends "that the symbolic approach, properly understood, can incorporate what is valid in the five models and at the same time correct what is misleading in them. These models, in turn, can contribute to the symbolic theory by further explicating what is required for symbol to

perience" and "new awareness" models fit him well. Revelation is an "inner experience" due to the internal capacity of the human for revelation and it is "new awareness" insofar as it enables "creatures to achieve a higher level of consciousness."[140] Interestingly, in Ratzinger's case the doctrinal view is less present than the dialectical and new awareness models. God's revelation is a dialectic between revelation and concealment (indeed, concealment is part of the revelatory process for Ratzinger), and it fits the "new awareness" approach to the extent that humans are seen as playing a part in the process through faith (which he understands to be the reception of the revelation).

Second, there are points of convergence between these three thinkers. Most significantly, Dulles, Rahner, and Ratzinger all suggest that revelation is the process, event, or means by which God communicates Godself. The three seem to be united in opposition to a strictly propositional view, according to which *information* is most important. This places the three in tension with some strands of conservative thought in which salvation consists in cognitive assent to a series of propositions and revelation is the communication of these propositions, most often in sacred texts. Although Dulles may be the more amenable to the propositional view than Rahner and Ratzinger (as evidenced by his work in apologetics), he is clear about his commitment to seeing revelation as primarily divine self-communication. Each of these thinkers agrees that God's very self is communicated primarily; information is secondary. This is understandable, however, given the second area of commonality: the incarnate Word as the preeminent form of revelation. Whereas Rahner discusses the "logos as unsurpassable" and Dulles and Ratzinger use "Christ" language more, the point is the same: however and wherever revelation is to be found, it is *most* (if not exclusively) found in Christianity's founder.[141] Furthermore, all three retain a healthy respect for the mystery of both the revelatory process and the content of revelation. Again, it is expressed in different ways, but none of the three suggests that what is revealed is God in God's absolute and unmediated essence. For Dulles, the symbols mediate; for Rahner, transcendental revelation always occurs in the categorical realm; and for Ratzinger, revelation includes a measure of concealment.

---

be truly revelatory" (Dulles, *Models of Revelation*, 141).

140. Ibid., 100.

141. See, e.g., Ratzinger, *Introduction to Christianity*, 198. Here Ratzinger quotes Rahner: "In the man Jesus, God has once and for all uttered himself: he *is* his Word and, as his Word, himself. Revelation does not end here because God deliberately puts an end to it, but because it has reached its goal; as Karl Rahner puts it, 'Nothing fresh is said, not in spite of there being still much to say, but because everything is said, indeed everything is given, in the Son of love in whom God and the world have become one.'"

Third, there are some tensions in these three approaches, some internal to these three thinkers and some when they are put into conversation with non-Catholics. Evangelical conservatives could press Dulles on whether his dismissal of the propositional approach is entirely consistent with some of his other philosophical and theological commitments. For example, Dulles criticizes the doctrinal approach for not most fully representing the material in the sacred texts; recall that he wondered whether scripture actually makes claims to infallibility. A propositionalist could bring up the issue of papal infallibility, asking whether the texts authorize any one human as having infallibility. The propositionalist will suggest that the stories found in the pages of their texts more often than not portray humanity as ignorant, sinful, and finite. The propositionalist will argue that contemporary views of revelation must protect it from the undue influence of tradition while at the same time creating a space for tradition inside it. Dulles gives insufficient attention to the potential of tradition to lead one astray in his defense of the infallibility of the magisterium.

Another tension one finds in these views of revelation has to do with the role of humanity in the revelatory process. Rahner suggested that revelation is present even when refused by the human, which justifies his notion of the "anonymous Christian."[142] This differs from the implication of Ratzinger's perspective in which revelation includes the recipient as part of the revelatory process. If revelation includes the recipient, it cannot be present when refused. With respect to "saving" revelation, Dulles would agree with Ratzinger on this point. In a November 20, 2002 lecture at Fordham University, "The Population of Hell,"[143] Dulles argues that "the constant teaching of the Church supports the idea that there are two classes: the saved and the damned."[144] If there are those who are damned, then there are those whom saving revelation does not reach. So it seems on the issue of who receives revelation, there is a discrepancy in these thinkers. This signals a need for contemporary models of revelation to posit a difference between revelations with soteric significance and those with non-soteric significance.

A final tension is related to the previous point, namely, that Dulles and Rahner have different understandings of the recipient's participation in the revelation. For Dulles, revelation was a participatory thing; it occurs from within, as "we must not be detached observers but engaged participants."[145] To the extent that Rahner's non-Christian (i.e., an anonymous Chris-

---

142. Rahner, *Theological Investigations*, vol. 6, 391–93.
143. Dulles, *Church and Society*, 387–400.
144. Ibid., 390.
145. Dulles, *Models of Revelation*, 133.

tian) participates in a world with various symbols, s/he will be unable to participate as an "insider" in the world of Christian symbols, in Dulles' view. Rahner might respond by noting that the revelation is there for the non-Christian and, consequently, the non-Christian *is* participating in it. Dulles would most likely not accept that a person is unknowingly participating in one symbolic world (the Christian world with its symbols of the cross, the Church, the Eucharist, etc.) when one is actively and knowingly participating in a quite different one.

LINGERING QUESTIONS

In sum, this chapter has explored the concept of revelation as understood by Avery Dulles, an explicitly orthodox Catholic philosopher and theologian, Joseph Ratzinger, a "teacher and guardian of the faith," and Karl Rahner, a monumental thinker with orthodox tendencies. After giving Dulles' typology of the "models of revelation," I showed how his "symbolic mediation" approach sought to mine all five models for their best and while avoiding their pitfalls. Moreover, we discussed how Rahner saw his view of revelation in both the transcendental and categorical realms as bridging the two unacceptable options of immanentism and extrinsicism. We also showed how Ratzinger maintains a view of revelation in which God is at once revealed and concealed. Last, there were some areas of agreement and disagreement, the latter of which gestures toward some questions a contemporary model of revelation must answer.

The preceding analysis invites further reflection, and the questions that linger are numerous. Although it is not the subject of this chapter or the book as a whole, what if the scope were broadened to include Catholics whose work could be considered progressive? Would revelation even be a major theme in their writings? Could more be said about the ways in which revelation relates to tradition, and does the fallibility of tradition change what one can say about how revelation happens? Is revelation always mediated, as Dulles suggests, or does it provide unmediated access to God or one's role in the larger narrative of God's workings in the world? How is revelation related to many other traditional systematic loci, in particular the three themes of creation, redemption, and consummation? Another question emerges from one of the other interlocutors, conservative Bernard Ramm. In some evangelical traditions, concepts of revelation are changing in ways that correlate to changes in the understanding of distinctively Christian religious ends, viz., salvation. Could such a correlation also exist in contemporary orthodox Catholic thinking? In short, what is the relation between gospel and revelation? Is it dialectical? Finally, and most importantly, does the category of "symbol" hold promise for revelation today among non-Catholics? If so, how? The three perspectives on revelation presented here raise these questions and many others, and they all will be fruitful avenues of further reflection in the constructive portion of this book.

At the close of this chapter, one can appreciate a common element in the views of revelation advocated by Dulles, Rahner, and Ratzinger, namely, the inability of God to be absolutely "pinned down" in human constructs. While it is true that revelation acts as the bridge from God to humanity, these three thinkers argue that we cannot—indeed, *must* not—think that it provides unmediated access to the inner life or essence of God. Anything other than mediation is thought to trivialize the significance of the Word's incarnation. Rahner himself maintained a Thomistic approach that respected the limitations of what one can and cannot know, and he sought to make clear that God is known precisely *as* a mystery. To view God as fully comprehensible is to idolize that which was thought to be God. Nothing can express God's absolute and unmediated essence.[146] This remains a great strength of these approaches with loyalty to Rome: the preservation of the mysterious element in and of the divine presence. In Ratzinger's words, "Revelation cannot be pocketed like a little book one carries around. It is a living reality which calls for the living man as the location of its presence."[147] Dulles, the primary focus of this chapter, is perhaps the clearest on the ineffability of God and revelation:

> Theological systems, with the help of theoretical models, illuminate certain aspects of a reality too complex and exalted for human comprehension. A given system, even though correct in what it affirms, will inevitably fall short of fathoming the mystery of the divine being or the divine activity. The classical [orthodox] theological tradition, with its doctrine of analogy, has consistently maintained this position. Revelation, as a divine mystery, surpasses all that theology can say about it.[148]

---

146. This is an area in which the Catholic thinkers are strong, and it is an area in which one of the postconservative evangelical thinkers I discuss—Stanley Grenz—is mistaken. Grenz is going to mention how revelation provides access to God's essential nature, whereas the Catholic thinkers are wise to remain Thomistic about this by saying we cannot know God's unmediated essence.

147. Ratzinger, *Revelation and Tradition*, 36.

148. Dulles, *Models of Revelation*, 32.

CHAPTER 2

The External Word
The Yale School and Revelation

LOOKING FORWARD

The second figure useful in our construction of an intellectually defensible and contemporary view of revelation is George A. Lindbeck, longtime professor at Yale University. Along with Hans Frei, Lindbeck is often considered a "founding father" of postliberalism.[1] The Yale School is not normally considered in conjunction with the revelation question, but its perspective needs to be heard. A short story illustrates why.

In 1995, evangelical flagship institution, Wheaton College, hosted a conference in which postliberals and evangelicals gathered to discuss areas of overlap, points of divergence, and paths for future inquiry.[2] The conference resulted in a book that includes a series of essays on this topic: *The Nature of Confession: Evangelicals and Postliberals in Conversation*. The papers delivered at this conference are fascinating, but one thing in particular is noteworthy for the purposes of this book, an event that occurred toward the end of the conference. The final session of the day was a panel discussion between George Lindbeck, Alister McGrath, Gabriel Fackre, and George Hunsinger. The last exchange between them concerned the issue of Christian particularity vis-à-vis the world's other religions, a topic on

---

1. Phillips and Okholm, *Nature of Confession*, 15.
2. Grenz and Franke, *Beyond Foundationalism*, ix.

which many philosophers of religion have had something to say. The two conservatives in attendance pressed Lindbeck for a reason why a person should choose Christianity instead of Islam. Lindbeck gave his answer, which is discussed below, but as they were all getting up from the table to leave, Lindbeck surprised those in attendance with an unexpected comment. He declared, "if the sort of research program represented by postliberalism has a real future as a communal enterprise of the church, it's more likely to be carried on by evangelicals than anyone else."[3]

Comments such as these have prompted conservatives to respond to Lindbeck's challenge by beginning to take up the mantle of postliberal theology in a postmodern context.[4] These sentiments also motivate evangelicals to mine postliberal theology for what it might offer philosophy of religion and theology today. This is precisely the case with this book.

This chapter does a number of things. First, it discusses the difficulty in defining what "postliberal" means and who qualifies as one. Second, it describes Lindbeck's context, the liberalism to which he and Hans Frei were responding. Third, after noting some postliberal family resemblances, the chapter explores Lindbeck's view of religion in general and revelation specifically, noting a distinction he makes between the *verbum internum* and *verbum externum*. Fourth, Lindbeck is put into conversation with two other postliberal thinkers, his "co-father" Hans Frei and one of his students, Ronald Thiemann. Finally, Lindbeck's view on revelation is evaluated with the help of some of his interpreters, especially on the implications of his view for proposals of religious pluralism.

DEFINING POSTLIBERALISM

Postliberalism, like Catholicism, resists easy categorization. Surely "postliberal" means "after" or "beyond" liberalism to some degree, but in what sense? In the past twenty-five years, this question has not been easily answered. A conversation hosted by the *Christian Century* illustrates the difficulty in defining postliberalism. James Gustafson asked, "Just what is 'postliberal' theology?"[5] In the next issue, William Placher answered Gustafson's question: "'Postliberalism' is the school of theology shaped by Hans Frei, George Lindbeck and some of their friends and students—also called 'the Yale school,' or 'narrative theology.'"[6] Gustafson was not satisfied with

---

3. Lindbeck, "A Panel Discussion," 253.
4. See, for instance, Grenz and Franke, *Beyond Foundationalism*.
5. Gustafson, "Just What Is 'Postliberal' Theology?," 353–55.
6. Placher, "Being Postliberal," 390.

this answer, and in the following issue presses Placher for more: "Placher missed what I asked for in seeking a definition[;] . . . a genealogy of any movement, theological, political, or scientific, does not define it."[7] Indeed, one has as difficult a time defining postliberalism as one does defining liberalism. George Hunsinger claims that "at best [the word 'postliberal'] represents a loose coalition of interests, united more by what it opposes or envisions than by any common theological program."[8] James Fodor suggests the individual thinkers are varied; they "are thus not finally reducible to 'postliberalism'—which is to underscore its character as 'a radical movement within a larger tradition.'"[9]

Be that as it may, Fodor[10] proceeds to outline some family resemblances in postliberal thinkers, some of which are found in Lindbeck's seminal 1984 monograph, *The Nature of Doctrine: Religion and Theology in a Postliberal Age*. These similarities include (a) the retrieval of tradition,[11] (b) attention to the context, (c) a narrative hermeneutic, (d) a linguistic method, (e) the regulative application of doctrine, (f) openness to other religious expressions, i.e., ecumenism, (g) performative, nonfoundational epistemology, (h) kerygmatic instead of apologetic tone, and (i), *ad hoc*, non-systematic responses to critics.[12]

In short, postliberalism is not a monolithic enterprise. However, there were major works leading up to Lindbeck's systemization of its central tenets[13] and its proponents share these common commitments. Three in particular deserve elaboration: (a) anti-foundationalism, (b) communitarianism, and (c) particularism or historicism. First, the postliberal project rejects the idea that there is a common epistemological foundation upon which one builds other claims; this is in contradistinction to the way conservatives apply sacred texts and liberals universalize human experience. Rather, Lindbeck notes that intelligibility—the goal for which foundationalism arose in the

---

7. Gustafson, "Liberal Questions," 422.

8. Hunsinger, "Postliberal Theology," 42.

9. Fodor, "Postliberal Theology," 229.

10. Ibid.

11. This aspect of postliberalism is so important that in "Theologies of Retrieval" John Webster considers it an appropriate heading for theologies like postliberalism. Cf. Lindbeck, *The Nature of Confession*, 221: "The atonement is discussed in this essay as an illustration of the thesis that premodern hermeneutics better accommodates differences without disunity than is possible in modern modes of interpretation, whether liberal or conservative. In the light of this and other considerations, it is argued that the retrieval of classical hermeneutics in a form suitable to the present is both possible and desirable."

12. Werpehowski, "Ad Hoc Apologetics," 282–301.

13. See, e.g., Frei's *Eclipse of Biblical Narrative* and Fackre, *Christian Story*.

first place—comes *not* from accepting universal foundations. Intelligibility comes from "skill, not theory" and "credibility comes from good performance, not adherence to independently formulated criteria."[14] Second, at variance with the modern preoccupation with the individual, Lindbeck says postliberalism is more social in nature. Religion is seen as "a communal phenomenon that shapes the subjectivity of individuals rather than being primarily a manifestation of those subjectivities."[15] Third, related to the idea of human social and communal existence is the postliberal emphasis on identity formation in the context of particular and historical communities: "Humans . . . receive their identity and experience reality within communities that live out of inherited understandings of life. Their overarching interpretations or world views are not interchangeable or reducible to one another and neither is the experience that occurs within them."[16]

The influence of Wittgenstein's philosophy on postliberal thinkers is quite obvious. Wittgenstein had said that language functions in a number of ways in different situations.[17] Language has plasticity similar to a dynamic city, "a maze of little streets and squares, of old and new houses, and of houses with additions from various periods; and this is surrounded by a multitude of new boroughs with straight regular streets and uniform houses."[18] Philosophy for Wittgenstein (and theology for postliberal thinkers) is a descriptive enterprise—it shows the ways language functions in communities—and the rules of thought in those communities are like "language games."[19]

Wittgenstein gives several examples that postliberals would embrace. Three will suffice: the beetle box,[20] the duck/rabbit figure,[21] and the last judgment.[22] With respect to the beetle box, Wittgenstein wonders whether people can generalize or universalize the experience of pain. He explains that each person has a box that contains what everyone refers to as a "beetle." People cannot see what others have in their box, only what is in their own. So, ultimately there's no way of knowing what people mean by saying that they, too, have a "beetle" in their box. Another example is the duck/

---

14. Lindbeck, *Nature of Doctrine*, 131.
15. Ibid., 33.
16. Davaney and Brown, "Postliberalism," 455.
17. Wittgenstein, *Philosophical Investigations*, 42e.
18. Ibid., 7e.
19. Ibid., 43e.
20. Ibid., §293.
21. Ibid., 166e.
22. Wittgenstein, *Lectures and Conversations*.

rabbit figure, a sketch that looks like either a duck or rabbit depending on the perception of the viewer. Those who view the image as a duck see a beak to the right and the head to the left whereas those who view it as a rabbit see ears to the left and a head to the right. Of course, others will say that there is a third "thing" that the object really is, independent of the viewer's interpretation. For Wittgenstein, however, there is in actuality no third thing. One final example, which is more apropos to religious discussion, is not found in the *Philosophical Investigations* but rather in his "Lectures on Religious Belief." Wittgenstein presents a conversation between one person who says, "I believe in an afterlife," and Wittgenstein, who reflects on how he could respond. He ends up concluding that different "languages" are used: "In a religious discourse we use such expressions as: 'I believe that so and so will happen,' and use them differently to the way in which we use them in science." He also says, "I think differently, in a different way. I say different things to myself. I have different pictures."[23]

These three examples drive home a central point for Wittgenstein, and a similar sort of thinking is found in postliberalism. The point is this: there is only so far one can go into questions such as these. We cannot explain ourselves completely to members of different communities who utilize different language games. One cannot go deeper in these instances; one reaches the "bedrock," and has to admit, "This is simply what I do."[24] In Wittgenstein's view, one cannot escape subjectivity, so he seeks to reformulate the question according to patterns of life, or "language games." Language and words function in individuals and communities differently, so ultimately there is no return to objectivity; indeed, it is lost. Postliberals attempt to pick up the pieces in philosophy of religion and theology in light of this loss of objectivity.

THE CONTEXT: THEOLOGICAL LIBERALISM

Although he is an historical theologian by training, George Lindbeck will be remembered most for his unique role in the development of this postliberal school of thought, a movement with important and lasting effects in philosophy of religion and theology. The impetus for postliberalism was, in a very real sense, an effort to move beyond the assumptions, methodologies, and conclusions of liberalism. Liberal theology is the context out of which postliberalism grew and the approach to which it responded. Like Catholicism

---

23. Wittgenstein, "Lectures on Religious Belief," 55.
24. Wittgenstein, *Philosophical Investigations*, 72e; 44e.

and postliberalism, liberalism "is notoriously difficult to define,"[25] and so the best one can hope for is to corral some family resemblances and try to find a trajectory.

Themes developed by three thinkers help describe it: Schleiermacher, Ritschl, and Tillich. First, in *On Religion: Speeches to its Cultured Despisers*, Schleiermacher asserted the primary of experience in his explication of the scope of religion, an internal intuition of the divine: "How then are you to name this . . . series of feeling? What life will it form? [Answer:] The religious. . . . The chief point in my Speech is now uttered. This is the peculiar sphere which I would assign to religion."[26] Second, if feeling is that which reveals the deity, then sacred texts, traditionally held as a standard on which theologies were based, are no longer operative to the highest extent in philosophical and theological adjudication. The primacy of texts is usurped by not only religious feeling/intuition but also ethical considerations and, as noted by Albrecht Ritschl, the "apostolic circle of ideas" discerned through solid historical research.[27] Third, liberalism can be characterized by a specific desire to make faith palatable to secular audiences; that is, liberalism has an apologetic impulse. Paul Tillich said his work was "an attempt to correlate the questions implied in the [cultural] situations with the answers implied in the [Christian] message. . . . It correlates questions and answers, situation and message, human existence and divine manifestation."[28]

Although more hallmarks of the liberal tradition could be mentioned, these three—the primacy of experience, reliance upon extra-textual material, and apologetic impulse—are characteristic of many of the liberal tendencies to which Lindbeck responded. He explicitly mentions them as constitutive of liberalism in *The Nature of Doctrine*. First, in his discussion of "the problem of assessment," Lindbeck mentions "the liberal commitment to the primacy of experience,"[29] and as he discusses judgments in terms of eschatological "faithfulness and accountability" he notes the following: "Liberals start with experience, with an account of the present, and then adjust their vision of the kingdom of God accordingly."[30] In fact, his repudiation of the "experiential-expressivist" approach itself betrays his commitment to replacing liberalism with his own "postliberal" perspective.[31] Second, on

---

25. Grenz and Olson, *20th Century Theology*, 51.
26. Schleiermacher, *On Religion*, 45.
27. Ritschl, *Christian Doctrine*, 282.
28. Tillich, *Systematic Theology*, vol. 1, 8.
29. Lindbeck, *Nature of Doctrine*, 113.
30. Ibid., 125–26.
31. See, e.g., *Nature of Doctrine*, 135, note 1: "[W]hat I have in mind postdates the

modernity's use of sources beyond sacred texts, Lindbeck suggests that with the exception of a brief neo-orthodox interlude, "the liberal tendency to redescribe religion in extrascriptural frameworks has once again become dominant."[32] Third, on the issue of liberalism's apologetic impulse, Lindbeck notes that the "liberal program is in one sense accommodation to culture, but it is often motivated by missionary impulses no less strong than those which send Wycliffe evangelicals overseas to translate the Bible into aboriginal languages."[33] Or, otherwise expressed, liberalism has an "apologetic focus on making religion more widely credible" as liberal foundationalists "identify the modern questions that must be addressed, and then . . . translate the gospel answers into a currently understandable conceptuality."[34]

So how did Lindbeck understand religion and revelation in light of these liberal tendencies? How did he seek to get beyond it? It is to Lindbeck's understanding of religion and revelation that this chapter now turns.

LINDBECK ON RELIGION AND REVELATION

Religion for Lindbeck is neither about cognitive assent to a body of philosophical propositions nor a matter of giving voice to universally recognized human experience. Religion is, rather, organizing bodies of beliefs and practices that function in particular ways in particular communities. In the recent edition of *The Nature of Doctrine*, Lindbeck retains this view of religion: "Religions are universal or 'comprehensive interpretive schemes' centered on that which is taken to be 'more important than everything else in the universe,' and [used in] organizing all of life, including both behavior and beliefs."[35]

With respect to revelation, *The Nature of Doctrine* elaborates on some key themes that provide Lindbeck's understanding of the issue, prominent among them his comments on the *verbum externum* and *verbum internum*. For Lindbeck, religion is

> above all an external world, a *verbum externum*, that molds and shapes the self and its world, rather than an expression of thematization of a preexisting self or of preconceptual experience. The *verbum internum* (traditionally equated by Christians with the action of the Holy Spirit) is also crucially important,

experiential-expressivist approach which is the mark of liberal method."
32. Ibid., 124.
33. Ibid., 129.
34. Ibid., 130, 132.
35. Lindbeck, "Afterword," 132.

but it would be understood in a theological use of the model as a capacity for hearing and accepting the true religion, the true external world, rather than (as experiential-expressivism would have it) as a common experience diversely articulated in different religions.[36]

In passages such as these, Lindbeck demonstrates his heritage in explicating the mediation of grace (as Luther did during the Reformation). For Lindbeck the mediation of grace is assured "not through introspection, but by turning to the *verbum externum* of the gospel."[37] It is clear that the referent of Lindbeck's "experientialist-expressivism" is liberalism, beyond which he hoped postliberalism would move. Moreover, it is also clear that Lindbeck is skeptical of the ability of one to find revelation in liberal emphases on the aforementioned "preexisting self or [in] preconceptual experience." Instead, Lindbeck sides with Luther (and Barth) insofar as he embraces an incarnate Word "available in the preached Word and the sacraments."[38] He suggests that the postliberal project is not so different from Aquinas and Luther on the issue of revelation and its place in philosophy of religion and theology:

> Both these thinkers . . . can be viewed as holding that revelation dominates all aspects of the theological enterprise, but without excluding a subsidiary use of philosophical and experiential considerations in the explication and defense of the faith. Similarly, a postliberal approach need not exclude an ad hoc apologetics, but only one that is systematically prior and controlling in the fashion of post-Cartesian natural theology and of later liberalism.[39]

If revelation is understood less as a matter of turning inward and more of the *verbum externum*, i.e., the external world of the incarnate Word and proclamation, what does Lindbeck say of a typically cited instantiation of "special" revelation, namely, sacred texts? Although the postliberal project draws heavily on some Barthian elements, the role of texts in religion and theology is one in which they depart. Whereas Barth held that scripture (and preaching) are derivative revelations of God's paramount revelation in the incarnate Word, Lindbeck suggests that Christianity's sacred texts are more like a world that provides meaning and interpretive tools for its readers. For Lindbeck and other postliberals, scripture "shapes our imaginations,

---

36. Lindbeck, *Nature of Doctrine*, 34.
37. Mangina, *Karl Barth*, 53.
38. Ibid.
39. Lindbeck, *Nature of Doctrine*, 131–32.

giving us a set of categories by which to interpret ourselves and the world ... creating its own privileged domain of meaning."[40] Or, in Lindbeck's famously asserted words, the Christian Bible is "able to absorb the universe" as it "supplies the interpretive framework within which believers seek to live their lives and understand reality."[41]

Lindbeck retained this view as time went on, and his former colleagues embrace it as well. A decade after *The Nature of Doctrine* was published, Lindbeck still argued for the contextual nature of revelation and how it functions in missionary and evangelistic settings. His words, similar to Wittgenstein's philosophy of language above, can be taken as a critique of philosophical argument intended to convert others:

> There is no single logic of coming [to faith]. There is a logic of belief. There is a structure of Christian faith. But the ways in which God calls us through the Holy Spirit to come to believe are so varied that you cannot possibly make generalizations. I would add: people are inevitably committed to working within a given conceptual cultural language system. We Christians think, look and argue from within the faith. There's no way of getting outside the faith to objectively compare different options.[42]

Nearly three decades after the first edition of his *Nature of Doctrine*, Lindbeck still argued that sacred texts give "privileged though rudimentary access to the ultimate interpretive framework, God's vision of the whole, which embraces all times and places. Changes in landscape and worldviews occur within believers' Scripture-dependent outlook, which, precisely because it is textually inscribed, remains basically unchanged."[43] One of Lindbeck's former colleagues, David Kelsey, still uses scripture in this way, as evidenced by his reflections on the doctrine of God in the 2011 Warfield Lectures at Princeton Theological Seminary[44] and his 2009 theological anthropology, *Eccentric Existence*.[45]

Lindbeck views revelation as part of the broader category of religion, so elucidating his views of revelation will include his view of propositional truth and adjudication, Christian particularly and salvation, and the issue of pluralism. One of the most difficult tasks of any view of revelation is to

---

40. Mangina, *Karl Barth*, 54.
41. Lindbeck, *Nature of Doctrine*, 117. Cf. pp. 116–21.
42. Lindbeck, "A Panel Discussion," 252.
43. Lindbeck, "Afterword," 135.
44. In particular, Kelsey describes his approach to scripture in the first three lectures.
45. Kelsey, *Eccentric Existence*, 132–58.

judge between competing putative revelations. Lindbeck's approach proves instructive.

The questions of truth and pluralism—so popular among philosophers of religion who hold a foundationalist epistemology—are closely related. It seems reasonable that "truth" claims, multifaceted as they are, must at some level have propositional content if they are to be useful tools for interreligious dialogue. As Lindbeck himself says, "If we are to do justice to the actual speech and practice of religious people, we must . . . not simply allow for the possibility that a religion may be categorically as well as symbolically or expressively true; we must also allow for its possible propositional truth."[46] It seems fitting, then, to give Lindbeck's account of truth claim adjudication, explore how these methodological comments impact various religious traditions, and present Lindbeck's amenability with proposals of religious pluralism.

For Lindbeck, there are two types of religious truth claims: "intrasystematic" and "ontological." The former is primarily a matter of internal coherence: "Utterances are intrasystematically true when they cohere with the total relevant context, which, in the case of a religion when viewed in cultural-linguistic terms, is not only other utterances but also the correlative forms of life."[47] Claims must cohere with other claims the members of a community make, as well as the practices and rituals that community performs. A claim is verified by its correlation to the material and lived patterns in the rest of the system. Moreover, it cuts both ways; claims are falsified when a certain proposition or form of life is contradictory with another proposition or action *in the system*. This first type of "truth" is not limited to religious inquiry, as "coherence is necessary for truth in nonreligious as well as religious domains."[48] Lindbeck stresses that this is not limited to philosophical propositions, for praxis can be consistent or inconsistent with the systematic framework of belief as well. Cognitive-propositional accounts of religion "cannot be detached from a particular way of behaving."[49]

Intrasystematic coherence is a necessary, yet insufficient criterion for a religious truth claim; one also needs the criterion of ontological correspondence to reality. A claim "is ontologically true if it is part of a system that is itself categorically true (adequate)."[50] Here, "adequacy" refers to categories

---

46. Lindbeck, *Nature of Doctrine*, 63.
47. Ibid., 64.
48. Ibid.
49. Ibid.
50. Ibid., 65.

"which can be made to apply to what is taken to be real."[51] Ultimately, however, Lindbeck only affirms "performance-propositional" truth claims, i.e., those in which the assertion affects positive behaviors commensurate with that which is being affirmed.[52] Again, recall the influence of Wittgenstein and his semantic delineations.[53] As Wittgenstein had noted, one eventually reaches bedrock; "this is simply what I do." Religious sentences merely "acquire enough referential specificity to have first-order or ontological truth or falsity only in determinate settings."[54] Lindbeck is quite clear on whether systematic theology is able to produce ontologically meaningful and true statements: "Here, in contrast to the common supposition, one rarely if ever succeeds in making affirmations with ontological import, but rather engages in explaining, defending, analyzing, and regulating the liturgical, kerygmatic, and ethical modes of speech and action within which such affirmations from time to time occur."[55] Put another way, doctrinal speech is useful for Christians, but it has little impact on questions of ontological truth and the impact of those questions on non-Christians. And revelation, Lindbeck might assert, is contextual like this.

If religious truth claims are not strong claims of the propositional sort, this raises the question of whether Lindbeck is willing to accord the Christian tradition any type of ontological uniqueness or particularity. The twentieth century was replete with thinkers asserting that God's revelation is absolutely unique; revelation was often thought of as synonymous with person of Jesus Christ.[56] Lindbeck, however, suggests that Christianity is governed by its own set of language rules and communal practices while making no universal or absolute claims regarding the tradition's sole validity. In his own words, "The theological and doctrinal uses of, e.g., 'Christ is Lord' are important . . . but they are not propositional."[57] Not only are they non-propositional, but also they are not useful unless they correspond to re-

---

51. Ibid., 48.

52. Ibid., 67.

53. Ibid., 69: "Just as grammar by itself affirms nothing either true or false regarding the world in which language is used, but only about language, so theology and doctrine, to the extent that they are second-order activities, assert nothing either true or false about God and his relation to creatures, but only speak about such assertions. These assertions, in turn, cannot be made except when speaking religiously, i.e., when seeking to align oneself and other performatively with what one takes to be most important in the universe by worshipping, promising, obeying, exhorting, preaching." See also ibid., 48–52.

54. Ibid., 68.

55. Ibid., 69

56. See Barth, Rahner, Ratzinger, and Ramm on this point.

57. Lindbeck, *Nature of Doctrine*, 68.

ligious practices. Lindbeck is not describing ultimate or absolute reality, and the difference between the cognitivist and the cultural-linguistic approach is primarily one of location in which "they are located on quite different linguistic strata."[58] The cultural-linguistic approach places a higher value on religious life and Christian practice rather than cognitive propositional approaches, for "propositional truth and falsity characterize ordinary religious language when it is used to mold lives through prayer, praise, preaching, and exhortation. It is *only* on that level that human beings linguistically exhibit their truth or falsity, their correspondence or lack of correspondence to the Ultimate Mystery."[59] In short, to the extent that the Christian tradition entails a set of religious truth claims it is neither uniquely nor objectively valid at all; it is merely one set of beliefs and practices among many.

Lindbeck offers us some helpful tools for understanding revelation today, tools that will be elucidated in chapter 4, but he lacks a basis on which to defend a distinctively *Christian* view of revelation. Ironically, he does not believe non-Christian religions have their own unique or valid religious ends, but rather he suggests they are subsumed under Christian religious end of salvation. In his writing beyond *The Nature of Doctrine*, Lindbeck proposes a "primarily futuristic eschatological theory" which he also calls "the futuristic *fides ex auditu* approach." In this eschatologically oriented perspective, "everyone will be explicitly offered salvation in the future."[60] He claims this view is "harmonized with Scripture" while also encouraging "Christian modesty and openness to dialog with, rather than proselytizing of, other religions."[61] He further asserts that his eschatological soteriology is "capable of maintaining the Christian imperative to preach the gospel to all creatures."[62] How these two seemingly irreconcilable differences—the imperative to proclaim Christianity to others and the lack of the tradition's particularity—can coexist is insufficiently defended.

What is more, Lindbeck takes the point further. Not only does a Christian framework lack the tools to deny its religious end (salvation) to those outside the fold, but it also lacks the ability to speak meaningfully about those traditions at all. Consider Lindbeck's comments on Western religious sensibilities compared with Eastern ones: "the means for referring in any direct way to the Buddhist Nirvana are lacking in Western religions and the cultures influenced by them and it is, therefore, at least initially puzzling

---

58. Ibid., 69.
59. Ibid., 69 (emphasis added).
60. Lindbeck, "Unbelievers and the 'Sola Christi,'" 182–89.
61. Lindbeck, *Church in a Postliberal Age*, 81.
62. Ibid., 81.

how one can say anything either true or false about Nirvana, or even meaningfully deny it, within these latter contexts."[63] Each religious tradition has its own language game, and translatability is severely limited. Lindbeck retained this view as time went on, and he provides a story that illustrates the lack of meaningful interreligious dialogue in the "Afterword" to *The Nature of Doctrine's* anniversary edition. He explains:

> A Buddhist and Christian group of five doctoral students persuaded me shortly after the publication of *The Nature of Doctrine* to lead them in reading and discussing sociological and philosophical theories of religion.... [In this group,] the Buddhist and Christian students checked to see if their maximally favorable redescriptions of each other's faith from within their respective outlooks were intelligible to their counterparts. Both parties failed this test in reference to assimilate God to Nirvana or Nirvana to God in terms that made sense to the other.[64]

Simply put, interreligious dialogue can only go so far. Interestingly, Lindbeck surely is a *Christian* thinker. The introduction mentioned that James Buckley described Lindbeck using distinctively *Christian* terms (e.g., "evangelical" and "catholic"). So for Lindbeck, the Christian story matters a great deal. But how?

Enter divine revelation, which demands faith in the triune God as a response.[65] It is true that Lindbeck configures faithfulness interreligiously: "One test of faithfulness for all of them is the degree to which descriptions correspond to the semiotic universe paradigmatically encoded in holy writ."[66] But Lindbeck does not go so far as to say that these faiths are objectively "true" or possess a greater degree of "truth" than the Christianity with which Lindbeck aligns himself. Therefore, one can conclude that Lindbeck's method supports proposals of pluralism in general by virtue of the fact that diverse communities with their own narratives create and sustain their own religious worlds. Since one lacks the ability to truly live in the philosophical or religious world of the other, one is in no position to deny the other's claims to truth. However, neither are they, he would claim, positioned to deny a Christian vision of the world.

---

63. Lindbeck, *Nature of Doctrine*, 48.

64. Lindbeck, *Nature of Doctrine* (updated edition), 137.

65. This is a point made by Dulles throughout his *Revelation Theology*. In tracing the history of theologies of revelation, Dulles also provides the historical understandings of "faith" that accompanied these views of revelation.

66. Lindbeck, *Nature of Doctrine*, 116.

One can follow this line of thinking further. Rather than inquire as to the "truth" of this or that faith tradition, Lindbeck might say that the question itself is wrongheaded. He might suggest that religious worlds—belief systems and their corresponding practices—are not the type of thing to which "true" and "false" apply in the same way that they would apply in, say, chemistry or mathematics. This would be akin to asking whether a fictional universe—Middle Earth, for instance—were "true." The question is a non-starter. The subject does not permit it.

On the relation of revelation to pluralism, Lindbeck says that each community has its own language, meaning, etc., through which it interprets the world and, in a sense, constructs it. He has also suggested that access to a revelation outside one's particular system is rare, if possible at all. Logically following, therefore, with respect to revelation, he notes that each "faith" has its own unique norm, its sacred text, and/or its communal apparatus of meaning-making: "This is true in some degree of all the world's major faiths. They all have relatively fixed canons of writings that they treat as exemplary or normative instantiations of their semiotic codes."[67] Each religion, Christianity included, has its own narratives. Whether his postliberal colleagues agree with this level of contextualism is quite another matter.

POSTLIBERALS IN CONVERSATION: FREI AND THIEMANN

There are many postliberals from whom to choose discussion partners for Lindbeck. Despite the difficulty one faces delineating clearly who qualifies as a postliberal, they were shown to share some similarities. Postliberals reason *after* modernity, after the confidence in rational objectivity and human progress collapsed. The central strategy of postliberals, therefore, was to return to a pre-modern reading of sacred texts, a reading that concentrated on their narrative quality. Lindbeck comments on who qualifies as postliberal: "Postliberals happen to be a collection of individuals engaged in what scientists call a research program . . . [which] can be characterized as an attempt to recover pre-modern scriptural interpretation in contemporary form."[68]

Since one of its "founding fathers" discusses pre-modern interpretation as the organizing center of postliberalism, at least one of the conversation partners should address this concern. Lindbeck's other "founding father" of postliberal theology is Hans Frei, whose *Eclipse of Biblical Narrative* is the only text that rivals Lindbeck's *Nature of Doctrine* as the seminal text

67. Ibid., 116.
68. Lindbeck, "A Panel Discussion," 246.

of the entire program. Frei's input is helpful not only for his stature within the postliberal school, but also because he highlights theological issues that become important in the constructive chapters of this book. Frei diverges from Lindbeck in important ways. George Hunsinger notes that Lindbeck and Frei represent the postliberal agenda in moderate and extreme forms.[69] Lindbeck is seen as the extreme form because in his understanding, truth depends on how well a concept or claim functions and not whether or not that claim is objectively true (if one can ask the "truth" question at all). Hunsinger goes so far as to call Lindbeck's approach a form of "neoliberalism . . . a revisionist extension within the established liberal paradigm."[70] Hunsinger is more sympathetic to Frei, whom he defends as modeling a moderate postliberalism that is open to not only intra-systematic religious truth claims but also "ontological truth statements."[71] In my estimation, Hunsinger's characterization is overly harsh since, as noted above, Lindbeck allows for ontological correspondence at some (small) level. But Frei makes an excellent conversation partner due to his more moderate version of postliberalism.

Frei's view of divine revelation is best seen in the context of his basic approach to the relationship between philosophy and theology. Reminiscent of the typological approach used by Niebuhr and Dulles, Frei offers a continuum that opposes two basic ways of legitimizing theological speech: on the one side, correspondence to external scientific and/or philosophical truths, and on the other side internal coherence with the grammar of practicing Christians.[72] Along this continuum are five viewpoints: two pure positions at both ends of the continuum and three mixed positions. Type One is a pure philosophical position represented by Gordon Kaufman (and Immanuel Kant before him), and it prioritizes external philosophical adequacy to the neglect of all internal self-description. Type Two is represented by David Tracy, who gives priority to external experience and tries to conform internal self-description to it. Type Three is represented by Friedrich Schleiermacher, who gives equal weight to both external and internal adequacy. Type Four is represented by Karl Barth, in whose writings Frei finds a greater emphasis given to internal self-description.[73] On the far end of the continuum—Type Five—one finds D. Z. Phillips, whom Frei accuses

---

69. Hunsinger, "Postliberal Theology," 42–45. Cf. Comstock, "Two Types of Narrative Theology," 687–717.

70. Hunsinger, "Postliberal Theology," 44.

71. See Frei, "Epilogue," 278–79.

72. Frei, *Types of Christian Theology*, 2–51.

73. Christian self-description tacitly contains norms, which are used to harmonize externals by "ad hoc procedures."

of ignoring any and all external correspondence to scientific or philosophical reality and attending exclusively to self-description.

Interestingly, using this typology Frei is able to show similarities that cut "right across the ordinary lines of conservative and liberal."[74] For example, in the same camp as liberal David Tracy one finds Carl Henry, a conservative who is discussed in the following chapter. Both Tracy and Henry argue that theology "must have a foundation that is articulated in terms of basic philosophical principles."[75] Another unlikely relationship is found in Schleiermacher and Barth, who are next to one another on the continuum. Frei would likely place Lindbeck with D. Z. Phillips in Type Five, the model which attends exclusively to self-description at the expense of correspondence to philosophical knowledge/truth. Frei sympathizes with Type Four, a mixed position between external philosophical correspondence and internal self-descriptive coherence (but not neutral). The two can overlap in Frei's view, and even conflict with one another. When they do conflict, Frei sides with the internal perspective.[76]

Frei does not explicitly discuss revelation as much as he does other systematic loci, and he never provides a systematic or constructive treatment of the subject. He is clear about where he stands: "I agree with the recently emerged consensus . . . that 'revelation' is not a wholly unambiguous or satisfying central concept for stating what Christianity is all about."[77] Frei sounds similar to Kelsey in his criticism of the topic and lack of confidence in its ability to generate useful insights. He says, "there is justice in the cognate criticism that . . . 'revelation' turns out to be so non-informative as to lack all intellectual content."[78] Instead, he prefers to speak of the "presence of God." He describes the decline of the notion of revelation historically in *The Eclipse of Biblical Narrative*: "No matter what its future, [revelation] has had more than two and a half centuries of preeminence. . . . There are signs that the day of its decline has arrived."[79] So according to Hans Frei, elaborating a doctrine of revelation was, in the 1970s and 1980s, problematic and unhelpful.

We take his context seriously and admit the difficulties and/or risks associated with pulling a perspective on revelation out of his work.[80] However,

---

74. Frei, *Types of Christian Theology*, 24.
75. Ibid.
76. Ibid., 43–44, 48, 51.
77. Frei, *Identity of Jesus Christ*, vii–viii.
78. Ibid., viii.
79. Frei, *Eclipse of Biblical Narrative*, 52 (quote inverted for emphasis).
80. This is more risky with Frei than it was with Lindbeck, because others have

even though Frei never treated the issue explicitly or wrote a constructive or systematic treatise on revelation, his body of work attests to its importance and to his own views on the subject. The young Frei, for instance, investigated revelation in a doctoral dissertation at Yale University—supervised by H. Richard Niebuhr—which centered on the early Barth's concept of divine revelation. Moreover, one can discern his view of revelation from an unpublished lecture he gave at Yale in 1975. His subject was "Contemporary Issues in Theology,"[81] and in this lecture he claims this: "The *great* pervasive issue [from] 1920–1970 was *what is revelation?*"[82] He also asked: "What kind of knowledge is it? Before Christians talked about God, they tried to settle (the) question of *knowledge* of God."[83] The following week he discussed the nature of revelation in an era after Barth's *Römerbrief*. Frei says, "relationship to God" is "totally indirect, across an absolute barrier man could not cross."[84] He then provides as detailed a statement on revelation as one can find in any of his writings, in which revelation is conceived much like a bridge:

> "Revelation" in [the] first place was contact with God [which] man cannot provide for himself: Not a heightening of ordinary insight. Secondly, revelation does not take away the barrier but miraculously crosses it: Man remains forever limited: Revelation (is) not direct, special or mystical insight. (It must always come to man as even "now"; Man never possesses it, only receives it. Revelation [is] never behind him.) Thirdly, revelation then means a trusting abiding in non-knowing of God. God is hidden in his revelation.[85]

One can also point to his early chapter in *A Handbook of Christian Theology*,[86] in which Frei argues that the Christian faith is solely founded

---

tried to discuss Frei's view of revelation and been met with serious criticism. For instance, Abdul-Masih's book, *Edward Schillebeeckx and Hans Frei* is faulted by Higton in *Modern Theology* (pp. 590–92) for confusing Frei's view of revelation with Barth's, on whom he wrote his doctoral dissertation.

81. Frei, "Contemporary Issues in Theology," January-March 1975 in Henderson, *Logic of Belief*, 10–11.

82. Ibid., Lecture 2. For another take on Frei's view of divine revelation, see Topping, *Revelation, Scripture, and Church*.

83. Frei, "Contemporary Issues in Theology," January 16, 1975.

84. Ibid., January 23, 1975.

85. Ibid.

86. Frei, "Religion (Natural and Revealed)," in Halverson and Cohen, eds., *Handbook*, 313–23.

on the event of the incarnated Word.[87] As noted by Frances Henderson, Frei shows different logics at work: ontological, epistemological, and grammatical. He believes revelation must be intelligible to its recipients, which means several things: (a) revelation is meaningful only "insofar as it is first of all 'hearable' (let alone 'heard') by its 'human recipients.'"[88] (b) Revelation must do more than give heretofore-inaccessible knowledge; it must actually communicate the revealing God. And (c) intelligibility requires the capacity to be formulated by humans in grammatical terms. Henderson summarizes Frei's view of divine revelation:

> If we assume an absolute dialectical distance between world and God, of course we could say nothing about God, had God not crossed that distance and revealed in this world. But nevertheless, we already have drawn up criteria for what qualifies as revelation. God may speak in freedom, when and how God chooses. But if God's speech is to qualify as "revelation," then . . . it is bound by some of the rules of conversation. We have to be able to hear the speaker in some sense to be "real." And we should be able to repeat back to the speaker the significant content of what they have said, but this time in our own words . . . [All] these "conditions" for revelation can be no human conditions imposed on the divine. The dialectic does not work in that direction: that would be the wrong grammatical order. Rather, they must be considered as conditions established by the divine itself, precisely in and with the moment of revelation.[89]

A number of items in this summary of Frei deserve attention and clarification: first, revelation is cast as an event, as something that happens in a "moment"; second, God does the revealing because in and of themselves people are unable to bridge the gap; third, revelation relates to a "conversation;" fourth and finally, after the revelation event the perspective of the receiver is changed to the extent that she understands what was revealed and can communicate it to others in her own vernacular. Contemporary models of revelation would do well to incorporate these insights.

Another postliberal figure worth considering is Ronald Thiemann, longtime Dean of the Harvard Divinity School and present Benjamin Busey Professor of Theology. Thiemann is useful due to his stark contrast with the theological program of Lindbeck and Frei on the issue of revelation. Instead of steering away from the "problem of revelation," he devoted an entire

---

87. Henderson, *Logic of Belief*, 13.
88. Ibid., 20.
89. Ibid., 20–21.

book to the subject, his influential *Revelation and Theology*. His argument proceeds in three basic stages: resistance to foundationalist epistemology, necessity of divine prevenience, and reconfiguration of the gospel as narrated promise.

Thiemann believes that many theologians have erred in their view of revelation because, among other things, they associate it with a foundationalist epistemology.[90] Instead of seeking some common foundation upon which other ideas are built, Thiemann finds himself in agreement with the anti-foundationalist philosophers who say that no experience exists prior to human interpretation; there is no "assumption-less" starting point. The problem of foundations, he notes, has plagued a long list of philosophers and theologians in the Christian tradition, and the foundations ranged from miracles to religious intuition. This has led some of his contemporaries' to abandon the idea of revelation altogether. This worries Thiemann, because only through revelation is one able to safeguard the *prevenience* of God: "God's prevenience must be established not only as an intelligible category within the discourse of the text but also as a reality which confronts the reader *through* the text."[91] In Thiemann's view, "a divine initiative precedes all our speaking and acting and responding."[92]

How does Thiemann get here, considering that he cannot "prove" God's prevenience from premises we all accept? Thiemann offers a "holist justification" for his view, and he suggests that this is the type of argument other thinkers should make.[93] Interestingly, he also says that this "holist" approach is found in Hans Frei, "especially in his as yet unpublished Shaffer Lectures."[94] Much of what Christians do and say would be sacrificed were God's prevenience abandoned in favor of a view in which our speaking and practice about God came before the divine initiative. So maintaining the reality of revelation, which preserves divine prevenience, is essential and worthy of rescue from those who would discard it.

Revelation, for Thiemann, is "narrated promise." In his view, understanding it in terms of "promise" seems to preserve the fact that *God* initiates, not humans. Humanity is simply responsible to respond after the promise is made. One learns about this promise through the narrative in Christianity's sacred texts of God's identity as the one who does the promising. Thiemann

---

90. Thiemann, *Revelation and Theology*, chs. 1 and 4. For a fine summary of Thiemann's whole book, see Placher, "Postliberal Theology," 349–50.

91. Thiemann, *Revelation and Theology*, 143.

92. Placher, "Postliberal Theology," 350.

93. Thiemann, *Revelation and Theology*, 171–72.

94. Ibid., 172.

dissects the Gospel of Matthew to show the divine initiative at work, a book in which the reader is invited into the story. A brief example will illustrate the principle at work: Thiemann says the author of Matthew's Gospel has an "artfully constructed conclusion" which "juxtaposes the promise of the one who claims that 'all authority in heaven and on earth has been given to me' to the doubting response of his disciples."[95] For Thiemann, this serves a literary function; it carries "the world of the Gospel narrative into that of the reader."[96] Thiemann continues:

> Matthew devises no dramatic confession of faith to conclude his story, nor does he introduce an explicit narrator to proclaim the Gospel's message. Rather, he uses Jesus' final act of promising to extend the Gospel's promise "to the whole world." Jesus, whose identity is depicted in the Gospel's narrative, now becomes the agent of promise as this story becomes a proclamation addressed to the reader. It is as if in this final episode Jesus directs his gaze for the first time outside the frame of the story and issues his promise directly to the reading audience. Thus the reader is invited to respond to this narrated promise by *entering the world of the narrative* and joining with those on the mountain who worship him.[97]

Summarizing Thiemann, one can say that he does not attempt to ground the discussion on either religious intuition or revelation itself, but rather sees revelation as part of theology proper, that is, the doctrine of God. He shows the coherence of his view with some other aspects of Christian teaching and living. Like Frei, Thiemann's approach offers a contemporary perspective of revelation some interesting pathways.

Lindbeck's utility is another matter. Try as he might to explain his version of postliberalism, his value lies primarily with the conversation he helped start rather than the contribution he made during it.

EVALUATION: LINDBECK'S INTERPRETERS AND THE ISSUE OF PLURALISM

In an effort to evaluate Lindbeck's view of revelation within his cultural-linguistic theory of religion, one wonders how he has been received, in particular by those who address the pressing issue Lindbeck's work raises

---

95. Ibid., 142.
96. Ibid.
97. Ibid., 142–43 (emphasis added).

about an important category in the philosophy of religion: religious pluralism. As will become clear, there is a correlation between Lindbeck's lack of confidence in the objectivity of Christian revelation and his willingness to entertain proposals of religious pluralism. Where the certainty of revelation's objectivity increases, the potential for pluralism decreases, and vice versa. Consider Lindbeck from the point of view of his critics.

First, Janine Hill Fletcher affirms some aspects of the Lindbeck's postliberal proposal, most notably his "approach to religious difference" in which "Christians can adhere to the traditional affirmations of how Christ's distinctive pattern reveals the mystery of God . . . [and] the incomprehensible mystery of God and diverse experience of God in various traditions."[98] However, she is critical of Lindbeck for not offering a venue in which transreligious discourse might occur: "What is *missing* from his theology is a way for people of differing faith perspectives to converse with and learn from each other."[99] In other words, in Lindbeck's cultural-linguistic approach, which asserts that members of distinct faith traditions are shaped by communal narratives and the practices flowing from them, the conversation between traditions is limited to the extent that members are not part of more than one faith community. Indeed, Fletcher suggests that in Lindbeck's view, "this [type of translatability] is rare."[100]

Of course, Lindbeck could reply to Fletcher that dialogue is actually enhanced between adherents of various religious traditions. Disparate religionists with a postliberal view lack the assumption that there is some common core in religious systems. In other words, "the partners in dialogue do not start with the conviction that they really basically agree . . . [and] they are not forced into the dilemma of thinking of themselves as representing a superior (or an inferior) articulation of a common experience of which the other religious are inferior (or superior) expressions."[101] The result is that "they can regard themselves as simply different and can proceed to explore their agreements and disagreements without necessarily engaging in the invidious comparisons that the assumption of a common experiential core make so tempting."[102] In the new "Afterword" to *The Nature of Doctrine*, Lindbeck points to a religion's "assimilative power" as a way to preserve "the independence of different religions . . . [while it] also liberates them from the isolationism and fideism that critics fear. The way is opened to meaning-

---

98. Fletcher, *Monopoly on Salvation*, 75.
99. Ibid (emphasis added).
100. Ibid.
101. Lindbeck, *Nature of Doctrine*, 55.
102. Ibid.

ful communication, including combative disagreement, about the full range of their similarities and differences."[103]

Second, S. Mark Heim interacts with Lindbeck in *The Depth of the Riches* by affirming his observation on the first-century Christian church:

> Those Christians, living as a minority in an intensely pluralistic world, invited all to accept the gospel of Christ as the way of salvation. Yet they also had abiding confidence that whatever the outward effects of their evangelism, God would 'do right' by all people.... Lindbeck's point is intriguing.... The attitudes he notes are real enough. We could go a good way toward supporting a similar disposition in Christians today if we were to develop a theological understanding that genuinely sees other religions as testimony to God's providential activity in the world, and sees in their religious fulfillments a tempered hope.[104]

Heim is, paradoxically, drawing on the portion of *Nature of Doctrine* that defends the Christian notion of salvation in other faiths, which is precisely the idea Heim is trying to overcome. To the extent that he affirms Lindbeck's understanding of historically conditioned belief structures, Heim seems to support Lindbeck's perspective on religious pluralism, even if they disagree on the soteriological point.

Third, Paul Knitter interacts with Lindbeck's work to a greater degree than both Fletcher's *Monopoly on Salvation* and Heim's *Depth of the Riches* in his *Introducing Theologies of Religions*. Knitter locates Lindbeck in his "acceptance model" in contradistinction with the "replacement," "fulfillment," and "mutuality" models.[105] He mentions that Lindbeck, and the postliberal project on the whole, is hesitant to admit to a common ground between the religious traditions: "If our language creates our worlds, and if our languages are different, then our worlds will be different, with no common ground between them."[106] Not only does Knitter highlight the lack of common ground in Lindbeck, but he also rightly draws attention to the issue of incommensurability, viz., "untranslatability."[107] For example, Knitter suggests it is "not possible, according to the postliberal viewpoint, to translate 'Buddhist' into 'Christian.'"[108] This is a function of Lindbeck's commitment to the notion of "intratextuality," a concept that posits a semiotic exclusivity

---

103. Lindbeck, "Afterword," 137.
104. Heim, *Depth of the Riches*, 271–72.
105. Knitter, *Theologies of Religions*, 173–237.
106. Ibid., 181.
107. Lindbeck, "The Gospel's Uniqueness," 423–50.
108. Knitter, *Theologies of Religions*, 182.

between religions by virtue of their own distinct languages, cultures, and subsequent meanings. Knitter plainly states that according to postliberalism, "the word 'compassion' has its meaning only within the Buddhist texts. In Christian texts, its meaning is vastly different."[109] A similar criticism may be made with respect to revelation.

Of course, we have already seen that Lindbeck recognized the issue of untranslatability in a postliberal approach to religion. But from the hypothetical exchanges between Lindbeck and the others, one can say a few things about what a contemporary proposal for revelation must offer: first, it must enable rather than blunt what Fletcher calls "translatability" between different religions, not as a denial of their differences, but rather to have some ground on which a substantive conversation about their differences can take place; second, Heim demonstrates that differences are no cause for demonization of the "other," and he shows that revelation is ultimately a mysterious phenomenon left to the providence of God; third, Knitter's point is similar to Fletcher's insofar as the criterion for adjudicating between competing revelations must work hard at overcoming the "untranslatability" problem.

There are other critiques that bear directly on the Lindbeck's view of revelation and religion (including the pluralism question), all of which have to do with his applicability to the practicing Christian community. First, Thiemann worries that the postliberal project as advocated by Lindbeck is guilty of paying too much attention to methodology and not enough to the practice of *doing* theology, making actual claims about theology's object, God: "There is, indeed, the real danger that in much of Lindbeck's essay talk about 'text' stands in place of talk about 'God.'"[110] Second, other thinkers say that when Lindbeck dismisses the experiential aspect of Christian living, his project lacks relevance; they criticize Lindbeck's "approach as being far too abstract to be of service to the Christian community. In refusing to take the claims of Christian experience as the primary data to be understood, Lindbeck insulates his proposal from being useful to the widest community of Christian believers."[111] Third, Joseph Mangina offers the same criticism of Lindbeck's work as Thiemann,[112] but adds that Lindbeck lacks a strong view of revelation like the one he finds in Barth. Says Mangina: "Without an account of God's prior action, the system of encoded human performance

---

109. Ibid.

110. Thiemann, "Response to George Lindbeck," 377–82.

111. Trembath, *Divine Revelation*, 187, note 33.

112. Mangina, *Karl Barth*, 55: "One of [postliberalism's] weaknesses is that it is often tempted to substitute talk about the church and about Christian practices for God himself."

simply collapses in on itself. In the end, something like an account of revelation is needed to display how the human activity of interpreting Scripture is a response to God's action towards us."[113] These three issues—linguistics substituted for God, irrelevance, and no strong perspective on revelation—bear on the issue at hand and are limitations of Lindbeck's proposal.

Or consider a critique of Lindbeck originating from conservative analytic philosophers. They will say, simply, that Lindbeck contradicts himself. On the one hand, Lindbeck tries to support the reality of a distinctively *Christian* narrative, which was not discovered by humanity's capacities alone but rather *revealed*. For he desires that all are beneficiaries of the Christian religious end, salvation (even if through an eschatological futuristic offer) and takes seriously the Christian practices of preaching and evangelism. On the other hand, however, one wonders on what ground he can apply these concepts onto members of the other faiths. That is, although "salvation" is available to those outside the Christian fold, by adopting a cultural-linguistic approach to religion, one could charge Lindbeck with relativizing his claims to such a degree that he is unable to consistently impose Christian concepts—salvation, Christ—onto adherents of other traditions.

One could state this objection using Lindbeck's own criteria for religious truth, intrasystematic coherence and ontological correspondence. Lindbeck's proposal lacks an adequate "intrasystematic coherence," which he could have maintained had he not attempted to defend salvation in other faiths. Moreover, Lindbeck's pluralism fails to fulfill the ontological correspondence criterion for religious truth claims by failing to take adequate account of the contradiction inherent in proposals of deep religious pluralism. Even if he had left his Christian notion of "salvation" out of the equation, proposals of deep religious pluralism will be seen by the philosophical "modern" Christian thinker (in contrast to the "postmodern") as self-defeating. If pluralists were to affirm all perspectives as equally valid, they would have to affirm the proponent of religious exclusivity. Pluralism cannot embrace exclusivism while maintaining its own identity and distinction. The best one can hope for is inclusivism. One could also reasonably suggest that if social construction has greater impact on belief structures than anything else and does not point toward that which is actually ultimately real or absolute, as Lindbeck seems to suggest, then the postliberal vision of communalism and relativity is also socially constructed. This objection would locate postliberalism amidst postmodernity's incredulity toward meta-narratives and point out that this, too, is self-defeating in the sense that it makes absolute claims about the lack of absolutes. Now to be fair, it is quite possible that Lindbeck

113. Ibid.

would affirm this charge, because he states that "what seems credible or incredible to contemporary theologians is likely to be more the product of their milieu and intellectual conditioning than of their science, philosophy, or theological argumentation."[114]

LINGERING QUESTIONS

This chapter has shown how Lindbeck's postliberalism responded to liberalism and its attending affirmation of the primacy of experience. It showed that revelation in the *Nature of Doctrine* is conceived intratextually as context-specific instantiations of the divine activity. Finally, it demonstrated that Lindbeck's view of revelation ramifies into issues of pluralism; he is less willing to assert the superiority of his own tradition based on revelation and, therefore, he seems willing to embrace a *de facto* measure of religious pluralism, as much as his more traditional interpreters—the kind one finds in chapter 3—will find it inconsistent or unhelpful. It is worth highlighting that while Lindbeck sought to correct the prioritization of religious experience, he also sought to prevent it from going too far. That is, he did not remove the value of human experience altogether in some search for an almost positivist view of revelation. In the next chapter, the reader will see such a move.

There are many lingering questions that may prove fruitful for further theological inquiry, areas that take as their starting point Lindbeck's work and the responses from his interpreters. First, what does the correlation of one's view of revelation and one's stance on religious pluralism look like when examined through other seminal figures such as those mentioned elsewhere in this book? Second, since much of this discussion about Lindbeck has involved the Christian religious end of "salvation," what is the relationship between revelation and salvation? Are there some revelations that concern salvation and other revelations that do not? Third, are there good reasons to try to salvage the "narrative" component in revelation that postliberal theology opens up? Fourth, can one extend Lindbeck's postliberal project even further into the idea of revelation in a way that goes beyond Thiemann and other postliberals (e.g., Gabriel Fackre)? Finally, how could the central revelational theme in postliberalism—narrative—relate to the one Dulles defended (symbol)?

In his new "Afterword" to *The Nature of Doctrine*, Lindbeck says he regrets not making more explicit the fact that his chapter on "Many Religions and the One True Faith" did not "sufficiently remind the reader that it treats

---

114. Lindbeck, *Nature of Doctrine*, 63.

interreligious relations not for their own sake but for the limited purpose of testing the nonecumenical plausibility of a theory of religion and doctrine developed for Christian ecumenical reasons."[115] If the text had been primarily geared toward proposing a philosophy or theology of religions, he would have devoted significant attention to how ecumenism interacts with interreligious relations and missionary evangelism, "both of which are major concerns"[116] of his. Lindbeck closes his reflection by noting, "These topics, however, call for another and very different volume that I definitely do not intend to write."[117]

At the end of chapter 1, Dulles reminded us that God is ultimately incomprehensible, ineffable, and mysterious. Lindbeck offers a similar exhortation. Simple though it may be, a central aspect of the discussion that can and should be affirmed by all is this: conversation, though limited by cultural and linguistic locatedness, is more fruitful than bloodshed. Religions possess great power to influence society for the good or for evil. It is the responsibility of all involved, in a culture of plurality, to strive for the good as they discern the ways in which God has communicated and the adequate response on behalf of revelation's recipients. Or, in the words of Lindbeck himself:

> In this new situation the only way to exert an effective Christian influence is for the church to serve human needs as humbly and self-forgettingly as did Christ himself. It must not use coercive measure by trying, for instance, to legislate Christian morals for society at large. Rather, it must encourage Christians to promote all worthwhile causes, from the artistic to the economic, whether these bear a specifically Christian label or not.[118]

---

115. Lindbeck, "Afterword," 138.
116. Ibid.
117. Ibid.
118. Lindbeck, *Dialogue on the Way*, 235–36.

CHAPTER 3

The Written Word
Evangelicals and Revelation

A RESPECTED MENTOR

The third person whose work is useful in understanding revelation today is Bernard L. Ramm, conservative Baptist thinker, apologist for the Christian faith, and faculty member at a number of Christian colleges. Along with Carl Henry, Ramm is often considered one of the great evangelical thinkers of the twentieth century, though for very different reasons than Henry. A brief story will illustrate Ramm's role in the larger narrative of twentieth-century thinking about revelation.

As a young professional, Ramm encountered Karl Barth in two ways. First, Ramm spent countless hours carefully reading Barth's *Church Dogmatics*, which taught Ramm that serious Christians can and *should* have great respect for the history of the Christian tradition when seeking to know God. Ramm came to see that Barth "did not believe in the 'tyranny of the time,' namely, that the old is wrong simply because it is old and the new is true simply because it is new."[1] Interestingly, second, Ramm also sat under Barth's tutelage personally. Ramm spent the 1957–58 academic year in Basel, where he listened to Barth lecture, faithfully attended his English language seminars, and visited Barth's home at the precise "posted" hour of

---

1. Ramm, "Helps from Karl Barth," 122.

2:00–3:00 p.m. on Saturdays. An inquisitive young Ramm would come with questions ready and paper for taking notes.

He soaked Barth's wisdom like a sponge. One event in particular was transformative, and it "stemmed from a passing remark Barth made to one of his questioners" in his home. Barth said "that if we truly believed we had the truth of God in Holy Scripture we should be fearless in opening any door or window in the pursuit of our theological craft. The truth of God can never be intimidated. If perfect love drives out fear, then the belief that we have the truth of God in Holy Scripture should drive out of our minds all intellectual fears about our theology." Before his personal encounter with Barth, Ramm "did fear open doors and open windows." But after this exchange, Ramm came to see that he "could fearlessly read, study, and listen to all options and opinions in theology." This is the great value of Bernard Ramm in a study of this nature on revelation: he represents the conservative "opening up" to mainline thinkers and advances in other disciplines. This was the impact Barth had on Ramm: "These literary and personal encounters with Karl Barth did materially change some of the ways I thought about theology, lectured on theology, and wrote theological books."[2]

This chapter does a number of things. First, it discusses some of the difficulty in defining what "evangelicalism" is and who qualifies as one. Second, it shows how Ramm's view of revelation emerged within a specific context of evangelicals coming out of hiding. Ramm emerged as a leading thinker among conservatives in part because he offered an alternative stance to modernity than that advocated by Carl Henry. Third, the chapter discusses Ramm's view of revelation. Fourth, it puts Ramm into conversation with two of his intellectual "heirs," as it were—Roger Olson and Stanley Grenz. Three points are made in the chapter: first, the concept of revelation has gone through something of a transformation in some strands of contemporary evangelical philosophy and theology in recent years; second, the shifts are due at least in part to the changing nature of the theological enterprise itself in evangelicalism and what is arguably most crucial to it: the gospel of Jesus Christ; and third, these changes have concrete implications for the way one understands and uses the Christianity's sacred texts. What is at stake here is the issue of *biblicism*, often thought to be one of four criteria for defining evangelicalism. If the assertions of this chapter are correct, the views of revelation advanced here represent an arc in evangelicalism vis-à-vis modern theology: from resistance and the offering of an alternative (Henry) to full participation and engagement with the broader-than-evangelical academic

---

2. Ibid., 121.

community (Grenz and Olson). The central figure in this arc, I will argue, is Bernard Ramm.

DEFINING EVANGELICALISM

In the chapter on Catholic views of divine revelation, the difficulty of defining what "Catholicism" is and who qualifies as one was noted. There is such great diversity in the various expressions of tradition today. Chapter 1 demarcated the field by dividing Catholics into two camps—orthodox and progressive—the former of whom offered a more fruitful path for exploring revelation. Postliberalism was even more difficult to define, so one can only describe some of the school's central features or "family resemblances." A similar move is necessary for evangelicalism, which also resists easy categorization, but is identifiable through some thematic emphases.[3]

However, the differences are substantial. More so than both Catholicism and postliberalism, evangelicalism is extraordinarily difficult to define due to the huge gulfs separating members who locate themselves under its umbrella. People who stand under the "evangelical" banner range from staunch conservative members of the Southern Baptist Convention to environmentalist advocates for wholesale change of public policy in favor of a liberal political agenda.[4] Evangelicals are on both sides of the abortion debate, political party affiliations, gay marriage issue, and foreign policy discussion. One can just as easily find an "evangelical" advocating for the end of what they take to be irresponsible and frivolous wars overseas as one could find an evangelical supporting the democratization of the world that comes dangerously close to support of manifest destiny. And just as members of the Catholic tradition recognize the diversity inherent in their own tradition—recall Reuther's comment that "Catholic does not equal the Vatican"—evangelicals do, too. Consider the harsh words one evangelical has for others evangelicals:

> I write as a jilted lover. The evangelical faith that nurtured me as a child and sustains me as an adult has been hijacked by right-wing zealots who have distorted the gospel of Jesus Christ, defaulted on the noble legacy of nineteenth-century evangelical activism, and failed to appreciate the genius of the First

---

3. I use the terms "conservative" and "evangelical" synonymously in this chapter when discussing Henry and Ramm; however, Ramm's interlocutors will attempt to demonstrate the inadequacy of "conservative evangelicalism," and therefore more appropriately are under the banner of "postconservative" evangelicalism.

4. Balmer, *Thy Kingdom Come*, ch. 5.

> Amendment.... The effect of this right-wing takeover has been a poisoning of public discourse and a distortion of the faith.[5]

Evangelicals of this sort would recast Reuther's comments for their own context by saying something like this: "evangelicalism does not equal the Religious Right." There is great diversity in the evangelical tradition, which prompts thinkers like Ray Anderson to claim, "no Christian theologian has a proprietary claim on the phrase 'evangelical theology.'"[6]

So why bother with evangelicals, a group so diverse that it seems to lack *any* ground on which to build a reasonable discussion? As a branch of Christianity, evangelicalism as a movement in a broader tradition seems no further toward self-discovery than it was fifty years ago.[7] The answer lies in the subject of this book—revelation. With the possible exception of Roman Catholicism,[8] it can be argued that writers in the evangelical tradition have either assumed or advanced the most robust doctrines of revelation of the past two hundred years, largely instantiated by their high views of scripture. So while "evangelicalism" is hardly monolithic, one can say with Gabriel Fackre that "common to its diverse expressions is the interiorization and radicalization of the formal and material principles of the Reformation," one of which is "the authority of Scripture."[9] Christianity's sacred texts are often thought to be God's "special" revelation, so it might be more appropriate to ask "Why *not* evangelicalism?" The selection of these thinkers in particular—Henry, Ramm, and Ramm's intellectual heirs—has mostly do with their ability to act as figureheads to three movements in evangelicalism vis-à-vis mainline academic philosophy and theology: resistance, engagement with caution, and full participation.

So how should one define "evangelicalism"? Like postliberalism, evangelicalism is more an attitude toward certain issues than a hierarchical or institutional affiliation. David Bebbington presents a commonly used fourfold

---

5. Ibid., ix.

6. Anderson, "Evangelical Theology," 480.

7. For instance, upon the founding of the evangelical magazine *Christianity Today* in 1955, Billy Graham said, "We seem to be confused, bewildered, divided, and almost defeated in the face of the greatest opportunity and responsibility, possibly in the history of the church." In 1999, *CT* editors show the movement's stagnation: "Though the specifics may have shifted since Graham's 1955 speech, evangelicals are still confused about their role in society, divided as a body, and even bewildered about what *evangelical* means." See "CT Predicts: More of the Same," 36–37. Cf. Grenz, *Renewing the Center*, 11.

8. See Chapter One of this book. See also Dulles, *Revelation Theology*, 136–70 and *Models of Revelation*, 131–54.

9. Fackre, *Doctrine of Revelation*, 154.

taxonomy of what evangelicals take to be important.[10] First, evangelicals are united by a stress on conversion. For example, almost halfway through the twentieth century, Anglican evangelical Max Warren said conversion was "the very heart of the Evangelical approach, the citadel of its doctrine, they key to its pastoralia, the method of its evangelism."[11] Decades later, a more conservative evangelical, also Anglican (J. I. Packer), agreed.[12] For many, this conversion is akin to a second birth, and the conversion experience is known as being "born again." Second, evangelicals are known for their activism, which at times is connected to social concerns and at other times is related to their desire for more converts. Third, evangelicals treat their sacred texts in a uniquely authoritative way. Popular evangelical preacher, Billy Graham, said in 1956 that he endorsed "Bible-centered preaching," coming out so strong in support of a biblical approach that he had to hedge against criticisms that he was advocating bibliolatry.[13] Finally, evangelicals tend to hold the crucifixion in high esteem. John Stott, a leading evangelical among Anglicans, said it was important to recognize "the centrality of the cross."[14] The focus on the crucifixion has, undoubtedly, contributed to evangelical preoccupation with soteriology, and one often finds penal and substitutionary models of atonement favored above incarnational or resurrection-based models.[15] Summarizing his argument, Bebbington notes that "All those displaying conversionism, activism, biblicism, and crucicentrism are evangelicals."[16]

However, Bebbington also recognizes the diversity in evangelicalism. After his brief survey of the various types, he is struck by "the sheer heterogeneity of the movement." Indeed, as Bebbington himself notes, "Evangelicals are remarkably diverse."[17] Part of the diversity is seen in competing views of revelation, which, in evangelical circles is similar to competing doctrines of scripture. As "biblicism" is one of the four hallmarks, some evangelicals elevate it over above the other hallmarks of the tradition. The central figure of this chapter, Bernard Ramm, sought to overcome biblicism in favor of a Barthian approach to sacred texts.

10. Bebbington, "Evangelicalism in Its Settings" and *Evangelicalism in Modern Britain*, ch. 1.
11. Warren, *What is An Evangelical?* 23.
12. Packer, *Evangelical Anglican*, 21.
13. Graham, "Biblical Authority," 6.
14. Stott, *Fundamentalism and Evangelicalism*, 28.
15. Bebbington, "British and American Evangelicalism," 366–67.
16. Bebbington, "Evangelicalism in Its Settings," 367, and *Evangelicalism in Modern Britain*, ch. 1.
17. Bebbington, "Evangelicalism in Its Settings," 366.

THE CONTEXT: EVANGELICALS COME OUT OF HIDING

Historian of religion in America, Randall Balmer, argues that an Arminian soteriology and its resulting postmillennialist eschatology was key to some major transitions in American Evangelicalism. After the Second Great Awakening in the nineteenth century, most postmillennialist evangelicals believed that the *parousia* was dependent on their efforts to construct the kingdom of God here on earth.[18] They worked toward this end, advancing the causes of abolition, public education, gender equality, etc. Only *after* the thousand years of peace would the incarnate Word return, it was thought. However, at the same time America was becoming more and more industrialized and urbanized. Working and living conditions were poor, and things appeared to evangelicals to be getting worse, not better. America "no longer resembled the precincts of Zion that postmillennial evangelicals had envisioned earlier in the century."[19] So they altered their eschatology to dispensational *pre*millenialism, in which true believers would be separated from nonbelievers in a "rapture" event. The world, once seen as the place for improvement, came to be seen—in the words of D. L. Moody—as a "wrecked vessel." Moody describes a revelation he received from God: "God has given me a lifeboat and said, 'Moody, save all you can.'"[20] This mindset began what Balmer calls a "theology of despair," which bifurcated American Protestantism into two camps: liberal Protestants who advocated a "social gospel" by continuing to work at reforming society, and more conservative evangelicals, who scaled back their work on social issues and pushed fervently for converts through missionary activity domestically and abroad. After all, if world was going to hell the focus should be on saving souls.

A subculture emerged and grew increasingly skeptical of philosophical, scientific, and other advances in the academy. Evangelicals continued to lose credibility in the mainstream, perhaps most publicly in the Scopes trial

---

18. Balmer, *Making of Evangelicalism*, 30–31: "Given the Arminian theology that dominated the Second Great Awakening—the doctrine that individuals could exercise their volition to initiate the salvation process—it should come as no surprise that the concomitant eschatology of the Second Awakening was postmillennialism, the notion that Jesus would return after the millennium. The corollary of postmillennialism was that believers bore the responsibility for bringing on the millennium by dint of their own efforts. Those who had appropriated salvation for themselves now looked to broaden their efforts and inaugurate the kingdom of God on earth, more particularly here in America. And this is precisely what they set out to do. . . . All of these initiatives were directed (at least in part) toward the goal of constructing the kingdom of God on earth."

19. Ibid., 33.

20. Ibid., 36.

of 1925 in which William Jennings "Bryan, and by extension all evangelicals, lost decisively in the larger courtroom of public opinion."[21] So they retreated further, serving only themselves and the causes they held most dear. Conservative evangelicals created their own denominations, congregations, missionary societies, seminaries, Bible institutes, Bible camps, and Bible colleges, "all in an effort to insulate themselves from the larger world."[22] By the middle of the twentieth century, evangelicals had a nearly fully formed subculture.

Not all evangelicals were equally pleased. In 1947, Carl Henry published a manifesto for re-engagement, *The Uneasy Conscience of Modern Fundamentalism*.[23] Henry called evangelicals to come out of hiding.

The work of Carl Henry responded to three issues. First, Henry was disappointed with American fundamentalists who had retreated from their surrounding culture. Instead, Henry suggested that evangelicals were called to actively resist by offering a plausible alternative to modernity's secular outlook. Instead of fleeting to its own sectarian haven, Henry advocated for evangelicals to return to the public sphere relying on the truth of their tradition and the reliability of their sacred texts: "The problem is not that biblical theology is outdated; it is rather that some of its expositors seem out of touch with the frontiers of doubt in our day."[24] Second, Henry worked in the wake of Rudolf Bultmann's project of demythologization and what he interpreted as Barth's misunderstanding of the character of the sacred texts. Therefore, Henry thought, "the hour is ripe now, if we seize it rightly, for a rediscovery of the Scriptures."[25] Third, in addition to evangelicals acting in "subevangelical"[26] ways and the loss of the Bible's authority, Henry lamented "the tragic losses . . . in mainline Protestantism,"[27] chief among them that "to its own peril the twentieth-century mindset had forsaken its rootage in the earlier commitment to divine revelation."[28]

Carl Henry was passionate about the subject of revelation, and there are several things one can say about Henry's view. First, for Henry divine revelation is entirely rational. Henry understood revelation as "that activity of the supernatural God whereby he communicates information essential

---

21. Ibid., 49.
22. Ibid.
23. Ibid., 50.
24. Henry, *Frontiers*, 140–41.
25. Henry, *Uneasy Conscience*, 9.
26. Henry, *Frontiers*, 140.
27. Grenz and Olson, *20th Century Theology*, 291.
28. Ibid.

for man's present and future destiny. In revelation God, whose thoughts are not our thoughts, shares his mind; he communicates not only truth about himself and his intentions, but also that concerning man's present plight and future prospects."[29] Here Henry's concept of revelation involves the dissemination of *information* and, hence, revelation is propositional in nature. This is the position *against* which the Catholic and postliberal theologians argued in chapters 1 and 2. Henry's most significant contribution to twentieth-century thinking about revelation, the six-volume *God, Revelation and Authority* can be read as an defense of the idea that "God's revelation is rational communication conveyed in intelligible ideas and meaningful words, that is, in conceptual-verbal form."[30] Due to the fact that revelation is God's rational communication in the form of propositional truth, this leads Henry to suggest that revelation is "objective, conceptual, intelligible and coherent."[31] In Henry's view, revelation is primarily rational and hence propositional because "rationality has its very basis in the nature of the Living God."[32] If revelation were not rational, humanity would be left with "a stuttering deity, a transcendental self who roams about in a super-rational sphere not fully subject to the categories of thought."[33] For Henry, "revelation is a mental activity."[34] Revelation is not primarily, as other thinkers have argued, God's self-communication or about establishing a relationship.

Second, characteristic of many conservative thinkers, Henry's view of revelation is virtually synonymous with his doctrine of scripture.[35] So important was Henry's bibliology that he suggested, "the doctrine of the Bible controls all other doctrines of the Christian faith."[36] For Henry, higher criticism and mainline Protestantism had failed to recognize essential truths about the texts, namely, their "historical and propositional revelation, plenary inspiration, and verbal inerrancy."[37] The Bible *must* be free of error if it has its source in God. For Henry, inspiration means "a super-

29. Henry, *God, Revelation and Authority*, III/457.

30. See, e.g., ibid., III/248.

31. Ibid., IV/426, III/173 and *Protestant Dilemma*, 99 in Grenz and Olson, *20th Century Theology*, 292–93.

32. Henry, "Fortunes of Theology," 30, in Grenz and Olson, *20th Century Theology*, 293.

33. Henry, *Protestant Dilemma*, 115.

34. Henry, *Towards a Recovery*, 55.

35. In fact, one of the contributing factors in his conversion from his youth as a nominal Episcopalian to a full-fledged evangelical was "a pilfered Bible" (Henry, *Confessions*, 47.).

36. Henry, *Frontiers*, 138.

37. Ibid., 134–35.

natural influence upon divinely chosen prophets and apostles whereby the Spirit of God assures the truth and trustworthiness of their oral and written proclamation."[38] God's superintendence means that the Christian texts are objectively true in all matters to which they speak, including science, history, geology, etc. For Henry, "the Holy Spirit superintended the scriptural writers in communicating the biblical message . . . safeguarding them from error."[39] Through the Bible, the Spirit of God "inscripturates divinely revealed truth in verbal form."[40]

Third, special revelation is intended to accomplish specific goals in accordance with the distinctively Christian religious end of salvation. Henry suggests "God willed to make himself known" in "his redemptive disclosure [which] is a revelation of grace. . . . When at his incarnation God the Son is forsaken by his own chosen people, the redemptive offer is extended to all men everywhere by divine mandate."[41] Special revelation, therefore, has soteriological implications; it is through the sacred texts that God reveals the answer to the question, "what must I do to be saved?" Knowledge of salvation from their existential situation (sin) is impossible through any other means than God's communication in the Bible, says Henry: "Indeed, only through special revelation do fallen human beings know the full implications of general revelation and human sinfulness."[42]

Fourth, Henry also comments about knowledge of God (in propositional form) ascertained through rational reflection on nature, i.e., through God's general revelation. However, he accepts general revelation only because special revelation (scripture) attests to as much (e.g., Ps. 19:1; Rom 1:19–20). For Henry, a "general revelation of the Creator in his creation is integral to Christian doctrine founded upon Scripture" and "anyone who denies this doctrine places himself not only in unmistakable contradiction to the Bible and to the great theological traditions of Christendom that flow from its' teaching, but also against the living God's disclosure in cosmic reality and in mankind to which Scripture testifies."[43] In addition to revelation in nature, God also reveals through morality, a principle Henry calls the "general anthropological revelation."[44] Morality, suggests Henry, shows God's activity "in the mind and conscience of man . . . who bears the rem-

---

38. Henry, *God, Revelation and Authority*, IV/129.
39. Ibid., IV/166–67.
40. Ibid., IV/129.
41. Ibid., II/87.
42. Ibid., II/86.
43. Ibid., II/83–84.
44. Ibid., II/87.

nants of the divine image even in his moral rebellion."[45] But while Henry accepted general revelation as a real form of God's communication based on his reading of scripture, he rejects any version of natural theology because that would elevate reason above God's revelation. Even while revelation is entirely a rational thing, if a battle exists between reason and revelation, Henry sides with revelation. He clearly warns about the dangers of any approach different from his own when he says, "a faith in God which tries to establish its case on any proposition derived from general anthropology or philosophy of history or any other basis than the revelation of God in his Word is in no sense on the road to monotheism but is already on a one-way street to atheistic humanism."[46] Otherwise expressed, "we reject natural theology because of the express nature of supernatural revelation."[47]

Fifth, Henry's understanding of his sacred texts, nature, and the rational character of revelation is rooted in prior assumptions about the nature of God. For Henry, God's omnipotence and omniscience safeguard the texts from errors: "If one believes in a sovereign divine mind and will, in God who personally speaks and conveys information and instruction, then the presuppositions of scriptural inspiration lie near at hand."[48] Henry's view of revelation, therefore, is rooted in the unlimited power and knowledge of God to accomplish what God will. If God desires to communicate a specific message, God's sovereign mind and will are not frustrated. His concept of general revelation is also dependent on divine attributes, particularly divine transcendence: "God's transcendence means that nature is always and everywhere open to his purpose, a purpose that he expresses freely either in repetitive cosmic processes and events, or in once-for-all acts."[49]

Finally, it is worth mentioning the obvious, namely, that Henry presupposes truthfulness of the Christian texts and can, therefore, be called "presuppositionalist."[50] Rational reflection on the content of scripture provides one with propositional truths about God. Henry summarizes his view as follows:

> Divine revelation is the source of all truth, the truth of Christianity included; reason is the instrument for recognizing it; Scripture is its verifying principle; logical consistency is a negative test for truth and coherence a subordinate test. The task of

---

45. Ibid.
46. Ibid., II/123.
47. Ibid.
48. Ibid., III/428.
49. Ibid., VI/50.
50. Grenz and Olson, *20th Century Theology*, 293.

Christian theology is to exhibit the content of biblical revelation as an orderly whole.[51]

According to Dulles' models of revelation, Carl Henry advocates the first model: revelation as doctrine. And he presents the conservative evangelical with one way of dealing with the surrounding culture. He did *not* advocate for a retreat from the world but rather engagement with it by providing an alternative to it. Bernard Ramm will take a different approach, not necessarily at first but throughout his own philosophical and theological journey.

RAMM ON REVELATION

Instead of a rationalistic approach to revelation, one finds in Ramm a non-rationalism that paved the way for thinkers like Roger Olson and Stanley Grenz. Whereas Henry offered an *alternative to* mainline academic inquiry into the subject of revelation, the mature Ramm represents an evangelical *engagement with* modern theology, particularly the work of Karl Barth. Interestingly, although Ramm eventually became quite fond of Karl Barth, early in his career, before Ramm studied personally with Barth in Basel, he emphatically rejected neo-orthodoxy as inconsistent with Christianity's sacred texts: "The Christ of atheism, of liberalism, and of Barthianism is not the Christ of the historical documents."[52] In what was roughly the midpoint of his career, Ramm began to admit the influence of Barth on his thinking, especially in the area of apologetics. In his Preface to *The God Who Makes a Difference*, for example, Ramm says that Barth's "massive doctrine of revelation . . . and his doctrine of the reality of God . . . are really apologetic treatises of the first order, and some of that material has filtered into these pages." And finally, toward the end of his career Ramm acknowledged that Barth "offers to evangelical theology a paradigm of how best to come to terms with the Enlightenment."[53] Barth influenced Ramm's thinking not only in apologetics, but also in forming an approach to revelation and scripture. Six of Ramm's mature ideas deserve elaboration in what follows: (a) evangelicals, fundamentalists, and the Enlightenment, (b) the non-rational character of revelation, (c) the definition of revelation, (d) general revelation, (e) the need for special revelation, and (f) the character of Christianity's sacred texts in light of higher criticism.

---

51. Henry, *God, Revelation and Authority*, I/215 (emphasis removed).

52. Ramm, *Protestant Christian Evidences*, 180 in Grenz and Olson, *20th Century Theology*, 307.

53. Ramm, *After Fundamentalism*, vi.

First, Ramm distinguishes evangelicals from fundamentalists by noting a disparate stance toward the Enlightenment. Fundamentalism, according to Ramm, "attempts to shield itself from the Enlightenment. It attempts to do its theological and biblical tasks as if the Enlightenment had never happened."[54] In contrast, "the evangelical believes that the Enlightenment cannot be undone. He must use the valuable tools of research developed during the Enlightenment, and he cannot ignore the entire change of the intellectual climate of Europe and America that the Enlightenment produced."[55] More specifically, the evangelical must come to terms with scientific history, the scientific method, higher criticism, modern standards of research, and "the possibility of false cultural assumptions infiltrating his theology."[56] Comments such as these are obviously indebted to the influence of Barth on Ramm, at least in part. These comments, found in *The Evangelical Heritage*, were written *after* Ramm's visit to Basel.

Second, contrary to Henry, whose rationalism nearly permeated his entire corpus, the mature Ramm can be seen as an apologist for "non-rationalism." This is not to say that Ramm was *ir*rational;[57] rather, it is to suggest that Ramm had a transformed epistemology. He understood the limits of human knowledge, language, and understanding that Henry's work did not. For example, when speaking about the nature of a "leap of faith," Ramm emphasizes that "we cannot rationally fully explain the incarnation. Therefore, in the language of logic, one must make a leap to affirm the incarnation. In this sense, *all* Christians leap! Roman Catholics! Fundamentalists! Evangelicals! Eastern Orthodoxy! If there is a revelation of grace, there must be a leap, for *grace defies rational explanation*."[58] Ramm worries about turning his tradition into a philosophical system, because "systems do not save; only the Gospel saves. When the appeal of Christianity is its appeal as a great intellectual system then faith has been converted into knowledge."[59] Instead, reason should be used in service to the gospel, suggests Ramm: "Reason is Christianized by the grace of God, the Holy Spirit, and the saving Gospel of

---

54. Ramm, *Evangelical Heritage*, 70.
55. Ibid.
56. Ibid., 70–72.
57. See, e.g., Ramm, *After Fundamentalism*, 67, in which he denounces irrational faith: "Not can one be a fideist and renounce all reason or logic, for that would make both God and his revelation irrational or something imperiously given. One must have a *Christianized* reason."
58. Ibid., 66 (emphasis added).
59. Ibid., 67.

Jesus Christ. Then that Christianized reason can do its utmost to explore the depths of Christian theology."[60]

Third, Ramm defines revelation by suggesting that it occurs in a variety of ways and places, not just in Christianity's sacred texts. Ramm suggests that God's revelation is found "in creation, in the nature of man, in the history of Israel and the Church, in the pages of Holy Scripture, in the incarnation of God in Christ, and in the heart of the believer by the gospel."[61] In these various means by which God reveals, Ramm also notes that there is a condescending character to the revelation, which he calls the "anthropic form" of revelation: "By *anthropic* we mean accommodated to man, his language, his culture, and his powers."[62] Ramm is clear that the type of knowing that results from revelation is not philosophical in nature; rather, it is spiritual. The spiritual nature of revelation is expressed using the "bridge" metaphor. In its simplest definition,

> revelation is God making himself known, and this "knowing" is a spiritual knowing. The Eternal Spirit creates a *bridge* from his infinitude to the finitude of man; he imparts to man a knowledge of himself, and through that knowledge creates a fellowship with the creature. . . . [Man] can know God only as God makes himself known to him.[63]

Here one sees echoes of Barth's *Römerbrief*. Interestingly, where Barth credits Christ, Ramm, like von Balthasar, credits the Spirit. Where Ramm does fully agree with Barth, however, concerns the theologian's task and subject matter. In Ramm's view, the theologian's task is to reflect on revelation, and to do so, "the theologian does not treat God *in himself*, but *God in his revelation.*"[64]

Fourth, Ramm's background led him to write extensively on the interaction of theology with philosophy and science, and his conclusions can be taken as a comment on the general revelation of God. The early Ramm believes that "both science and theology are fundamental human pursuits. Both science and theology deal with the same universe. . . . If it is one universe then the visible and the invisible interpenetrate epistemologically

---

60. Ibid.
61. Ramm, *Protestant Christian Evidences*, 302.
62. Ramm, *Special Revelation*, 33.
63. Ramm, *Witness*, 31 (emphasis added).
64. Ramm, *Special Revelation*, 14. This is similar to the way our three Catholic thinkers understood revelation: it provides not access to God's essence, but rather to God as God chooses to be revealed. Grenz is the only figure in this book who will suggest that God's essential nature can be known through revelation.

and metaphysically."[65] The more mature his work, however, the less willing Ramm became to accept the compatibility of science and faith. He even became less willing to accept science as a conversation partner for theology. In his final book, Ramm says "scientific research and scientific theorizing are Pelagian in principle. They presuppose that if experimentation is carried on under very strict rules and theories are formulated with utmost rational care, scientists will arrive at truth. [However,] science allows for no cosmic demon . . . nor fallen humans who prefer deceit or error to truth."[66] Yet Ramm retained the idea that God reveals Godself through general revelation: "General revelation is God's witness to himself for all men" and is general in the sense that for *all* people it is a "general kind of revelation" in which "no voice is heard."[67] Types of general revelation include the beauty of the created world, reason, and morality.[68]

Fifth, while general revelation is directed to all people through various created media, special revelation is more specific. Special revelation is aimed at a particular audience for a specific purpose. For example, Ramm says special revelation "is God's word in a concrete form to a specific person or group."[69] He cites as an example the Sermon on the Mount.

Time is significant in Ramm's discussion of revelation, and it leads to a further distinction beyond the general/special one. In *Special Revelation and the Word of God*, Ramm argues that revelation before the fall, "before the entrance of sin . . . is called *prelapsarian* or *preredemptive* revelation" and after the fall is "either *soteric* or *postlapsarian* revelation."[70] For Ramm, therefore, there is a connection between the time in which a revelation is offered and its salvific effect. Revelation that happens before the fall is "general" and revelation that happens after the fall is "special," even while general revelation is still present. These distinctions play a part in the constructive portion of this book, in which a rethinking of the general/special distinction is offered.

Finally, Ramm's notion of what is the most significant form of special revelation shifted over the course of his career as well. Whereas he initially sought to offer an apology for the utility of his sacred texts qua revelation, Ramm assumes a Barthian stance toward the end of his career. Typical of the early Ramm who equated the Bible with revelation, he asserts "divine

---

65. Ramm, *Science and Scripture*, 37.
66. Ramm, *Offense to Reason*, 153–54.
67. Ramm, *Special Revelation*, 17 (emphases removed).
68. Ibid.
69. Ibid.
70. Ibid., 18.

revelation has priority over human philosophy. No philosophy is more fundamental than Holy Scripture nor has a position prior to divine revelation. ... Christian revelation is the higher critic of all philosophies whenever they impinge on the knowledge of God."[71] The mature Ramm views the Bible as "a record, a book, a document. It possesses no magical powers to influence the human mind.... Without the Spirit it is a dead letter."[72]

By affirming the instrumental character of sacred texts through which the Spirit reveals the Word to humanity, Ramm was put at odds with the rationalism of Henry. He explicitly declares his view as "contrary to *any* sort of theological rationalism ... which attributes an independent power to the words of Scripture separate from the Holy Spirit."[73]

After having taken away the power of Christianity's texts to convict their readers or hearers by their own authority, Ramm is positioned to engage with the biblical scholarship to which Henry offered an alternative. Ramm made clear that the Bible, while important to the Christian thinker, is not her/his sole determinant of philosophical and theological truth. Scripture is a tool in the hands of a divine Revealer. Unlike Henry, Ramm was open to the possibility that higher criticism had something to offer evangelicals: "Whenever biblical critics seem to make a real case in which there is close to universal, international agreement, the evangelical has no other course than to assent."[74] For Ramm this was not to say that the evangelical must concede to critics that scripture's value is purely historical. Moderating a middle position between fundamentalists and liberals, Ramm suggested the following:

> The literary character of special revelation suggests [a] very important matter for the proper understanding of Scripture. If the Scriptures are fundamentally in the form of literature (and also of history), then they must be judged and assessed by the standards of judgments of literature, not by rules or principles foreign to them. At this point *Biblicism* and *criticism* can fail to come into proper focus. Biblicism may fail to see the literary character of Scripture and treat Scripture like a code book of theological ordinance. Criticism may be so preoccupied with the literary aspects of Scripture that it fails to see the substance of which literature happens to be the vehicle.[75]

71. Ramm, *God Who Makes*, 36.

72. Ramm, *Witness*, 63–64.

73. Ibid., 64–65.

74. Ramm, *His Way Out* (Introduction). Cf. Grenz and Olson, *20th Century Theology*, 300.

75. Ramm, *Special Revelation*, 68.

The mature Ramm emphasized that Christianity's scriptures are used by God to effect salvation by revealing the Word incarnate in Jesus Christ. Scripture, contrary to rationalistic fundamentalists or critical liberals, is both information *and* encounter, and "the disjunction presented so frequently in modern theology between revelation as either 'information' or 'encounter' is false. . . . The structure of special revelation calls for a hard event *and* a hard word of interpretation. There cannot be a hard event with a soft interpretation."[76]

In sum, whereas Carl Henry offered an alternative to modern thinking on revelation, Ramm is thoroughly engaged with it. Ramm's view of revelation is unlike the presuppositionalism of Henry, who operated with the assumption that Christianity's sacred texts were fully truthful in all matters to which they speak. Instead of presuppositionalism, the early Ramm's philosophical and theological method is more like evidentialism.[77] He sought to correlate science and religion, showing that both emerge from one God and are therefore both vehicles through which humanity is made aware of God's design in the universe. The mature Ramm, however, mitigated the force of these claims by suggesting that the texts have an instrumental power directed by God in the manner God determines for the results God desires. By drawing on Barthian themes, Ramm's intellectual arc paved the way for contemporary evangelical thinkers to be significant contributors to conversations happening in mainline academic circles.

EVANGELICALS IN CONVERSATION: OLSON AND GRENZ

Ramm's openness to mainline thinking has had a profound effect on subsequent thinkers in the evangelical tradition. Two will be explored here, Roger Olson and Stanley Grenz, the former of whom uses the term "postconservative" to describe his work and the latter of whom does not. Olson is a professor of theology at Baylor University, and Grenz held his longest faculty stint as professor of theology at Carey Theological College in Vancouver with brief sojourns at the University of Winnipeg, Baylor, and Mars Hill Graduate School. While Grenz and Olson have collaborated on several

---

76. Ibid., 158. Ramm emphasized the same point in *Evangelical Heritage*, 130, but here he is skeptical of neoorthodox theology to be sufficiently distinct from Bultmann and existentialism: "Extreme breeds extreme. When neoorthodox and existentially oriented theologians deny propositional revelation and assert that revelation is only confrontation with God or a divine-human encounter, then the evangelical pushes to the other extreme and declares all revelation is propositional. *Both alternatives are false*" (emphasis added).

77. Grenz and Olson, *20th Century Theology*, 301.

publications, and although Grenz has collaborated with other self-confessing "postconservative" theologians,[78] before his untimely death in 2005 he "was reluctant to have the label applied to him or his theological work."[79]

Olson's view of revelation is described below in six stages: (a) the erosion of foundationalism, (b) "post-rationalist"[80] theology, (c) his definition of revelation, (d) the idea of general revelation, (e) the need for special revelation, and (f) the Bible as literature.

First, Olson responds to two specific problems he sees in theologies resting on foundationalism: accommodation and arrogance. The type of thinking that yields "a systematic vision of reality that is comprehensive and coherent both internally and externally with the whole of experience" is wrongheaded.[81] Ironically, Olson faults Henry's foundationalism for giving away too much—pandering even—to the Enlightenment. In Olson's view, Henry "represents an accommodation to a passing cultural phase—modernity—and a stumbling block to relating theology to postmodernity."[82] The irony is that conservative evangelicals are accusing postconservatives of the same accommodation.[83] Olson replies that they are not accommodating to modernity or postmodernity, but rather seeking to understand the Christian vision of the world in a new situation. Moreover, Olson is responding to the arrogance Henry's rationalism communicates, "the rationalistic hubris implicit in foundationalism that leads inevitably to doubt when people see that the foundations are not as certain as the practitioners claim."[84]

Second, if Henry was rational and Ramm was non-rational, Roger Olson may be said to emphasize the *post*-rationalist nature of revelation. Insofar as rationalism contributes to propositional views of revelation, Olson rejects it as inadequate. Drawing on contemporary work in the philosophy of language, Olson suggests that "straightforward assertions of simple facts may not be the only conveyers of truth; truth may be communicated even more effectively in some cases by means of images, symbols, and stories." Some statements *do more* than communicate facts; these "speech acts . . . alter reality; they make things happen." Rationalism, as Olson sees it, fails to take these advances into account. Olson says rational defenses of

78. For example, Grenz co-wrote *Beyond Foundationalism* with Franke, author of *The Character of Theology: A Postconservative Evangelical Approach*.

79. Olson, *Reformed*, 15.

80. This term is my own to show a distinction from that of Henry and Ramm. To my knowledge, Olson does not use it of himself or his work.

81. Olson, *Reformed*, 130.

82. Ibid., 131.

83. See Erickson, *Evangelical Left* and Olson's response in *Reformed*, 12.

84. Olson, *Reformed*, 131.

propositional accounts stem "more from the Enlightenment than from the gospel or even Christian tradition." Where rationalistic evangelicalism sought modernity's highest prize—"the communication of objective facts as the highest form of language"—Olson wants to explore "other modes of revelation as valuable for theology and look into the possibility that theology itself may do more with words than simply communicate facts."[85] One such mode of revelation is narrative, on which postconservatives and postliberals have much in common.

Third, instead of rational propositions, Olson suggests that revelation can be defined as follows: "The heart of revelation, for narrative theologians, lies in its stories."[86] Relying on the work of postliberal theologians such as those mentioned in the previous chapter—Hans Frei and George Lindbeck—Olson uses the Yale School and its attending emphasis on narrative to put forward a postconservative view of revelation: "postconservative theology's conviction [is] that revelation is more about transformation than information, although it contains the latter."[87] And drawing on other evangelical postliberals, e.g., Henry Knight, Olson suggests that "the primary form of revelation for us—whatever its original forms in history may have been—is literature.[88]

Fourth, Olson does not discuss general revelation much in the two works that describe his postconservative approach. One would expect as much in consideration of the fact that the emphasis is on the transformative power of the Christian story instead of merely the communication of information in propositions. Of course, Olson and the postconservatives do not deny that there is general revelation in the created order. But whereas general revelation may be said to communicate information about God and God's attributes sufficient to make one accountable, a postconservative will value *transformation* more than *information*.

Fifth, Olson and other postconservatives have attempted to move beyond the rationalistic interpretation of conservative evangelicalism and fundamentalism, so he comments on the need left by general revelation. Olson agrees with Carl Henry and a bearer of his intellectual legacy today, Paul Helm, by affirming a distinction between general and special revelation and how special revelation is the primary source: "Most conservative evangelical theologians would agree with Henry and Helm: divine special revelation, in contrast to general revelation in nature, is theology's primary

---

85. Ibid., 154.
86. Ibid., 163.
87. Ibid., 165.
88. Ibid., 168.

source and norm and is the communication of information for the purpose of creating knowledge. Of course . . . postconservatives wonder if knowledge is the only or best means of transforming persons."[89] Herein lies Olson's vision of why special revelation is needed: only through it will persons be transformed. Olson describes what it means to be "evangelical" in such a way that the necessity of special revelation is shown: "Being evangelical includes being committed to the authority of God's Word. Why? Because we believe it is true. Why? Because it brings us to Christ who has saved us and lives in our lives."[90] Special revelation is necessary because only through it do people have access to the gospel.

Finally, though Olson affirms the Bible as a primary form of special revelation for the Christian, in the view of postconservatives Scripture is treated less as a book of propositions to be defended against the modern critiques and more as a means through which God transforms. Stories are transformative in postconservativism, and as such, "the Bible is more like a great nonfiction novel than like a book of philosophy. It contains philosophy (or at least something like it), but only within the framework of a grand narrative. It is an epic more than a textbook of information and ideas."[91] If the primary form of revelation is narrative, then Olson claims, "The Bible is first and foremost great literature. And great literature transforms more than informs."[92] If one fails to see the narrative character of the texts, one comes close to denying its special status in the Christian life. To those propounding a bibliology in which information alone is valid, Olson poses a question: "if a system of doctrine could be constructed that perfectly reflects biblical revelation in all its factual assertions, would the Bible no longer be necessary?"[93] Rather than a document full of either propositions or narratives that can be propositionalized, the Bible is the means by which God transforms people.

Olson rejects foundationalism, propositionalism, and rationalism as unfortunate accommodation to the Enlightenment. Rather than viewing revelation as a means to attain information, Olson and other postconservative thinkers suggest that revelation is a body of narratives geared toward transformation. Olson thinks—with postliberals—that narratives and stories can not only communicate, but also "make things happen."

---

89. Ibid., 54.
90. Olson, *How to Be Evangelical*, 40.
91. Olson, *Reformed*, 165.
92. Ibid., 168.
93. Ibid., 163.

Stanley Grenz also makes an interesting evangelical conversation partner. As noted above, Grenz resists the label "postconservative." Interestingly, however, his work is postconservative in a manner befitting the label, for he consciously and explicitly tries to move beyond theological conservatism. In *Renewing the Center*, for instance, Grenz talks about his desire for the evangelical community:

> The postmodern condition calls Christians to move beyond the fixation with a conflictual polarity that knows only the categories of "liberal" and "conservative," and thus pits so-called conservatives against loosely defined liberals. Instead, the situation in which the church is increasingly ministering requires a "generous orthodoxy" characteristic of a renewed "center" that lies beyond the polarizations of the past, produced as they were by modernist assumptions—a generous orthodoxy, that is, that takes seriously the postmodern problematic. Therefore, the way forward is for evangelicals to take the lead in renewing a theological "center" that can meet the challenges of the postmodern, and in some sense post-theological situation in which the church now finds itself.[94]

It is easy to see why Olson views Grenz as "the epitome of a postconservative evangelical theologian."[95] Even still, for personal or professional reasons, Grenz did not adopt the label. It could be the case that, perhaps like Telford Work, Grenz's writings are thoroughly postconservative but he is not ready to adopt the label because "postconservativism is not a radical enough name for 'evangelical theology after modernity.' A better one," says Work, "would be postliberalism. Why? Because postliberals abandon the Enlightenment project that sparked the whole fundamentalist-modernist controversy, and thus both contemporary liberal theology and contemporary evangelical theology." Whatever the reason, and one will never know, Grenz sympathized with Work's retort: "Don't Call Me Postconservative."[96] His request notwithstanding, it will soon become clear how much he has in common with those who self-identify as postconservative.

A few things can be said about Grenz's view of divine revelation. First, Grenz does not treat divine revelation as a locus in and of itself, and he does not give it methodological priority. Often when he discusses revelation he does so in conjunction with a doctrine of Scripture. In *Theology for the*

---

94. Grenz, *Renewing the Center*, 331.
95. Olson, *Reformed*, 15.
96. Review of Olson's *Reformed* in *Christianity Today*, Feb. 25, 2008.

Community of God, as Grenz describes the "nature and task of theology,"[97] he says he refuses to preface his systematic theology "with elaborate attempts to establish the resourcefulness of the Bible as the foundation" of his efforts because "all such attempts to establish the role of Scripture in theology . . . are ultimately unnecessary."[98] Rather, one can assume the authority of Christianity's sacred texts from the outset. There is an "integral" relationship between theology and the faith community, and the collection of Christian texts is "universally acknowledged" as a foundational document for the Church. The message in the texts is the "central norm for the systematic articulation of the faith of that community."[99] If one defines theology as reflection on community faith, one need not defend the sources that already function authoritatively in the community.

Second, Grenz accepts that revelation is real, and he offers a definition of it: "We may define revelation as the divine act of self-disclosure which makes known God's essential nature."[100] He elaborates on the idea of revelation by locating it historically. For Grenz, ultimately "revelation stands at the eschaton, at the grand climax of human history."[101] In Grenz's view, a "grand eschatological event will inaugurate a glorious state of affairs, for it will constitute God's ultimate self-disclosure."[102] This connection between eschatology and revelation is due to Grenz's view that "history is God's chosen medium of revelation."[103] This idea obviously has roots in Grenz's academic background; he studied with Wolfhart Pannenberg, whose *Revelation as History* advances similar themes. According to Pannenberg, God's self-revelation is not direct but rather indirect,[104] fully comprehended only

---

97. Grenz, *Community of God*, 16–20.

98. Ibid., 17.

99. Ibid.

100. Ibid. One could press Grenz on whether we can know anything about God's essence. Any good Thomist—Dulles, Ratzinger, Rahner, Ramm, von Balthasar, etc.—will deny that we can know something of God's essence. Barth suggests that we can know God in God's revelation, God as God has chosen to reveal Godself to us, not God in Godself. This will again be touched upon latter in the book as I take up the question of whether access to God is mediated or immediate, and when I discuss the nature of God and the God/world relationship with which this view of revelation relates best. (My guess is that Grenz simply inserted an inappropriate word rather than suggesting that we can know God's essence. I base this conjecture on his later comments that revelation in history is mediated.)

101. Ibid.

102. Ibid., 266.

103. Ibid., 393.

104. Pannenberg, *Revelation as History*, 125 ff.

in the eschaton, "at the end of the revealing history."[105] Grenz says—like Olson—that God's revelation in history is "mediated" to us through an act *and* our interpretation. "This understanding implies that the focus of divine revelation is not what we may call 'brute historical facts'... but rather 'interpreted facts.'"[106] Pannenberg said the same thing decades earlier: "History is not composed of raw or so-called brute facts. As the history of man, the history of revelation is always bound up with understanding, in hope and remembrance."[107] For Grenz, revelation is also a reality today because "it has appeared proleptically (in the manner of foretaste) in human history."[108]

Revelation is connected to the idea of sacred texts insofar as they are a record of God's people in relationship to God. They are a story of generation after generation of God's people who were confronted repeatedly with a self-disclosing God. So the Bible is the "foundational" witness to the self-revelation of God and a record of how the ancient people of God responded to God's calling to be a covenant people. The events narrated in the Hebrew scriptures as well as the New Testament are foundational for Christian thinkers. In Grenz's own words, "The foundation of Christian theology lies in these paradigmatic events and their use in the community of faith as set forth in the Bible."[109] Borrowing from Lindbeck, Grenz believes that the narratives serve a "regulative" function.[110] The task of the theologian is to "explore, order, and systematize" the ancient "symbols and concepts into a unified whole—a conceptual framework—for the sake of the community of faith which they serve."[111]

Third, Grenz is thoroughly trinitarian. He discusses revelation in the context of theology proper, pneumatology, and christology. In theology proper, it is characteristic of God to make Godself known, even in creation. He cites Aquinas and the Psalmist as evidence: "The heavens declare the glory of the Lord."[112] In his christology, Grenz specifically discusses "Jesus as the Revealer of God."[113] The incarnate Word's capacity as the revealer of God moves christology from merely functional to ontological because the "revealer cannot be separated from what is revealed" and "as a consequence

---

105. Ibid., 131.
106. Grenz, *Community of God*, 394.
107. Pannenberg, *Revelation as History*, 152.
108. Grenz, *Community of God*, 17.
109. Ibid., 18.
110. Ibid. Cf. Lindbeck, *Nature of Doctrine*, 18.
111. Grenz, *Community of God*, 18.
112. Ibid., 48.
113. Ibid., 264.

of this connection, Jesus participates by necessity in the essential nature of the one he reveals."[114] Jesus' identity as the revealer of God has objective and subjective meanings. Objectively, the picture of God Jesus gives accurately portrays who God is, and each part of his ministry is revelatory: "His teaching informs us about God; his character shows forth the qualities of God; his death reveals the suffering of God and his resurrection vividly declares the creative power of God."[115] The portrait of God this creates is one of love, and not just any love. This love is related to the Christian religious end, that is, this love is absolutely salvific.[116] Subjectively, the incarnate Word dwells among us and introduces God to us. The character of the Word "must be 'formed' in us. . . . As this transpires, we truly become the image of God."[117] Moreover, the incarnation supplements whatever fragmentary revelation is found in creation; the prior "hidden" God was forever manifested in our presence for everyone to see in Christ.

Last, Grenz discusses revelation in conjunction with his doctrine of the Spirit. In Grenz's view, the Spirit plays a vital role in revelation's reception. He goes so far as to say that "The Bible [is] the Spirit's book. Scripture is ultimately a function of the Spirit. It finds both its source and its abiding importance in the activity of the one who breathes it."[118] For Grenz the main bridge between revelation and the Bible as the instrument of our knowledge of God is pneumatology. Like Olson, Grenz departs from the rationalism and propositionalism of Carl Henry. Divine revelation is seen as God's self-disclosure, not merely cognitive or propositional statements. Even still, revelation is connected to knowledge of God insofar as it aids in the epistemological process of coming to know God.

In sum, Olson sought to replace the rationalism of Carl Henry with a post-rationalist approach in which God is powerful to act through narratives, and this is the process of revelation. In Grenz, a similar thing is happening, but revelation was oriented toward the eschaton and scripture defended in the context of pneumatology.

---

114. Ibid., 264. If John the Baptist can be considered a revealer of Jesus, I would disagree with Grenz on this point. The revealer can reveal something different than itself. Revelation, as I argue in chapters 4 and 5, can but does not necessarily have to include self-communication.

115. Ibid., 265.

116. Ibid: "It seeks to lost, suffers with the afflicted, and redeems the fallen. God's love is likewise jealous, as is evident in the picture of Jesus as the righteous Judge."

117. Ibid.

118. Ibid., 392.

EVALUATION: THE ISSUES OF BIBLICISM AND GOSPEL

Two things become clear in the following evaluation of Ramm and his intellectual heirs: first, the confidence conservative evangelicals once had in scripture's accuracy on non-faith matters has eroded; and second, this changing perspective on revelation is related to a more fundamental shift in the perception of the gospel among evangelicals. Bernard Ramm is the central figure in the evangelical arc this chapter describes. When evangelicals came out of hiding, Ramm eventually fully participated in conversations with mainline thnkers as opposed to Carl Henry's counter-cultural proposal for revelation.

Henry, Ramm, Olson and Grenz agree on some significant issues. First, all proudly self-identity as "evangelicals," which, using the taxonomy Fackre mentioned in the beginning of the chapter, means at a minimum that they are committed to justification by faith and the authority of Christianity's sacred texts. It also means that they hold crucicentrist atonement theories and are concerned with activism and conversions (if Bebbington's taxonomy is used). Second, all four responded to the theological climate around them, though in different ways: for Henry, the task was to offer an *alternative* to the modern thinking of Bultmann, Barth, and others; for the mature Ramm, the goals was to *mediate* between evangelicalism and modernity (particularly Barth) in order to emphasize revelation's power to be both *information* about God and *encounter* with God; for Olson and Grenz, the task is to restate Christianity in a postmodern context, which means rethinking social-locatedness and the limits of rationalism. A third shared view in Henry, Ramm, Olson, and Grenz concerns the reason for which special revelation is needed: the Christian religious end of salvation. All four argue that special revelation is needed because in it one gets access—in whatever form the access will take, be it propositions, transformation, or both—to salvation.

There are good reasons to suspect that the changes in revelation in evangelicalism are due to a deeper, more significant shift in the understanding of the gospel itself, a divergence in the answer to the Philippian jailer's question, "What must I do to be saved?" Their soteriologies, therefore, are useful for understanding their perspectives on revelation.

First, Henry's view of revelation as rational communication of propositional information (the presuppositionalist approach) is symptomatic of his soteriology, which is understood as a cognitive assent to a set of propositions. Henry comments at great length that the offer of salvation must be "personally accepted," because "without personal appropriation God's promise of rescue in and of itself saves no one."[119] Despite Henry's asseveration that salvation is "not by good tidings alone," he rejects theories in which "God is said to communicate himself, not truths about himself"[120] as he finds in Barth. For Henry, the Bible "teaches as a truth of revelation that unrepentant sinners have enough knowledge to render them culpable."[121] Special revelation provides the information necessary for salvation, and a human's response is either to believe what information the revelation gives or deny it, in which case the sinner is damned for unbelief. For Henry, Christianity's sacred texts qua special revelation attests to the character of the requisite knowledge for salvation: "The Bible does not empty the reality of spiritual life simply into a relationship of trust, but insists also on the indispensability of spiritual knowledge."[122]

Second, Ramm's soteriology toward the end of his career is notoriously hard to pin down. Early in his career Ramm had argued strenuously for the truthfulness of Christianity, and his early work on the subject is not unlike that of Henry's soteriology. However, one notices a shift in "mood" or "attitude" in Ramm's soteriology throughout his career. Whereas Henry had emphasized personal assent to sufficient propositions, the mature Ramm instead begins to concentrate on the figure of Jesus, and what Jesus has accomplished. He shifts to emphasize more what God did *for* sinners than what is required *of* sinners in response. His tone is appreciative rather than fear invoking or judgmental, both of which one might accuse Henry.[123] To

---

119. Henry, *God, Revelation and Authority*, II/38.

120. Ibid., II/42.

121. Ibid., II/44.

122. Ibid. Unfortunately, Henry does not sufficiently differentiate "spiritual" knowledge from other knowledge of a, say, scientific or theological variety.

123. For example, in 1959 Ramm described the way salvation might come to a person in *Witness*, 68: "Our salvation may come to us in a number of ways: it may come by a quiet reading of Scripture; by the customary preaching of the minister; by the impetus of an evangelistic service; by the personal word of a Christian; or by an accident of life which throws us unexpectedly into the hearing of the gospel. *When we believe*, the truth of the gospel is sealed in our hearts by the Holy Spirit. We not only believe but we have a conviction in our hearts that we have believed the truth. Our divine Lord has given us a divine salvation by the instrument of a divine message and by the efficacious administration of the Holy Spirit. The entire set of concepts is permeated with the veracity inherent in deity. But when we seek to discover the source of the message, we invariably find our way to Sacred Scripture. The sermon, the song, the tract, the personal witness, the Christian sacrament, all have their root in Sacred Scripture. We are led and driven to the conclusion that the source of the message which saved our souls is higher than the medium which brought the message. We are thus driven beyond minister, sermon, and sacrament to Holy Scripture as the ground (not the cause, which is the Holy Spirit) of our certainty, as the truth of God, and the authority for our faith and of our faith" (emphasis added).

be sure, Ramm still differentiated himself from liberalism, in which "there is no God who by the incarnation takes our cause upon himself; no theanthropic person who goes to the cross and takes our judgment and contradiction upon himself, who goes through death and emerges risen from the dead to share with us his victory over the grave."[124] But Ramm's focus was on God's role and less on the human response. Here again one sees the obvious influence of Barth on Ramm's thinking. In fact, toward the end of his career he is difficult to pin down because he attempted to put Barth's soteriology in perspective against those who charged him with universalism. Ramm defended Barth by reasserting that we do not know who is saved and who is not: "To affirm that God will only save some is a bit of knowledge none of us have."[125]

Third, Olson and Grenz are intellectual descendants of Ramm insofar as they emphasize God's work and not human response. In Olson's view, conservatives "prefer to believe in and look for a transcultural expression of the gospel [because they think] theology ought to be global rather than local."[126] But with the advent of postmodernity, Christians are no longer able to claim the type of absolutist knowledge of God that Henry's propositionalism maintained. According to Olson, "authentic evangelicalism is defined by its centrifugal center of powerful gravity and not by outlying boundaries that serve as walls or fences. The center is Jesus Christ and the gospel. . . . People gathered around the center or moving toward it are authentically evangelical: people or institutions moving away from it or with their backs turned against it are of questionable evangelical status. But it is not a matter of 'in' or 'out' as there is no evangelical magisterium to decide that."[127] To his own claim that the Bible "brings us the Christ who has saved us and lives in our lives," Olson asks, "How do we know? Because an entire population across centuries has witnessed to its life-transforming power."[128] For Olson, soteriology is "Christianity's essence" defined as "transformation over information."[129] Grenz agrees, as shown in his definition of conversion: "We may define conversion as that life-changing encounter with the triune God which inaugurates a radical break with our old, fallen existence and a new life in fellowship with God. This transforming encounter with

---

124. Ramm, *Witness*, 121–22.
125. Ramm, *After Fundamentalism*, 167.
126. Olson, *Reformed*, 24.
127. Ibid., 60.
128. Olson, *How to Be Evangelical*, 40.
129. Olson, *Reformed*, ch. 2.

God lies at the foundation of our Christian experience."[130] In the moment of salvation, one is transformed from old life to new. Furthermore, for Grenz the action is all God's; the divine working underlies any human response.[131] Like Olson, Grenz does not say the cognitive component of the gospel is entirely absent; rather, he mitigates Henry's propositionalism by advocating a "both and" rather than an "either or." He says, "we acknowledge this gospel message as true, not only in some general sense but also as applicable to our situation."[132] For postconservatives, conversion is only one stage in a three-part salvation process. Salvation also includes sanctification, in which one is transformed into Christlikeness, and glorification, in which the Spirit's work of renewal is completed "at the end of the age."[133]

Take note of the shifting soteriology. Once seen as a cognitive assent to the "four spiritual laws" disclosed in God's revelation, the view that the gospel involves more than the mere apprehension and personal appropriation of propositional data is growing. To be sure, there are large numbers of Christians still operating under the Henry-like notions of revelation and soteriology, as evidenced by missionaries and evangelists overseas or apologists in debate with the now defunct "new atheism." However, postmodernity has occasioned a re-evaluation of the types of twentieth-century evangelicalism that depend on Enlightenment standards of rationality. The mature Ramm's willingness to engage *with* modern thinking instead of offering an alternative *to* it has paved the way for contemporary thinkers like Roger Olson and the late Stanley Grenz to be dialog partners with mainline academics in a variety of contexts on a host of issues.

There are some implications of this sort of thinking for evangelical theology and philosophy of religion. First, one can point to a shift in mood or spirit, as attempts at proving God's existence through rational argumentation take a backseat to encouraging transformation individually and corporately. In *Christianity Today's* 2014 Book Awards, for example, the winner of the "Apologetics and Evangelism" category took a decidedly different approach than old school apologetics. Francis Spufford argued in *Unapologetic* how "despite everything, Christianity still makes surprising emotional sense," not rational sense. Moreover, the book that earned an Honorable Mention touted *The End of Apologetics*, in which Myron Bradley Penner examines what it means to have "Christian witness in a Postmodern Context." Henry-like attempts to offer a fully rational argument for Christian

---

130. Grenz, *Community of God*, 405.
131. Ibid.
132. Ibid., 409.
133. Ibid., 433.

truth claims are disappearing in favor of those that appeal to Christianity's transformative power.

Second, the style of argumentation of analytic philosophy of religion has lost some of the power it used to command, as Enlightenment standards of reason and evidentialism have given way to postmodernity and all its advances. This is not to say that reason itself is no longer useful (how could it be?), but only to say that when "truth" itself is being understood in different ways, there are consequences for those whose practice it is to discern the truth in analytic philosophy of religion. As an example of this dynamic in action, consider Eleonore Stump's recent monograph on the problem of pain, *Wandering in Darkness*. The next chapter says more about this book; suffice it to say here that Stump views storytelling as a more effective tool for discerning the truth than analytic philosophical argumentation, at least on the problem of pain.

Third, if methods for justifying what is "true" are changing, in a post-rationalist era one might suggest (contrary to the history of philosophy) that a criterion for a claim's truthfulness is its ability to foster transformation. And "transformation," it may be argued, is about the "good" more than the "true." Instead of holding one transcendental as absolutely most valuable—the "true"—a space is created by postconservatives for equal value to be placed on the "good" or the "beautiful."[134] Arguments, therefore, may involve the utility of principles to impact transformation in the world and in individuals rather than in their logical coherence, a possible implication one might call "religious neo-pragmatism."[135]

LINGERING QUESTIONS

Are these so-called "advances" in revelation beneficial? The arc represented by Henry, Ramm, Olson, and Grenz raises some serious questions, as does the work of each theologian on his own. Beginning with Henry, one might ask how he avoids circular reasoning by basing his views of the sole authority of the Bible on the sole authority of the Bible.[136] (The same criticism can be used for divine attributes, for if Scripture's author is God and God's at-

---

134. See, for instance, Whitehead, *Adventures in Ideas*, 265–72.

135. Neo-pragmatism is a term already in use. In 1995, Richard Rorty discussed issues related to this possible implication. See Rorty, "Response to Hartshorne," 135: "I linguisticize as many pre-linguistic-turn philosophers as I can, in order to read them as prophets of the utopia in which all metaphysical problems have been dissolved, and religion and science have yielded their place to poetry."

136. See Davis, *Debate*, 49–51.

tributes are derived from Scripture, is this not begging the question?) Henry held strict propositional ideas of revelation and salvation, using logical consistency as revelation's test for truth, and one could ask how this almost scientific defense of his view of revelation coincides with other sciences that call the "inerrancy" position into question: geology, biology, history, etc. One could press Olson and Grenz on whether transformation is primary: if transformation is the gospel to which narrative revelation points, what special status is given to Christianity? Presumably, one could be transformed to live an ethical or godly life by any number of non-Christian occasions or issues, and a person could in fact never recognize God's role in the transformation. Does this matter for revelation? Can one receive revelation and adjust one's life without ever recognizing its source?

Finally, one could question the arc itself. If it is true that there's a correlation of shifts in evangelical perspectives of revelation and soteriologies, what is the cause of its shift beyond reactionary countermoves? Is the current trend of "postconservative" evangelicalism simply the impact of postmodernism corrupting it? Perhaps just as Henry's accommodation to the Enlightenment is wrongheaded, so too is the postconservative accommodation to postmodernity. It is almost certain that postmodernity will give way to another phase of intellectual history, though no one is quite sure what that will be. In that new phase, it seems likely that younger philosophers of religion and theologians will criticize postconservatives of accommodation to postmodernity, does it not?

Criticisms of Ramm belong at the end for a simple reason. In short, his later work provides a helpful and instructive mediation between historical tradition and unavoidable advances. Though the early Ramm agrees with Henry with respect to the "inerrancy" position,[137] he recognizes that the incarnate Word is the central feature of the Christian faith and the central revelation of God. He criticizes evangelical biblicists of forgetting this: "The temptation of biblicism is that it can speak of the inspiration of the Scriptures *apart from* the Lord they enshrine. . . . There can be no formal doctrine of inspiration; there can only be a Christ-centered doctrine of inspiration."[138] The mature Ramm emphasized God's activity in salvation and revelation, noting both an *encounter* with God and *information* about God. So while it may be unfashionable these days to maintain a "middle of the road" position, perhaps Ramm's balance is the most appropriate position given the shifting nature of intellectual inquiry as shown in the diversity of opinions throughout the history of Christian thought. At any rate, the questions

---

137. See, e.g., *Protestant Biblical Interpretation*, ch. 8.
138. Ramm, *Special Revelation*, 117.

raised by the work of each individual thinker and the arc of which they are a part are many, and they point towards some things a contemporary doctrine of revelation should address.

With respect to biblicism, the evangelical trajectory opens up new possibilities. Ramm has paved the way for contemporary thinkers to re-imagine the ways in which Christianity's sacred texts function authoritatively in Christian communities. The "point and shoot" theory of revelation is loosing ground, as it should. It does not respect the narrative quality of the sacred texts. But herein lies a challenge: if they are to remain faithful to their heritage, evangelical Christians should no more disregard the Bible than they should entirely commit to an inflexible or unbending interpretation of it. We are shown through this evangelical arc—of which Ramm is the central figure—that a contemporary perspective of revelation must seek to both preserve the uniqueness of these sacred texts and be conversant with advances in other disciplines. If higher criticism is showing evangelicals that inflexible biblicism is wrongheaded or impossible, evangelicals should evaluate the extent to which this impacts their views of the Bible as revelation.

Evangelicals who endorse a close-minded biblicism must come to terms with tensions in the text itself and adjust their views accordingly. They must ask themselves hard questions, like: How is the Bible useful for someone who is illiterate, as many have been in the history of the Christian church? What about issues in translation or areas in which scholars are unsure of what the original text actually said? A contemporary model of revelation (and inspiration) must take into account that specific words have a function in the communication of ideas and stories. Inspiration and revelation thus include, but are not limited to, the Bible. God, the infinitely skilled communicator, may use *any* tool as a proverbial microphone. These are subjects treated more fully in chapters 4 and 5.

One result of this evangelical arc is, interestingly, a growing resurgence of the evangelicalism of the nineteenth century mentioned above: young, socially active, progressive evangelicals who have serious commitments to social justice, the environment, and other progressive causes.[139] In short, they are interested in *transformation*. By emphasizing God in the transformation process instead of the necessary human response, evangelicals have used the figure of Jesus as the centerpiece of their social justice work. Christ is a reason for building bridges between disparate racial, socioeconomic and even religious groups instead of cause for division. For example, a recent Bob Jones University graduate participated in the Interfaith Youth Core, which

---

139. Balmer, *Thy Kingdom Come*, 145: These evangelicals "believed that they, as followers of Jesus, could bring on the millennium now—right here on earth and, more specifically, right here in America—by dint of their own efforts."

gathers young women and men together for the purpose of solving social problems. In the past thirty years, many young evangelicals have followed the lead of Jim Wallis (founder of *Sojourners*) and Tony Campolo (founder of *Red Letter Christians*). Roger Olson shares their sentiments: "I believe if Jesus were here today he would identify with the poor and oppressed more than with the wealthy and powerful."[140]

In close, it is appropriate to mention all four of these figures encountered the work of Karl Barth: in Henry's case, the task was to refute him; for Ramm, it was at first refutation, then cautious appreciation, and finally acceptance; and in the postconservatives, Barth is encountered in his continuing legacy as the greatest Christian thinker since the Reformation. It seems appropriate, as the reader transitions out of the exegetical portion of the book into the constructive part, to recall an episode from the life of Barth. The narrative reminds one of the necessities of humility and humor as one navigates through challenging intellectual times:

> During Barth's 1962 tour of the United States, a student asked him what had been the most momentous theological discovery of his long life. [He gave] a naïve answer, but not inaccurate as a summary of the central message of the *Church Dogmatics*. His answer was "Jesus loves me, this I know, for the Bible tells me so."[141]

---

140. Olson, *How to be Evangelical*, 202.
141. Mangina, *Karl Barth*, 9.

PART TWO

PART TWO

CHAPTER 4

The Big Picture
Toward an Integrative Model of Revelation

A SUMMARY THUS FAR

The preceding chapters have explored the notion of revelation in three thinkers who were active in the late twentieth century and whose writings exercise influence today. Their views were put into conversation with some other thinkers in the branch from which the thinker came and the exchange was used to ask questions that their work raises on important issues related to divine revelation (e.g., tradition, pluralism, soteriology and biblicism). In each figure one gains something valuable for understanding revelation, including an important central revelational theme that figures into the model of revelation this book advances.

In chapter 1, Avery Cardinal Dulles represented a Catholic view of revelation, the "symbolic mediation" approach. Dulles' central revelational theme is "symbol," according to which revelation is mediated through signs that mysteriously work on humanity in a way that eludes precise description. Dulles said revelation happens in three steps: first, we are attracted to a symbol; second, we surrender to its power; and third, we receive the revelation. The whole process is participatory, and Dulles believes it is thoroughly in line with Christianity's sacred texts. While revelation results in new knowledge, Dulles also argues that it has transformative effects on people's behaviors and commitments. Dulles reminds us that we must be ever cautious to avoid dogmatic assertions about an ultimately ineffable God. He also wisely suggests the incorporation of "symbols" into the idea of revelation, a move that finds resonance in the proposal offered here. Where Dulles falls short, however, is where postliberalism is strong: Dulles made little use of the category of "narrative" in his proposal of revelation despite the fact that it has been a major theme in theology of the past three decades and is also being used by some philosophers of late.

In chapter 2, George A. Lindbeck represented a postliberal perspective on revelation, and postliberals are known for proposing "narrative" as a central theme. Lindbeck found liberal theology's inward experiential turn unhelpful for finding or understanding revelation, and instead saw the incarnate Word available in preaching and the sacraments, both of which are externally oriented activities. Like Dulles, Lindbeck reminds the reader that revelation is participatory. Insofar as Christianity's sacred texts act as revelation, they are a world into which a reader immerses herself and lives out their worldview and its principles derived from their narratives. On this much Lindbeck, postliberals in general, and postconservative evangelicals (e.g., Roger Olson) are in agreement: scripture's value lies in its stories. Narratives are heuristically powerful devices, and the postliberal school shows that a contemporary view of revelation must incorporate them in some way. Therefore, not only does the view proposed in this chapter take seriously the concept of symbol, but it also suggests that narrative is a useful concept in the idea of revelation. One is reminded, however, that Lindbeck struggled to show how revelation can be understood in a distinctively *Christian* way and he offers few reasons why the Christianity's sacred texts should still be considered theologically unique among all of the other sacred texts of the world.

In chapter 3, Bernard L. Ramm represented an evangelical stance on divine revelation. The stance Ramm advocated, however, is not "the" evangelical stance any more than Dulles' view is the Catholic view or Lindbeck's is the postliberal view. Catholicism, postliberalism, and evangelicalism are traditions that house enough diversity to only make possible discussion of family resemblances among their members; hence, each chapter provided two interlocutors to round out the discussion. Conservative evangelicalism offers the opportunity to explore "scripture" as the central revelational theme, and Ramm shows the reader ways to hold scripture in high esteem without burying one's head in the sand when it comes to other disciplines. Carl Henry, it was noted, viewed revelation through the lens of what may be called "extreme rationalism," which also impacted his approach to scripture. It may be that Henry is more representative of everyday evangelicalism than Ramm, who adopted a middle position in which God uses various media for the ends God seeks in the way God determines. Ramm reminds evangelicals of the necessity of open communication with not only those who disagree but also those working in other fields. Ramm became increasingly sympathetic to some modern yet non-evangelical thinkers. He viewed their approach as better than those who would offer "counter-culture" perspectives without seriously entertaining the work of others. Ramm also argued that our focus should be on the Revealer more than the means through which the Revealer works.

One wonders how Ramm would respond to the notion of "symbol" as Dulles has defined it and "narrative" as used by some postliberals. This chapter suggests that "symbol" and "narrative" deserve a second look by conservative evangelicals. Neither Ramm nor most conservatives offer a way to conceive of revelation broadly enough to be of ultimate concern for others. Conservative Christians, one might argue, lack the ability to speak meaningfully to not only members of other faith traditions, but also moderate and liberal Christians. What is more, many do not recognize the problem of "pervasive interpretive pluralism" even within their own walls. This is the opposite criticism from Lindbeck, whose approach was so broad as to not really give his tradition any distinct voice. Ideally, revelation should be understood by Christians in such a way that it has a distinctive voice while also being of interest to other types of Christians and non-Christians. In short, therefore, Ramm's view was too narrow. Ironically, the openness to non-evangelical contributions is laudable. He reminds one of the irenic spirit with which others should be approached.

REVELATION: SENSES AND TYPES

Let's step back a moment and talk about the word "revelation" itself. How does one find it used in everyday speech? One can imagine it used to describe a particularly moving aesthetic endeavor: "This painting is a revelation!" Or one can imagine it used in reference to a changed perspective brought about by a turn of events in a narrative: "Jones' sacrifice gave Smith a revelation of his character." Variations of the word can also be used in other ways, too. "Brenda revealed to her brother Sam that their father was still alive," for example, in which case the revelation is more about information than anything else. It seems that Ramm was right about at least this much: the concept of revelation can be used in many ways.

The temptation when describing distinctions in the concept of revelation is to view those distinctions as binaries. For example, revelation must be transformative *or* informative, propositional *or* narratival, symbolic *or* literal. Perhaps it is the case, however, that the different ways the term is used draw attention to the fact that revelation is a concept with remarkable flexibility, and one can discuss it by mapping onto it various *continua* instead of dualistic binaries. It is true that the same word "revelation" is used to describe experiences in which a person's life is changed and a deposit of information in a written document. But surely there are gradations in these uses. What is "transformative" exists on a continuum; one can be more or less transformed. Similarly, some revelations will supply their receiver with more or less information, more or less epistemic content, than others.

One continuum has to do with the content sense of the word revelation in juxtaposition to the event sense of the word. In one sense, people use the word revelation to describe an event. When used in this way, revelation is an action-oriented word, a *verbal* noun in function (in which case it is synonymous with "a revealing," also a verbal noun). The "event" sense of revelation can be thought of as simply "a revelation," like in the painting example above, or a revelation *of* something or someone. Something *happens* when a person encounters the painting. Something *happened* when Smith saw Jones' sacrifice. These "happenings" are revelatory; the events uncover something that had previously been hidden. When it is used in this "event" sense, revelation is thought of as an experience or an encounter between a person and something or someone else. It is an event that happens between a revealer and a person to whom the revelation comes.

It is also common to find the word "revelation" used in a more narrowly nounal sense. The "noun" sense of revelation describes content, a deposit of information, or message in which case it is synonymous with "that which has been revealed," or simply, "the revealed." The "content" sense of revelation is a revelation *that* such and such is true, an insight. In a sense, content revelation is an after-the-fact recital of the knowledge gained in some other event. In the Brenda/Sam example above, what is revealed is information, the fact *that* Brenda and Sam's father is alive. Brenda found out that her father was alive through some previous event, but her communication of that event to her brother is informative. For Sam, however, the revelation of this information *is* the event. The type of revelation varies according to the person receiving it.

These two senses of the way the word "revelation" is used have implications for the extent to which revelation's receiver participates in the event revelation and/or communicates the revelation to others. In the event sense of the word, revelation's receiver does participate in the revelation, but s/he may not be able to communicate the revelation to others. Aquinas, for example, had an experiential revelation after which he simply stopped writing. Presumably God showed Thomas something or someone that was beyond words, in light of which all else seemed like straw.[1] Thomas' inability to convey what exactly happened, however, does not mean it was not a revelation of God. (Nor would it discount his experience if he were able to communicate what happened.) The point is that the event sense of revelation is always participatory and only sometimes communicable.

Contrarily, in the content sense of the word, revelation's receivers may not have participated in the event revelation but are surely able to communicate the information the event gave to others. Essentially, this revelation amounts to a body of knowledge, the communication of which can take many forms (written, spoken, performed, etc.). Creeds can be said to function in this way. Although those who recite them were not present during their writing or the events they narrate, through them Christians have been communicated with. The Church receives the story from those who did participate in the construction of the creeds. In short, content revelation is transmittable; it can be communicated to others whether or not a recipient participated in the event.

Event revelations always add at least some new information and they are always participatory, but they are only sometimes transformative and sometimes communicable. Content revelations always add at least some new information and are always communicable but they are only sometimes transformative and sometimes participatory. The differentiation here is suggests that the way people use the word "revelation" gives voice to two distinct, yet related, concepts of revelation: one that centers on content of revelation but only after and secondary to the other, which centers on the experience of receiving the revelation (the "event"). While both have a vital function in the lives of revelation's receivers, and both can work in cooperation, the event is logically prior.

INTEGRATING THE CENTRAL REVELATIONAL THEMES

Each of the three interlocutors supplies a central revelational theme around which their view of revelation revolves. Dulles' approach centered on the use of "symbols" which mediate the divine presence. Lindbeck's approach has been amplified to defend "narrative" as the central revelational theme. And finally, Ramm never left behind his affinity for "scripture" qua revelation, as is the case with many evangelicals. So we have three concepts: symbol, narrative, and scripture. The question at this point becomes how these three distinct approaches can be put into conversation with one another. To

1. Davies, *Aquinas*, 9.

what extent are they incommensurable? Can some meaningful integration of the three be advanced, and does one central revelational theme deserve primacy? If so, there are three options: a scripture-centered approach to revelation, a narrative-centered approach to revelation, and a symbol-centered approach to revelation.[2]

The scripture-centered approach to revelation suggests that the Christian texts are the primary tool of revelation and the authoritative means through which God reveals truth to human subjects. Narrative is valuable as a revelational theme only insofar as it is found in scripture or authorized by it. Advocates of a scripture-centered perspective on revelation will likely perceive "symbol" as too vague a concept unless, of course, the symbol is "natural" (i.e., found in nature), in which case it would fall under the blanket of Paul's comments in Romans about revelation in nature, which many scripture-centered people endorse. Again, however, in this scenario "symbol" would be a concept authorized by scripture, and without textual authorization it would not be accepted.

The problem with a scripture-centered view of revelation is that it cannot adequately account for all of the ways God reveals. Not only is it unable to account for all the ways that scripture itself says that God reveals, but it is also unable to account for all of the ways that those who hold a scripture-centered view of revelation want to endorse. This is why Ramm's intellectual arc is so valuable: he came to learn that scripture-centered perspectives on revelation cannot capture all the manifold ways God reveals to human subjects. For example, the concept "scripture" or "written Word" is of no use to someone without the faculties to comprehend written words. Certainly the conservative would not accept some of the implications of a

---

2. There is a fourth central revelational theme one could mention, a christocentric approach. However, as David Kelsey reminded us in the introduction, this is problematic: "Especially in the latter half of the twentieth century, it has been argued that 'revelation' really means 'the person of Jesus Christ' who is revelatory not because his message discloses something God seeks to communicate to humankind, but because his person, his very 'self,' is the very presence of God's own self, so that Jesus Christ reveals, not information about God, but God Godself. And he alone is God's self-disclosure. All other ways in which 'revelation' (and related terms) have been used in Christian practices and beliefs are to be interpreted in relation to this christocentric sense of 'revelation,' yielding a single, comprehensive, coherent, systematic doctrine of some one thing called 'revelation.' It is arguable that such systematizing is accomplished only by forcing irreducibly different notions onto a procrustean bed. . . . It is dubious whether the confusions apparently endemic in systematically christocentric doctrines of revelation *can* in principle be sorted out." From Kelsey, *Eccentric Existence*, 911. To this I would add: for Christians, it makes sense to imagine Christ as the "content" of revelation but this does not give us clarity on how revelation occurs or what nonchristological revelations, if they exist, would entail.

scripture-centered approach to revelation, one of which is especially troubling: that illiterate peoples, unlike those who can read, have no immediate access to God's revelation, which would preclude most of the Church throughout her history from receiving revelation. Instead, commonsense suggests that the same revelation can be communicated in different ways, in which case some category broader than "scripture" should be the central revelational theme. If truth can be communicated in other ways, there exists a broader revelational theme under which one can place scripture.

Second, one could take a narrative-centered approach to revelation in which case narrative is the overarching genus while symbol and scripture are species under it. In a narrative-centered view of revelation, scripture is only useful to the extent that it contains a series of stories that can be situated in the larger narrative of God's work in the world. A narrative-centered approach to revelation is appealing for a number of reasons elaborated on later in this chapter, chief among them that narratives help one make sense of the world. Further, stories resonate with something deep within most people: stories can do things many other forms of communications cannot.

However, when narrative is the central revelational theme, it faces a similar dilemma as scripture: there is no room for other types of revelation. In other words, "narrative" cannot account for the ways in which God reveals outside of the framework of storytelling, for example, through propositions or commands. Can the category of "narrative" fully capture *all* that was revealed in the Decalogue, through the Sermon on the Mount, or any other occasion in which more is being communicated than a story? To be sure, although narrative deserves further attention, especially among evangelicals, it is still not a broad enough category to capture all of the ways in which God reveals to humanity.

The goal is the broadest category possible to place at the "top" of the model, as it were. The model should be headed by a "catch all" category that can account for *all* of the possible ways God can reveal. And both scripture and narrative limit divine revelation, the former more than the latter. Both are worth exploring as examples of revelation, but they must be placed into the category of a larger central revelational theme.

Therefore, third and finally, one could take a symbol-centered approach to divine revelation. Dulles defined a "symbol" as an "externally perceived sign that works mysteriously on the human consciousness so as to suggest more than it can clearly describe or define."[3] He proceeds to describe a symbol as "a sign pregnant with a plenitude of meaning which

3. Dulles, *Models of Revelation*, 131.

is evoked rather than explicitly stated."[4] The category of symbol may be understood as limited or broad. When the category is limited, it is more nearly in line with what Dulles calls "signs," the specific and tangible things one can see and touch, e.g., a cross or a dove. But the category can be broadened beyond the easily graspable. For example, Dulles stretches the definition of "symbol" to include more obscure concepts, like the "kingdom of God"[5] or "light."[6] This broader understanding of symbol gives reason to suspect that a symbol-centered approach is most useful for an integrative perspective on revelation.

In short, symbol is the broadest category we have without becoming so broad as to render "revelation" void of meaning. Symbols carry meaning with them. The category of symbol subsumes scripture and narrative, as well as other ways God reveals (e.g., traditions, propositions, commands, etc.). While it is true that if one stretches the category too far it will loose all meaning, it is also true that if one hopes to adequately represent the diverse ways in which God can reveal, as broad a field as possible is necessary. So the word "symbol" designates a variable, an open space to house anything through which God decides to reveal.

There are three ways that Dulles' notion of symbol should be broadened if it is to stand in place of a variable. First, symbol should include not only *externally* perceived signs that work on the human consciousness, but also *internally* perceived signs that do the same. Surely there are instances in which the sign itself may be inside the subject's own consciousness, not external to it. Second, the category of symbol would also benefit from an extension in the impact that Dulles assigns it. Whereas Dulles says a symbol's impact is evocative, a broader concept of symbol suggests that it is primarily evocative, not solely. Revelation must also account for the communication of truth in such a way that no emotion is evoked. A third broadening of the category of "symbol" has to do with symbolic communication's "polysemic character," according to which symbolic communication "suggests more than it clearly states."[7] If symbol stands in place of a variable, surely one would want to open up the possibility for God, at least some times, to reveal exactly what is clearly stated. It is not, as Dulles suggests, "always" the case that revelation suggests more than it clearly states.

The point with these three extensions of Dulles' symbolic mediation approach is that if the category of symbol is broadened to account for any

---

4. Ibid., 132.
5. Ibid., 135.
6. Ibid., 139.
7. Ibid., 136.

type of symbol, tangible and intangible, then it is the best and broadest category to put at the "top" level in this model of divine revelation.

NARRATIVE AS THE PRIMARY SYMBOL

Conservative evangelicals would likely accept symbol as I have defined it here, since it amounts to not much more than placeholder for some variable. They will simply insert "scripture" into the open space. So part of the task of this book, part of the argument for a symbolic approach to revelation, includes creating a conceptual space within which a conservative can appreciate narrative as the primary symbol. Creating a space for narrative in non-postconservative evangelicalism involves calling attention to recent shifts in the tasks of philosophy and theology, as well as paying attention to what scholars are learning in other areas that might bear on the revelation question. Narrative is not a new subject in theology; sophisticated systematic explorations of it have been around for nearly forty years. (The common use of narrative in philosophy of religion is a more recent development.) However, non-postconservatives are hardly on board with the conversations happening in the mainline.

This book attempts to propose a model of revelation that goes against that tendency toward exclusivism. Again, Ramm proves instructive in this regard. My thesis is that we would do well to view narrative and scripture as revelatory symbols, the former of which should be seen as the primary symbol. It's an integrative approach termed "narrative symbolism." In what follows, the style of argumentation is intended to get conservatives on board. The next section discusses the features of narrative symbolism and the final section of this chapter explores the ways in which this view of revelation is able to maintain the uniqueness of Christianity's sacred texts.

Recent Shifts in the Field

Bringing conservatives to the mainline table involves showing them some of the ways in which the discipline of theology has changed and how narrative might be a helpful conversation partner for it. By seeing the ways in which the discipline itself has changed since Dulles, Lindbeck, and Ramm were most prolific, one will be better positioned to discern how the idea of revelation can be explored in ways that were unavailable to conservatives of forty years ago or more. While there are certainly a host of changes one can mention and a huge history from which one can draw, here the discussion is limited to theology during the past half-century and three basic shifts in emphasis: (a) away from methodology, (b) toward praxis, and (c) into other disciplines.[8]

First, some thinkers suggest that the work of theologians today differs from that of their predecessors insofar as it considers method a lesser priority than the actual "doing" of theology. In *Ethics After Babel*, Jeffrey Stout warned that a preoccupation with method contributed to theology's failure to speak meaningfully to its academic, public, and ecclesial neighbors. In Stout's view, academic theology was not a "distinctive contributor" to its surrounding culture because "preoccupation with method is like clearing your throat: it can go on for only so long before you lose your audience."[9] It can become a vicious cycle: as theology becomes less and less relevant to the public, many theologians respond by arguing for their right to be heard by delving into methodological concerns, i.e., the intelligibility and plausibility of their speech, a practice still common among evangelical philosophers of religion who work in apologetics.[10] However, when scholars wrote for scholars on methodological issues, doing so only marginalized theology further, pushing it toward the "sidelines" and away from the concerns its public shared.

Losing the audience worries Miroslav Volf, who observes that theologians, "like the street-corner preachers of yesterday . . . find themselves talking to a crowd too hurried to honor them with more than a fleeting glance."[11] Stout's assessment of the situation was resisted by some thinkers like Stanley Grenz and to some extent even Volf himself.[12] Nevertheless

---

8. The claims of this section are, admittedly, oversimplification of a complex interplay of thinkers and their ideas. However, I include them because while they may be oversimplifications, they are made by some of the leading figures on the theological scene today. For example, many of the aspects of theology's shifting emphases in this section are also found in Tanner, "Shifts in Theology," 39–44, and "How My Mind," 40–45.

9. Stout, *Ethics After Babel*, 163.

10. For example, see William Lane Craig's recent works on the plausibility of the Christian worldview.

11. Volf, "Theology, Meaning & Power," 45. Cf. Clayton, *Transforming Christian Theology*, 65–66: "Don't just talk about it; Do It! . . . There is a danger in spending all one's time describing the space in which theology might be done, but never getting around to actually doing any theology. Sadly, many people who are called theologians succumb to this temptation. Metaphorically speaking, they are like builders who talk about why houses should be build but who never actually get around to building any . . . Academic theologians call this discourse about 'The House That Nobody Built' *theological methodology*."

12. Volf argues that the "throat-clearing" analogy is problematic because if anything, "theological method is more analogous to the strategy of an oration than to the clarity of a speaker's voice; learning proper method is more like taking lessons in public

many mainline theologians, consciously or not, adjusted their focus away from methodology. If one can speak of a general shift in emphasis, many theologians followed William Placher's admonition to "abandon their preoccupation with methodology and get on with the business of really doing theology."[13] To be sure, it may be the case that the contrast between methodology and the "doing" of theology is overstated, as it fails to account for different audiences (the academy and the church). But a shift is still there, even when repackaged in terms of audiences: one could suggest that theologians of the past thirty years have become more concerned with making their insights accessible to and content reflective of the struggles of the public and Church. Conservatives are only beginning to get on board in this regard.[14]

Second, theology today largely differs from the theology of fifty years ago in its concern for praxis. Refining theological methods became less important in part because there were more pressing concerns to which mainline theologians wanted to respond: racism, classism, and sexism, for instance. The three major strands of liberation theology—black, economic, and feminist—stand out in this theological trajectory,[15] yet many other academic theologians have taken up their mantle as specific social concerns figure heavily into their theological constructions.[16] One might argue that when some theologians began to shift their focus from method to the doing

---

speaking than like clearing the throat." Volf, "Theology, Meaning, & Power," 45–46. Volf adds another criticism of Stout's perception, with which Stanley Grenz agrees. According to Grenz, "in contrast to this latent modernist assumption, conceptions of method emerge online in the context of an interrelated web of beliefs. Method is not simply a self-sufficient programmatic enterprise that can be readily abstracted from the rest of theology. Rather, decisions made about the method of theology both *inform* the entire conceptualization of a theological model and are themselves *informed by* the theological conclusions that emerge from that model." From Grenz and Franke, *Beyond Foundationalism*, 12.

13. Placher, *Unapologetic Theology*, 19.

14. K. Smith, J. Lalitha, and L. Hawk, *Evangelical Postcolonial Conversations: Global Awakenings in Theology and Praxis* (Downers Grove, IVP Academic, 2014).

15. See, for example the following seminal works in these three types of liberation theology: Cone, *Black Theology, Black Power* and *Black Theology of Liberation*; Roberts, *Africentric Christianity*; Cleage, *Black Messiah*; Gutierrez, "Two Theological Perspectives," and *Theology of Liberation*; Johnson, *Quest*; Hopkins, "Black Theology of Liberation"; McDougall, "Feminist Theology"; and Greene-McCreight, *Feminist Reconstructions*.

16. It is not uncommon to find any combination of social locations addressed in contemporary theology—black and feminist combine to form womanist, feminist and Latin American combine to form mujerista; Asian-American; post-colonial; etc. These types of theologians would argue that this is precisely the point: each person and community has their own social location, their own history, and their own unique insights to contribute.

of theology, they renewed their prophetic voice to their culture in a manner befitting the legacy of public theologians Reinhold Niebuhr and Dietrich Bonhoeffer. Again, conservatives have only recently begun to address social concerns in the way the post-Second Great Awakening evangelical activists did.

Of course, this relationship was a two-way street in the mainline. On the one hand, by focusing less on theoretical issues—e.g., those involved in discussions of method—mainline thinkers were freed up respond to practical issues of their culture in a new way. On the other hand, as mainline theology became decreasingly concerned with method, its "starting point" shifted at some level from an older paradigm of "using theology to evaluate culture" to a new paradigm of "using culture to evaluate theology." Many mainline theologians today believe that orthopraxis precedes orthodoxy.[17] The idea that right practice precedes right theology is foreign to conservative cultures in which believing the right things is more soteriologically important than living the right way.

Third, mainline academic theology today differs from theology of the mid-twentieth century insofar as it is has become increasingly interdisciplinary. Like Carl Henry, many conservatives today still view theology as the explication and systematization of Christianity's sacred texts. Today mainline theology not only interacts with its surrounding culture in ways geared toward social transformation but it is also open to other academic avenues of inquiry, and the interaction with other disciplines is another two-way street. On the one hand, some thinkers say theology is validated among the other disciplines because it no longer needs to defend its right to exist or be seated alongside other disciplines. According to Kathryn Tanner, "appeals to specifically Christian sources and norms of insight and the advocacy stance assumed by many theologians are less suspect than they used to be, now that the tradition-bound, culturally influenced and politically invested character of even the 'hard sciences' has become an intellectual commonplace."[18] The burden of proof that theology once bore alone is lessened "because every discipline finds itself in the same seemingly inescapable

---

17. According to Gutierrez (*Theology of Liberation*, xxix), theology is "a critical reflection on Christian praxis in light of the word of God." Bonino (*Doing Theology*, 81) elaborates the sentiment well: "Theology, as here conceived, is not an effort to give a correct understanding of God's attributes or actions but an effort to articulate the action of faith, the shape of praxis conceived and realized in obedience. As philosophy in Marx's famous *dictum*, theology has to explaining the world and to start transforming it. *Orthopraxis*, rather than orthodoxy, becomes the criterion for theology."

18. Tanner, "How My Mind," 40–41.

circumstance to some degree or other."[19] Shifts such as these are no doubt due to the embrace of postmodern ways of knowing, which hold claims to universality at a distance. Moreover, the theological "pump" had been primed for these types of inquiries since Tillich's "method of correlation" answered questions raised by culture using traditional Christian symbols.[20] Theology is validated among other disciplines, and now has more power to speak with and to them.

On the other hand, non-philosophical and non-theological disciplines are given heretofore-unparalleled weight in mainline theological adjudication. That is, not only can theology speak into and shape other academic disciplines, but also other academic disciplines can speak into and shape what mainline theologians say. In the past three decades, Tanner notes that "primarily methodological preoccupations have given way before more substantive efforts to rethink a theological vision of reality with a more hard-hitting potential to direct thought and action differently, in conversation with academic dialogue partners far beyond the usual philosophical ones."[21] In other words, one of the ways that theology has changed is its incorporation of insights gleaned from other disciplines, and it uses those disciplines to re-imagine the traditional claims, symbols, beliefs, and practices of Christian faith.

It is this last feature of theology today—its dialectical relationship with other academic disciplines—that helps us see narrative's potential as the primary symbol. Evangelicals are fond of the idea that "all truth is God's truth," so theology's interdisciplinarity gives them an opportunity to test this thesis. Three examples will suffice to show the principle in action.

Shannon Craigo-Snell re-imagines ecclesiology with the help of theater/performance studies. If people attend a church, they face a problem: "What will I get in exchange for my time? My theological standards are high. Will the preacher offer theological reflections that pass muster? Will the service give adequate attention to the diversity of the Christian tradition and the nuances of biblical hermeneutics?"[22] As a constructive theologian, Craigo-Snell first describes the challenge before her:

> One of the exciting characteristics of constructive theology is that it often involves creative engagement with other academic disciplines. Constructive theologians draw on the ideas and insights of other fields of knowledge in order to think more fully

19. Tanner, "Shifts in Theology," 41.
20. Tillich, *Systematic Theology*, vol. 1, 59–65.
21. Tanner, "Shifts in Theology," 39.
22. Craigo-Snell and Monroe, *Living Christianity*, 123.

and more creatively about particularly theological questions. One of the primary conversation partners for theology over the centuries has been philosophy. In the modern era, history has been a valuable interlocutor. Now theologians engage the world of sociologists, theorists, economists, physicists, and myriad others.[23]

Craigo-Snell begins by reframing the question from what it means to *be* church to what it means to *do* church, since church "is a way of living in the world that shapes and is shaped by our embodied and communal lives" and not "just something we think about."[24] As something people do, church is a performance, and all performances have three things in common: they are events, they involve interaction, and there is an aspect of "doubleness," a gap between the ideal and the performance of the ideal. Craigo-Snell qua constructive theologian explains and models a view of the church in which Peter Brook's *The Empty Space* generates insights on how meaning is "conveyed and created in embodied, communal performances."[25] She concludes that church, like theatre, should not be overly tied to tradition; rather, it should be holy, rough (reflecting the "messy realities of life"), and immediate (a place where a "magic" encounter between divine and human is possible).[26] Being open to other disciplines—this case theater and performance studies—generates new theological insights and renews age-old theological commitments.

Kathryn Tanner provides several examples of interdisciplinary theological thinking. In *God and Creation in Christian Theology*, Tanner analyzed the way theologians talk about God, yet found discourse analysis insufficient for her second project, *The Politics of God*. For this book, Tanner needed to mine sociology and anthropology to argue her normative case for "how beliefs about God and creation *should* shape Christian lives."[27] In *Economy of Grace*, Tanner also incorporates insights from other disciplines into her theology: "The inequalities of global capitalism was the specific challenge that called for a systematic rethinking of Christian themes and their implications for economic matters."[28] In Tanner's book, *Christ the Key*, she builds on her own past work[29] to re-evaluate traditional Western notions of the

23. Ibid., 125.
24. Ibid., 125–26.
25. Ibid., 128.
26. Cf. Craigo-Snell, *Empty Church*, 113–44.
27. Tanner, "How My Mind," 42.
28. Ibid.
29. See, e.g., Tanner, "Incarnation, Cross, and Sacrifice," 35–56.

atonement. Traditional atonement theories wrongly elevate God's punitive nature instead of God's grace. So instead of the crucifixion and resurrection, atonement is provided by the Word's incarnation.[30] Whatever one thinks of this view, the point is this: contemporary mainline theologians do not hesitate to reshape traditional understandings of God and the world in light of the contemporary situation and insights from other academic disciplines.

Mainline theologians are also conversant with the emerging field of trauma studies, a sub-discipline of psychology. Two of the main figures are Shelly Rambo and Serene Jones. In *Spirit and Trauma*, Rambo asks how trauma theory might shed light on the Christian claim that new life arises out of death. Says Rambo: "Witness is a germ organic to Christian theology [but] the study of trauma moves us to rethink witness, particularly as it relates to witnessing the suffering that remains. Current studies in trauma complicate interpretations of witness, by turning us to a 'crisis of witness' at the heart of our central narrative of death and life, cross and resurrection."[31] Similarly, Jones asks how memory, action, and love are affected by violence, individual or collective. In *Trauma and Grace*, she asks how violence—whether it is the experience of marginalized persons, veterans of war, physical or sexual abuse—reshapes what we say about Jesus' death. The whole book can be seen as an attempt to explore how God loves a world broken by violence and other assorted harms we perpetuate against one another, but its starting point is the experience of violence.

These dialogue partners—performance studies, economic theory, and psychological trauma—are but three of the myriad disciplines that offer mainline theologians opportunities to explore their subject from a new angle. The move into other disciplines sometimes changes what the theologians say, or at least how they say it.

Conservatives could benefit from systematic theology's increasing interdisciplinarity. As mentioned above, there is still a large contingent of conservatives who define "systematic theology" as the practice of taking all of the propositions in the Bible or propositionalized material therein to form a vision of this or that theological idea based on that material.[32] They will also define "biblical theology" as the practice of taking a portion of scripture—a

---

30. Some theologians have gone so far as to criticize the traditional view as a form of "divine child abuse." This idea, only alluded to by Tanner, is found in other feminist and womanist writers. For a survey of recent critiques of the traditional view, see Van Dyk, "How Does Jesus Make a Difference?" 210–14.

31. Rambo, *Spirit and Trauma*, 16.

32. See, e.g., Grudem, *Systematic Theology* and Estep, Alison and Anthony, *Theology for Christian Education*, 13–14.

specific book, for instance, or a specific biblical author—and explicating a theological issue in light of that passage.

To me, these definitions seem patently wrongheaded. The term "biblical theology" should refer to the practice of taking into account the entire Bible (hence the title "biblical" instead of, e.g., "Johannine" or "Pauline") while systematic theology supplements the truth of scripture with insights generated in other disciplines (philosophy, history, etc.) to form a coherent (*and biblical*) theological statement. Limiting the purview of systematics to the biblical alone is overly restrictive.

Of course, the move toward interdisciplinarity is broader than systematic theology, as a few examples illustrate. The study of international politics impacts what biblical scholars say about the New Testament.[33] Reading history (e.g., Holocaust material) prompted at least one philosopher of religion to advocate a "theodicy of protest" in which God is put on trial, "and in that process the issue of God's wasteful complicity in evil takes center stage."[34] And some analytic philosophers are changing the idea of God based on where they sense "reason" inevitably leads.[35] One could speculate that the move towards interdisciplinary scholarship has impacted every "religious" discipline—biblical studies, philosophy of religion, comparative religions, religious ethics, history of Christian thought, etc.—and those beyond the academic study of religion.[36]

Whatever one makes of the preceding assertions based, at least in part, on the insights generated from other disciplines, one can appreciate the new insights they offer conservative thinkers. If nothing else, they give conservatives an opportunity to refine what they think and why, and explore whether and how their formulations, inherited or constructed, are palatable today. This is not to say, of course, that simply because a particular issue is unappealing or traditional that it is to be discarded. Like Ramm, we can learn from Barth that what is traditional is not necessarily worse and what is novel is not necessarily better. It is merely to affirm that there are opportunities afforded to the conservative when s/he explores other avenues of inquiry. This is the first reason to consider narrative as the primary symbol: theology today allows us to ask the question of its utility on the revelation question. But should we? Does narrative deserve to be the primary symbol

---

33. See, e.g., Kittredge, Aitken, and Bradshaw, eds., *Bible in the Public Square*.

34. Roth, "Theodicy of Protest," 10.

35. Rae, *Analytic Theology*, 6.

36. See, e.g., Frodeman, Klein, and Mitcham, eds., *Oxford Handbook of Interdisciplinarity*.

in divine revelation? To answer this question we will begin by exploring the nature of humanity.

The Anthropological Starting Point of the Question

In his *Institutes of the Christian Religion,* Calvin famously remarked that knowledge of God and knowledge of the human are interconnected: "Without knowledge of the self there is no knowledge of God . . . [and] without knowledge of God there is no knowledge of self."[37] This idea is not limited to the Reformation; similar approaches went before and similar approaches have been used since.

So who are we? What do we do? And does what we do show us what the primary symbol of revelation should be, what God is like, or at least how we should speak about God?

Consider a few perspectives on the matter of human identity and action. Hayden White says, "Far from being one code among many that a culture may utilize for endowing experience with meaning, narrative is a metacode, a human universal on the basis of which trans-cultural messages about the shared reality can be transmitted . . . the absence of narrative capacity or a refusal of narrative indicates an absence or refusing of meaning itself."[38] Victor Turner claims, "We must concede [narrative] to be a universal cultural activity, embedded in the very center of the social drama, itself another cross-cultural and transtemporal unit in social progress."[39] According to Kenneth Burke, "We assume a time when our primal ancestors became able to go from sensations to words. . . . When they could duplicate the experience of tasting an orange by saying 'the taste of an orange,' that was when story came into the world."[40] Gregory Bateson goes so far as to broaden narrative to non-human creatures: "Thinking in terms of stories must be shared by all mind or minds, whether ours or those of redwood forests and sea anemones."[41] And finally, Barbara Hardy says, "We dream in narrative, daydream in narrative, remember, anticipate, hope, despair,

---

37. Calvin, *Institutes,* 1.1.1–2. See also Zimmerman, *Recovering Theological Hermeneutics,* 30.

38. White, "Value of Narrativity," 6.

39. Turner, "Social Dramas," 167.

40. Kenneth Burke, "Logology: An Overall View." This is from a personal correspondence with Walter Fisher in Fisher, *Human Communication as Narration,* 65, 83n62.

41. Bateson, *Mind and Nature,* 14.

believe, doubt, plan, revise, criticize, construct, gossip, learn, hate and love by narrative."[42]

Narrative is a central feature of being human. More than just a "feature" of being human, however, narrative has a role in constituting humanity. Alasdair MacIntyre is well known for this and other theses that bear on the "revelation" question. In his influential book, *After Virtue*, MacIntyre says that the self is made up a series of connected narratives, which, together, constitute a lived, larger narrative. Only against this backdrop does human communication and activity become intelligible. In MacIntyre's words, "the act of utterance becomes intelligible by finding its place in a narrative."[43] Intelligibility is what separates the rational bulk of humanity from the non-rational (psychotic humans and/or animals). When we encounter an action or utterance that is unintelligible given what we know at the time, we are "baffled." As humans, we operate in a world of intelligibility: we detect patterns, we find meaning, and we see order in the world at every turn, including in the narratives of our lives, both large and small. Even when we are presented with material that resists narrative categorization, we look for it nonetheless: "The characterization of actions allegedly prior to any narrative form being imposed upon them will always turn out to be the presentation of what are plainly the disjointed parts of some possible narrative."[44] We seek narrative meaning and unity in the material with which we are presented.

The human tendency to look for narrative meaning is being confirmed by the so-called "hard sciences," in which we are learning about the human ability to detect patterns. Michael Shermer argues that a central feature of "the believing brain" and the human that houses it is "patternicity."[45] Humans have become "skilled, pattern-seeking, causal-finding creatures. Those who were best at finding patterns . . . left behind the most offspring. We are their descendants."[46] Shermer goes so far as to suggest that this is not only "why people believe weird things. It is a theory to explain *why people*

---

42. Hardy, "Poetics of Fiction," 5, in MacIntyre, *After Virtue*, 197.

43. MacIntyre, *After Virtue*, 196.

44. Ibid., 200.

45. Shermer, while useful in the detection of patterns and the formation of beliefs, is also overly narrow in his understanding of the social and theological location of this author. He suggests that in evangelicalism one *must* work to convert others and there is no separation of church and state. Both of these caricature evangelicals; even still, his area of specialty is useful for this discussion. See Shermer, *Believing Brain*, 42–43.

46. Shermer, *Why People Believe*, xxix. See also Shermer, *The Believing Brain*, ch. 4: "Patternicity."

believe things. Full stop."⁴⁷ Our mind works to integrate "inputs from all of the senses into a meaningful narrative arc that makes sense of both senseful and senseless data."⁴⁸

One of the patterns humanity seeks is one's place in a larger context, and it contributes to one's satisfaction in life, as advances in positive psychology are telling us. One of the fathers of positive psychology, Martin Seligman, suggests that recognition of one's place in the larger picture/narrative—what he calls "transcendence"—is essential for happiness.⁴⁹ Similarly, Christopher Peterson, who is part of the "Values in Action" classification system that intends to complement the *Diagnostic and Statistical Manual* of the American Psychiatric Association with findings of positive psychology,⁵⁰ says transcendence is one of the things "right" about healthy people. The ways in which one finds transcendence vary; it could be appreciation of beauty and excellence, gratitude, hope, humor, and/or spirituality.⁵¹ These are aspects of the human experience that "forge connections to the larger universe and provide meaning."⁵² Examples from positive psychology, therefore, include "knowing where one fits into the larger scheme."⁵³

Some philosophers of religion are recognizing and incorporating narrative into their understanding of God and God's relationship with humanity. For example, in *Existential Reasons for Belief in God*, Clifford Williams offers "a defense of desires and emotions for faith." To defend the idea that belief in God satisfies emotional and existential needs, Williams first discusses what those needs are. Among his list of universal human needs are self-directed needs (e.g., meaning) and needs directed at something external

---

47. Shermer, *Believing Brain*, 60. The full quote: "There was a natural selection for the cognitive process of assuming that all patterns are real and that all patternicities represent real and important phenomena. We are the descendants of the primates who most successfully employed patternicity. Note what I am arguing here. This is not just a theory to explain why people believe weird things. It is a theory to explain *why people believe things*. Full stop. Patternicity is the process of seeking and finding patterns, connecting the dots, linking A to B. Again, this is nothing more than association learning, and all animals do it. It is how organisms adapt to their ever-changing environments when evolution is too slow."

48. Ibid., 144.

49. Seligman, *Authentic Happiness*, 154–58. For a summary of the relevant portion of Seligman's book by one of his graduate students and now colleagues, see Rashid, "Authentic Happiness," 73–74: "The third component of authentic happiness in Seligman's theory is the meaningful life. It consists of attachment to, and the service of, something larger than oneself."

50. Peterson, "Classification of Strengths," ch. 2.

51. Peterson, "The Values in Action," 33.

52. Ibid.

53. Ibid.

(e.g., awe).[54] One of the self-directed needs is particularly important: "a larger life ... a more expansive life"[55] in which we desire to feel "awe for the grand landscapes, magnificent works of art and beautiful prose; appreciative understanding for the emotional life of our acquaintances; exhilaration at discovering something new about the beginning of the universe or the workings of culture; moral awe at observing goodness. Our desire for these emotions is a desire for a richer life, one that has a wider array of the emotions we regard as significant."[56] These are instances in which we get out of the quotidian and see ourselves as part of something larger.

What are we to make of these seemingly disparate phenomena? Seeing oneself in a larger context, narrative as a constitutive feature of being human, theological and anthropological epistemology as related, and the seemingly innate ability to find meaning and patterns in the world ... Do these hold any promise for the idea of revelation in which symbolism is the primary and central revelational theme? Given these things, what *ought* revelation look like?

In my view, an integrative approach to revelation looks like *narrative symbolism*. This will likely make non-postconservative readers uncomfortable. Unless reflecting on aesthetics, the idea of narrative may be uncomfortably "loose" or "fluffy" for those whose daily language is precise and concise. This need not be the case. On one level, narrative is useful for illustrating philosophical principles or providing cases for reflection. For example, recent philosophers have explored Wittgensteinian ethics using literary examples.[57]

However, the utility of narrative goes further than that, beyond mere illustration. Narrative also supplements philosophy where standard philosophical ways of knowing fall short. Consider Eleonore Stump's bold assertion in *Wandering in Darkness*, her recent effort to find satisfactory solutions to the problem of pain. She says "one idea ... for addressing the shortcomings of analytic philosophy while preserving its characteristic excellences is to marry it to the study of narrative" because "philosophical reflection on suffering is better with the help of a story."[58] As we have seen above, narratives do more than just illustrate; they explain and constitute. I

---

54. This distinction he gets from Westphal in "Religion as Means" and "Prayer and Sacrifice" in *God, Guilt, and Death*, 122–59.

55. Williams, *Existential Reasons*, 23.

56. Ibid.

57. See, for instance, see O'Neill, "Power of Example," 5–29, for a discussion about literary examples in twentieth-century Wittgensteinian ethics. Here narratives are used to prompt ethical reflection on particular cases in ethics.

58. Stump, *Wandering in Darkness*, 25.

believe Stump is correct when she asserts, "there are things to know which can be known through narrative but which cannot be known as well, if at all, through the methods of analytic philosophy."[59] This is not to treat a narrative as if it were structured as a syllogism. It is to accept a narrative in its messiness, which Stump calls its "disorderly richness."[60] After all, life is like that, as noted by Isak Dinesen: "All sorrows can be borne if you . . . tell a story about them."[61]

Are there different ways of knowing? If so, surely not all forms of knowing are equally applicable to the problem of revelation. Stump argues that narrative epistemologies are as legitimate as analytical ones, and with respect to our specific subject in this book, Pascal agrees: "it is the heart and not the head which finds its reason in revelation."[62] And as H. R. Niebuhr concurs, "the reason which is correlate with revelation is practical reason, or the reason of a self rather than of impersonal mind." This "implies that the conflict of practical reason is with practical irrationality as pure reason is at war with irrationality in the head and not with reason in the heart."[63] Narratives help us know things, they aid our understanding, and they resonate deep within.

Revelation is, among other things, a form of communication between one mind and another, between God and humankind. When reflecting on our understanding of human communication, Walter Fisher suggests that for a very long time the "rational world" paradigm dominated, according to which knowledge is acquired through propositions, premises, arguments, conclusions, etc. In the rational world paradigm, certain rules govern what we can say or not say. This relates to what Lindbeck referred to as the "cognitive-propositionalist" version of theology in which "church doctrines function as informative propositions or truth claims about objective realities. Religions are thus thought of as similar to philosophy or science as these were classically conceived . . . [and this version of theology has] affinities to the outlook on religion adopted by much modern Anglo-American analytic philosophy with its preoccupation with the cognitive or informational meaningfulness of religious utterances."[64] Many conservative

---

59. Ibid., 26.

60. Ibid., 27.

61. Passage found in Thiele, *Heart of Judgment*, 263, in Stump, *Wandering in Darkness*, 25.

62. Cf. Niebuhr, *The Meaning of Revelation*, 94.

63. Ibid.

64. Lindbeck, *Nature of Doctrine*, 16.

foundationalists find themselves in basic agreement with this approach, as we see in Carl Henry and those of his ilk.

But this approach is loosing ground, as not all philosophers of religion and theologians these days are equally enthusiastic about using philosophy as theology's "go to" conversation partner. Some argue, in fact, that propositionalism is actually dangerous for theology. In *Reforming the Doctrine of God*[65] F. LeRon Shults argues that we must not "strip away the symbolic and analogical dimensions of religious language to get at the clear and distinct ideas supposedly found in divine revelation."[66] There is, Shults suggests, a Cartesian anxiety in conservative thinking about revelation that owes to the work of Francis Turretin and Charles Hodge, both of whom sought to give the Christian tradition a solid basis in response to Enlightenment skepticism. A propositional approach to religious language "presupposes a basic dualism between God and the world, between two 'universes' that can be spanned by language, although one is 'much' larger."[67] The highly propositionalist, rationalistic, and univocal view of religious language, one might say, carries too much metaphysical baggage and does not do justice to God's transcendence.

Many philosophers of religion, theologians, and those outside the fold of so-called religious disciplines argue that there are "narrative" ways of knowing, which can supplement rationalistic approaches to knowledge that characterize propositionalized scripture.[68] Narratives teach us, as Roger Schank and Tamara Berman tell us: "As we experience life, we form increasingly complex memory structures that explain how the world works. . . . Our memory structures are experience-based, or 'case-based' which means, in essence, that they are story-based [and] we make modifications to our memory structures when we have expectation failures, and the modifications are related to our accepted explanations for the failures. It is the modification of our memory structures, our mental representations, that constitutes learning."[69]

Stories can do things that propositions cannot. This is one of the strongest features of postconservative evangelicalism and postliberal thought,

---

65. Shults, *Doctrine of God*.

66. Olson, *Reformed*, 155.

67. Shults, *Doctrine of God*, 206.

68. To be sure, when the narrative paradigm conflicts with the principle of non-contradiction or the principle of sufficient reason, this book sides with standard philosophical ways of knowing. Absurdity is absurdity, even when encountered in a story. But this is not to preclude narrative from being a way of knowing things for which there has not been yet shown satisfactory "scientific" explanations. In these cases, narratives can reveal truth where explanations are not yet—or may never be—present.

69. Schank and Berman, "Pervasive Role," 301–2.

and it builds on narrative hermeneutics and advances in philosophy of language: "Perhaps propositions cannot express everything story can express. Perhaps a propositional system of thought . . . cannot exhaust the tasks and goals of proper Christian theology."[70] After all, the term "narrative" is related to the Latin *gnarus*,[71] so perhaps story is simply an alternative—yet complementary—mode of knowing. One of narrative's functions is the facilitation of knowledge. Narrative "does not simply mirror what happens; it also explores and devises what can happen. It does not merely recount changes of state; it constitutes and interprets them as signifying parts of signifying wholes (situations, practices, persons, societies)."[72]

There are countless examples of the power of narrative to advance knowledge and/or understanding. Although one can know quite a lot of Kathryn Tanner's positions by reading her academic body of work, one gains a new sort of understanding when one reads her autobiographical essay in which she narrates the multi-year journey that explains how her mind has changed: the figures to whom she was responding, the influences from whom she learned, the personal struggles at the time of writing, etc.[73] This also applies to Jürgen Moltmann,[74] Stanley Hauerwas,[75] or ancient figures like Augustine, whose *Confessions* opens up a new array of insights into his views.

Philosophy of religion and theology face the same situation: although one can know a lot about God and God's relationship to the world through propositions, these ideas are given life when applied to situations, that is to say, when conveyed through stories. Narrative is not second-rate philosophy, but rather a much-needed supplement to first-rate philosophy. Lindbeck himself said that people "know" in many ways; for example, "Whether it will be possible to regain a specifically biblical understanding of providence depends in part on the possibility of theologically reading Scripture once again in literary rather than non-literary ways."[76] The so-called "radical orthodox" thinkers would agree, as God is seen not only as the savior of souls, but also as the savior of reason itself.[77] Gary Saul Morson explains: "I

70. Olson, *Reformed*, 154.
71. Prince, *Dictionary of Narratology*, 60.
72. Ibid.
73. Tanner, "How My Mind."
74. Moltmann, *A Broad Place*.
75. Hauerwas, *Hannah's Child*.
76. Lindbeck, *Nature of Doctrine*, 119. Methods of reading Scripture are important in contemporary discussions of providence, as noted by Wood, "Providence," 101.
77. See, e.g., Milbank, *Theology and Social Theory*; Pickstock and Ward, eds., *Radical Orthodoxy*. For a short summary, see Abraham, "Existence of God," 21.

do not view literary works as applied or sugar-coated or unrigorous philosophy, but as a specific form of philosophic thought in the broad sense. They philosophize not with a hammer but with a feather. . . . Not just individual works but also whole literary genres could profitably be viewed as 'forms of thought.'"[78]

At this point a caveat is necessary: the stress on narrative is due to the hesitancy of some conservatives to explore the category in philosophy of religion and theology, not because propositional approaches to truth are entirely deficient. Both ways of knowing work in cooperation, but not to the exclusion of the other in crucial elements. If propositionalism strips away the mysterious, analogical, symbolic, intuitive, and transcendent parts of God and God's revelation, narrative provides a helpful corrective to remind humans on an experiential and affect-oriented level of their place vis-à-vis God, which in turn should foster transformation. If narrative strains credibility or resists plausibility, propositionalism provides a helpful corrective to remind humans of the errors of their fanciful imaginations and that "truth" is an important goal.

So in answer to the basic question, "why narrative symbolism?" one can respond that narrative brings an integrative, aesthetic and authentic dimension to the discussion about revelation that other ways of knowing (e.g., philosophical precision and scriptural propositionalism) cannot. It is truer or closer to life than abbreviated arguments or passages plucked out of context. Indeed, Walter Fisher suggests that narrative is the most appropriate heading for *all* human communication. If we do not invest in the category of narrative, we risk "a fossilized view of the world, unable to account for the richness of the reality in which we live our lives."[79] Or, in the words of Bas van Fraassen: "The world in which we live is a precious thing; the world of the philosophers is well lost for love of it."[80] We will return later in the book to the sort of knowledge that is conveyed by means of narrative; for now, we will explicate the features of this "narrative symbolism" as a model of revelation.

WHAT DOES NARRATIVE SYMBOLISM LOOK LIKE?

In narrative symbolism, God primarily reveals through the symbol of narrative. Divine revelation in this case is an event in which God interrupts and reforms one's subjectivity by situating and/or meaningfully connecting all or

---

78. Morson, *Narrative Freedom*, 4–5.
79. Stump, *Wandering in Darkness*, 27.
80. Fraassen, *Empirical Stance*, 18. Cf. Stump, *Wandering in Darkness*, 27.

part of one's story to a larger narrative of God's work in the world. It is when a "part" sees itself as it really is, only a part in relation to either the Whole or a larger part of some as-of-yet unknown whole. I would suggest that this model of revelation, which emerges from the best of our three thinkers and advances in other disciplines, is helpful to overcome some of the missteps of non-postconservative thinkers. This configuration is able to withstand criticism from the two audiences of this book: (a) those who would give up the idea of revelation or a Revealer, and (b) those who would bury their heads in the sand without entertaining challenges to their biblicism.

If "narrative symbolism" involves an event in which individual stories are meaningfully situated in a larger narrative, then it requires several features, some explicit and others implicit (see figure 4.1). The explicit set of necessary features includes the following: first, the person to and for whom the revelation occurs; second, the story of the individual; third, a larger narrative into which the story of the individual is situated; fourth, something or someone who places the smaller story into the larger narrative; and fifth, a sign that initiates the revelation. The implicit set of necessary features includes the following: sixth, self-awareness on the part of the individual; seventh, difference between the smaller story and larger narrative; eighth, unity between the smaller story and the larger narrative; ninth, the linear passage of time; tenth, willingness to participate in the revelatory event; and finally, a meaningful connection between the narratives.

In what follows I will elaborate on each feature. The reader would do well to keep in mind that narrative approaches to theology in general and revelation specifically are not new territory for scholars. Rather, in what follows I argue that recent advances in the fields of those who study narratives give the decades old idea new life and, therefore, deserve a second look by conservative thinkers.

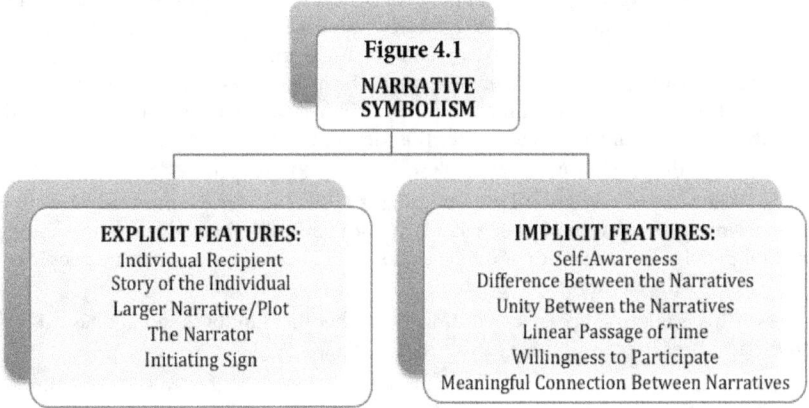

Explicit Features of Narrative Symbolism

Some aspects of the aforementioned definition of revelation require little explanation, e.g., individuals who receive divine revelation. It is more complicated to explore what makes a "story" such that an individual would have one, how stories relate to a larger narrative, what sorts of things initiate a revelation, and what sort of being guides the process or reveals using narratives. Call the individual the "narratee," the one to whom a story/narrative is communicated[81] or the "implied reader."[82] In this view of revelation, the narratee also functions as a character in the narrative; therefore, she can also be referred to individually as an "actant" in the story and collectively as the "dramatis personae"[83] if several people receive the same divine revelation.[84]

Second, each individual has a history, a present, and a future. These constitute portions of the individual's "story." But what does this mean? "Story" and "narrative," although generally used synonymously (as they have been in this book thus far), are actually distinct concepts, and the distinction is vital for understanding what happens in the event of narrative symbolism.

As mentioned above, theology today interacts with other disciplines more than ever before. Since the publication of Lindbeck's *Nature of Doctrine*,[85] an entire field—narratology—has emerged that explores what makes a "story" and its relation to other types of communication and other kinds of events.[86] As an academic discipline in its own right, narratology

---

81. Prince, *Dictionary of Narratology*, 57.

82. Note, however, that Prince takes pains to distinguish these two concepts (*Dictionary of Narratology*, 43). The differences are largely technical, but even Prince allows that separating the two is sometimes problematic. For our purposes, we will use "narratee" and "implied reader" interchangeably.

83. Propp, *Morphology*. For a lengthy discussion of the ways in which these terms have been understood by narratology's early influences including Propp, see Prince, *Dictionary of Narratology*, 1–3, 23, 43, and 57. The distinction between "actants" and "dramatis personae" is the difference between the approaches of Propp and Greimas. In my estimation, not much hinges on their minor disagreements; rather, the use of specific types of characters is useful for this view of revelation, not what we call them. For more on these definitions, see Cobley, "Narratology" (online).

84. The view of revelation I am outlining is individualistic. Communal revelation would simply be the reception of a similarly- or identically-themed revelation among several people. The dynamics of the revelation do not change when several people receive the same revelation.

85. This is not to suggest a correlation, but rather that Lindbeck did not have access to the advances in literary theory this paper discusses.

86. As is the case with all academic disciplines, there is a great variety of opinions and perspectives on the concepts and ideas within its purview. I acknowledge this, and

"examines what all narratives, and only narratives, have in common as well as what enables them to differ from one another qua narratives, and it aims to describe the narrative specific system of rules presiding over narrative production and processing."[87] For all the talk of "narrative theology" and Lindbeck's comments that evangelicals are the future of postliberal theology, there has, in my opinion, been insufficient interaction between conservative philosophers of religion and systematic theologians on the one hand and narratologists on the other. The primary goal of narratologists is obviously the study of narratives. While its beginnings are traced back to the early twentieth century, as a specific field it only achieved systematic treatment in the late twentieth century (and is still hotly debated among literary theorists). To be sure, there is a growing body of interdisciplinary work between narratology and other disciplines (e.g., biblical studies[88] and homiletics[89]); however, to my knowledge no conservative has applied narratological principles as understood by the leaders in the field to the idea of revelation, with one notable exception: Gabriel Fackre. In *The Doctrine of Revelation*, Fackre offers "a narrative interpretation" of the concept of revelation. While I share Fackre's overall aim, his project differs from the one I offer here in three important respects, which become clear in the pages that follow.

So, close attention to the insights of narratologists offers valuable insights to philosophy of religion and theology, particularly for reflection on the idea of revelation. Our discussion partner will be Gerald Prince, one of the most prominent and prolific narratologists working today.[90]

Very often narratologists work with narrative, plot, story, *fabula*, *sjužet*, and discourse. Some definitions are necessary at this point, and in my judgment it is best to let Prince speak for himself regarding the meanings of these terms, much to the burden of the reader. (For a visual representation of the next several paragraphs, see Figure 4.2.)

---

so do its leading figures. That is to say, this presentation of narratology's salient features of general emphases is not to suggest that all narratologists do the same sort of work or that they all reach the same conclusions. Rather, I present one of the field's leading thinkers here, Gerald Prince, and his perception of the field itself, which includes his place in the field but not at the expense of fairly presenting the views of those with whom he disagrees.

87. Prince, "Narratology," 524.

88. See, e.g., older monographs such as Crenshaw, *Samson*; Fishbane, *Text and Texture*; Gunn, *Story of King David* and *Fate of King Saul*; Sasson, *Ruth*. See also the more recent Tolmie, *Narratology and Biblical Narratives* and Stibbe, *John as Storyteller*.

89. See, e.g., Brown, *Transformational Preaching*, 397–462.

90. Castle, *Blackwell Guide*, 119: "Structuralist narrative, or narratology, remains a vital field of scholarly research and advanced teaching, with Gerald Prince dominating the field in the U.S."

Prince and other specialists in narrative studies tend to view "narrative" as the broad category into which all of the other terms and concepts are placed. As the larger category, narrative is "the recounting (as product and process, object and act, structure and structuration) of one or more real or fictitious events communicated by one, two, or several (more or less overt) narrators to one, two or several (more or less overt) narratees."[91] Simply put, "narrative" is the umbrella term under which the rest of our concepts are placed.

In Prince's narratology, the term "story" means two things. On the one hand, "story" can be differentiated from other concepts with which it is often conflated such as "narrative" and "plot." This sense of "story" refers to the chronological ordering of events in a narrative, and it basically asks, "what happened?" Used in this way, "story" involves *fabula* and *sjužet*, terms borrowed from Russian formalism. *Fabula* is "the set of narrated situations and events in their chronological sequence [or] the basic story material"[92] and *sjužet* is "the set of narrated situations and events in the order of their presentation to the receiver."[93] This sense of story means that all stories are narratives, but not all narratives are stories. On the other hand, "story" refers to one of three methodological approaches to linguistic systems.[94] The second approach is also called "narrative discourse," and instead of asking, "*what* happened?" it asks, "*how* did the author show us what happened?" A third methodological approach is a hybrid of both approaches that attempts to bring together the *what* and *how* questions.[95]

Prince offers a fivefold definition of "story" that takes into account both senses of the word. He says story is (a) the content plane of narrative as opposed to its expression plane, (b) the basic material arranged into a plot as opposed to the plot itself, (c) an arrangement of events with an emphasis on chronology as opposed to causality, (d) a causal sequence of events

---

91. Prince, *Dictionary of Narratology*, 58.

92. Ibid., 30.

93. Ibid., 87.

94. For more on this usage of "story," see Benveniste, *Problems in General Linguistics*. Prince describes Benveniste's theory as follows: "According to Benveniste, and along with discourse (*discours*), [story is] one of two distinct and complementary linguistic subsystems. Whereas discourse involves some reference to the situation of enunciation and implies a *sender* and a *receiver*, story or history (*histoire*) does not. Compare 'He has eaten' or 'I've reminded you of it many times' with 'He ate' or 'She reminded him of it many times.'" From Prince, *Dictionary of Narratology*, 91.

95. Prince, "Narratology," 525. Since this book is an exploration of the concept of revelation, it is an exercise in the "how" question rather than the "what" question. It asks how an author/narrator conveys a narrative and how the reader/narratee responds to it. One could say, therefore, that this project performs an analysis of "narrative discourse."

pertinent to a character or characters seeking to solve a problem or reach a goal, and (e) one of two distinct and complementary linguistic subsystems (the other being narrative discourse).[96] Definitions (a) and (e) relate to story as one of the three methodological approaches to narratives, and definitions (b), (c), and (d) show the story's relationship to plot, *fabula*, and *sjužet*.

Prince gives several relevant definitions of "plot": "the arrangement of incidents; the situations and events as presented to the receiver," in which case plot is synonymous with *sjužet*; "the global dynamic (goal-oriented and forward-moving) organization of narrative constituents which is responsible for the thematic interest (indeed, the very intelligibility) of a narrative and for its emotional effect"; and last, "a narrative of events with an emphasis on causality, as opposed to story, which is a narrative of events with an emphasis on chronology."[97] In Prince's view, the story dictates what happened, but the plot provides causal links between what would otherwise be disparate events.[98] He gives an example to illustrate the principle: "'The king died, and then the queen died' is a story, whereas 'The king died, and then the queen died of grief' is a plot."[99] Although Prince does not go so far as to suggest it, one can perhaps think of the plot as answering the "why?" question since it adds causality to the events. (Question: *why* did the queen die? Answer: grief.)

One can further understand the concepts of narrative, story, plot, *fabula*, and *sjužet* in relation to each other. The *fabula* is related to story insofar as they are both concerned with the basic content of the story

---

96. Prince, *Dictionary of Narratology*, 91. For our purposes, we will not attempt to resolve definitions (c) and (d) above; the seemingly contradictory nature of under-emphasizing causality in (c) and seeking causal sequences in (d) is not the purpose of this section. I mention Prince's definition only to set the stage for how some aspects of story relate to the issue of divine revelation, not to resolve conceptual tangles in which current narratologists find themselves.

Moreover, there are other narratologists who are less concerned to separate these ideas into distinct categories. Consider Roger Schank and Tamara Berman, who say that "a story is a structured, coherent retelling of an experience or a fictional account of an experience. A satisfying story will include the following elements: themes, goals, plans, expectations, expectation failures (or obstacles), and perhaps, explanations or solutions." Quote taken from Schank and Berman, "Pervasive Role," 288. In my view, Prince offers the most helpful narratological view for explicating the concept of revelation today, since he presents distinct categories that turn on the issue of causality and ordering.

97. Prince, *Dictionary of Narratology*, 72.

98. Prince credits E. M. Forster with the observation that story is not the same as plot; story turns on chronology and plot turns on causality. See Prince, *Dictionary of Narratology*, 91, 72. See also Forster, *Aspects of the Novel*.

99. Prince, *Dictionary of Narratology*, 91.

ordered chronologically. *Sjužet* is related to "plot" insofar as both convey the significance of the narrative: *sjužet* does this by presenting the material in a specific way (which may or may not present material in the strict chronological ordering of the events), and plot does it by showing the causal connections in the chronology. Whereas "story" is the basic material of a narrative (the *fabula*) arranged or conceived chronologically, plot explores the relationship between these events in terms of causality and is presented to the receiver in a specific way that may or may not reflect the chronological ordering (the *sjužet*).

On this narratological reading, the significance of an event is conveyed in two ways: (1) *what* is revealed to the narratee and (2) *how* it is revealed to the narratee (i.e., by the causality implied in the plot and by the order in which the event is received by the narratee).

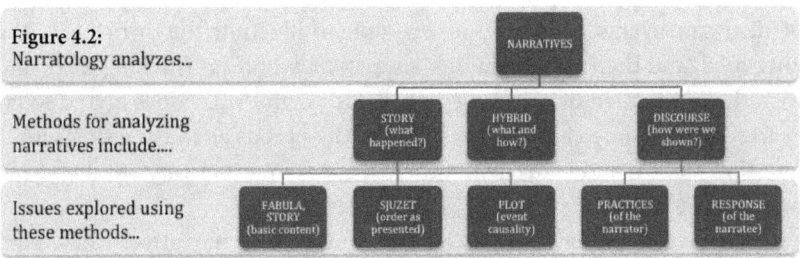

Figure 4.2:
Narratology analyzes...

Methods for analyzing narratives include....

Issues explored using these methods...

These observations culled from recent literary theory are relevant for proposals of revelation in which narrative figures heavily. I defined narrative symbolism as an event in which God interrupts and reforms one's subjectivity by situating one's story in a larger narrative for this very reason: the smaller "part" is a story, lacking its fullest significance until it is placed in the context of a larger narrative. The smaller story is placed in the larger narrative when the Narrator, discussed below, shows causality and presents the events to the narratee in a unique and purposeful (though not necessarily chronological) order to the narratee. At that time, when the smaller story is placed in the larger narrative, it becomes a "plot" because it has been shown to have greater significance than the smaller story had on its own. The larger narrative is the plot and the smaller part that finds itself in the plot is, until it is situated, only a story. It takes the right combination of causality (plot) and ordering (*sjužet*) for the narratee to ascertain the revelation's significance. A narrative symbolism perspective on revelation suggests that revelation adds plot to an individual's story (*fabula*); it adds causality to the chronology; it adds "why" to the "what."

Narratologists also consider a reader's or narratee's response to the material. If one had never read or heard two seminal Christian creeds, for instance, they would likely serve as an interesting example of the story/plot dynamic described above.[100] The Apostles Creed mentions that Jesus Christ "suffered under Pontius Pilate, was crucified, dead and buried." This provides a story of events that happened: suffering, execution and death, burial. The story in the Apostle's Creed mentions nothing of their significance for people who take this creed to be authoritative. Upon a plain reading, "the events as such seem not to point beyond themselves."[101] Question: *What* happened? Answer: Christ suffered, died, and was buried. Contrast this with the Nicene Creed, which states that Christ "for us men, and for our salvation came down from heaven" and was "crucified for us under Pontius Pilate, suffered and was buried." The Nicene Creed adds causality to the Apostle's Creed. Question: *Why* did Christ die? Answer: For us and for our salvation. "The saving significance of the whole sequence of events in general and of Christ's crucifixion in particular is explicitly stated" in the Nicene Creed; "it was for us, for our salvation, that all this happened.... It tells not just the story of Jesus Christ; in doing so it tells our story as well as his."[102] The *pro nobis* is the essential ingredient in turning the story of the crucifixion into the plot of the redemptive workings of God; indeed, much is added by suggesting that Christ died "for us." The same goes for narrative symbolism: it adds causality (plot) and a specific ordering (*sjužet*) to what are otherwise a series of less significant, perhaps even disparate events.[103] According to Luke Timothy Johnson, the Nicene Creed "does not propose a philosophy of life but tells a story with characters and plot. It is a story about God and the world, about God's investment in humans and their future."[104]

The recipient of narrative symbolism does not previously know the larger chronology or causality, including the events happening beyond her immediate field of vision or beyond her comprehension. Yet in the moment of revelation, a fuller picture is created in the mind of the receiver such that more connections are made and more reasons are given.[105] Narrative sym-

---

100. Evaluating the "reader response" allows us to get beyond traditional and/or historically-bound interpretations of these creeds. The idea of comparing the two creeds (though not necessarily in this way) comes from Dalferth, "Christ Died," 299–300.

101. Dalferth, "Christ Died," 299.

102. Ibid.

103. Of course, one could claim that this is too simple a contrast because the creeds seek to answer different problems or challenges. To follow this line of thinking: The Apostles Creed emphasizes the "facts" of Christ's life whereas the Nicene Creed emphasizes these facts' salvific character. The argument I am making here is not hurt, but strengthened by this addition. Salvation is the reason for the facts, the meaning behind the events. As I have outlined here, this is how plot works.

104. Johnson, *Creed*, 58.

105. One can draw a correlation between this aspect of the model of revelation

bolism offers meaning in situations by reaching the receiver in a purposed moment and in a purposed way (*sjužet*) to make clear the larger chronology and/or causality of events, the larger narrative into which her story fits, and the way in which her story fits into it. Prior to the event of revelation, the narratee may think she knows something of the reasons for why life is the way it is; she thinks she understands the plot of her life. But through narrative symbolism, God interrupts her subjectivity and reforms it. In revelation God shows the true plot—the ways in which her story fits into the larger narrative of God's work in the world—again and again, as often as God wills. With each revelation, she is reminded that her "story" is but one small part of a much larger narrative. With each revelation, the subplots of isolated incidents are situated in the larger plot; as a consequence, her entire life becomes fuller, richer, and more beautiful.

Two qualifications are needed at this point: first, the recipient of revelation in narrative symbolism does not necessarily need to recognize that God is the revealing One, an idea elaborated on in chapter 5; second, the plot does not necessarily have to complicate situations or events. In fact, divine revelation properly understood will simplify life for the narratee by making clear the "real" or "true" reasons for situations or events, thereby removing confusion or making unnecessary what would otherwise be a frustrating attempt to understand that which has not been illuminated yet requires illumination.[106] Narrative symbolism simply requires that individuals have

---

I defend here and Alasdair MacIntyre's understanding of history. The idea of "story" suggests an undeveloped or underdeveloped narrative to which plot adds causality. This is similar to MacIntyre's understanding of "intelligibility," which comes as a result of the larger picture in *After Virtue*, 199–200. Here MacIntyre says "what I have called a history is an enacted dramatic narrative in which the characters are also the authors" and we identify "the intelligibility of an action with its place in a narrative sequence."

106. Whitehead said that, "Rational religion appeals to the direct intuition of special occasions, and to the elucidatory power of its concepts for all occasions," which is a similar concept to the one I am defending here. However, the rejection of a necessarily complicating emergence of plot is what will differentiate this view from that of process theologians who assert that the world is, moment-by-moment, gathering more complexity. Rather, the view I endorse suggests that complication and complexity is what results from an incorrect or misguided notion of causality and divine action. Revelation as I am defending it here will simplify the life and perspective of the narratee/receiver, not complicate it. Moreover, I should elaborate on my claim that the plot shows the reasons behind "specific events" in the narratee's own life as well as the plot of her life as a whole. This is meant to hedge against the idea that the view I'm defending does not allow for different stories at different times for different audiences for different purposes. If what I am saying here is correct, this is *precisely* how divine revelation works. Each revelation is tailored specifically for individuals and communities and so there *are* different times, stories, audiences, and purposes at work. With respect to the epistemological question raised by this account—which would go something like this,

"stories" which can be situated in larger narratives, which leads to our next feature.

Third, there must exist a larger narrative into which the smaller stories of individuals are situated in the revelation event. This is not unlike what MacIntyre describes in *After Virtue* as the "setting." He says setting is a "relatively inclusive term" that has a variety of instantiations: an institution, a practice, or a milieu.[107] Despite its diverse manifestations, all "settings" are identifiable as having some similar characteristics: "It is central to the notion of setting as I am going to understand it that a setting has a history, a history within which the histories of individual agents not only are, but have to be, situated, just because without the setting and its changes through time the history of the individual agent and his changes through time will be unintelligible. Of course one and the same piece of behavior may belong to more than one setting."[108] This multi-layered approach to "histories" and "behaviors" are also applicable to the concept of revelation as narrative symbolism.

One is tempted to view smaller stories as those in which the action is minimal, the stakes are low, and the impact is marginal. One is also tempted to view large events as the opposite: high action, high stakes, and high impact. But the significance, size and shape of narratives vary; they are relative to context, situation, and duration of time. There are different levels of narratives. The same event that is small in one situation may be large in another. Therefore, the event that constitutes a divine revelation in narrative symbolism may be seemingly trivial or monumental. Its action, stakes, or impact does not matter, only that there are always two levels operating—a smaller story and a larger narrative.

On this view of revelation, the nature of smaller and larger narratives impacts the story/plot distinction as well. Any story that becomes a plot through the specific ordering of events and causal relationships therein is, in another sense, still a story. The process of converting story to plot, situating the smaller story amidst a larger narrative, is ongoing.[109] In light of this,

---

"how do we know that God uses something or someone as a symbol instead of us just thinking God did so?"—I direct the reader to the criteria outlined in chapter 5. For the purposes of my account, there are clear differences between revelations originated with God and those originating elsewhere (e.g., originated in/with ourselves).

107. MacIntyre, *After Virtue*, 192.

108. Ibid.

109. This process is ongoing until, of course, one reaches the question of a meta-narrative. In the next chapter I will address whether God's relationship to humanity fits into one grand meta-narrative or more than one narrative with distinct and irreducible narrative logics.

we must say that many, if not all, situations are potentially at once story and plot, smaller story and larger narrative. As the narratee seeks more significance and meaning, the explanations of causality and ordering she once had are less satisfying than they once were, so the plot then reverts back to "story" status while still being "plot" from the perspective of "the way things were." Story and plot are tools to elucidate what God may be up to in one's life.

Of course, if one thinks one has pinned God and God's intentions down, eventually one realizes that whatever insight was just reached is still just a smaller part of the narrative told by an ineffable, mysterious, transcendent Reality. Barth is helpful in this regard as a reminder: "It is not God who stands before us if he does not stand before us in such a way that He is and remains a mystery to us. Mystery means that he is and remains the one with whom we know only because He gives Himself to be known. . . . We cannot think of being able to explain our knowledge of God in any way from itself instead of its object. We cannot imagine any possibility or actuality or ordering of our knowledge of God apart from that which God Himself has established."[110] In narrative symbolism, the explanations God offers are always real and true, yet always incomplete. They can never capture the fullness of the plans, majesty and glory of the One who gives them, which brings us to our next explicit feature of narrative symbolism.

Fourth, this model of revelation requires something or someone to interrupt and reform the receiver by situating her smaller story into a larger narrative. Since our subject is "divine" revelation and not merely the "disclosure of information" or "revelation in general," there must be a "larger narrative giver." This is in strict opposition to some sort of "*agentless* revelation," as described by the great philosopher of religion Nicholas Wolterstorff in his *Divine Discourse: Philosophical Reflections on the Claim that God Speaks*.[111] Someone places the smaller story into the larger narrative. Call this the "Narrator." Not only must the Narrator exist, but also the Narrator must place the smaller story into the larger narrative in the consciousness of the narratee. If a person has a "story," however small and containing whatever content, it is as a result of some prior "story giver" who has given this smaller story a place in the larger narrative.[112] Moreover, the Narrator is the author of the larger narrative(s) into which the smaller story is situated.

110. Barth, *CD*, II/1, 41.

111. Wolterstorff, *Divine Discourse*, 23. Wolterstorff discusses a form of revelation he calls "*agentless* revelation," and clearly that is not what I have in mind here. However, in the "sin" section of the next chapter I show how revelation may be impacted by a human's refusal to give herself over to the power of the symbol to initiate divine revelation.

112. The issues that may arise as a result of approaching the problem of revelation

A brief excursus is needed at this point to further describe the nature of the Narrator (i.e., God) in narrative symbolism. Our comments on the nature of God here will include discussion of (a) God and agency, (b) the God/world relationship, (c) God and time, (d) God as the greatest conceivable being, and (e) God as Christians understand God, viz., as a Trinity. I will not be arguing at length for any of these claims, but merely outlining the specific view of God that informs and is informed by this proposal.

I have discussed narrative symbolism as an *event* in which God situates individual smaller stories in larger narratives, but more should be said about the nature of God as a person as opposed to understanding God *as the event* of situating. The idea that God *is* an event is not without precedent in theology. Hans Urs von Balthasar understood God to be an "eternal happening,"[113] in which "God *is* an *event* of love."[114] According to Antonio López, beings "can be considered events inasmuch as they appear proceeding from being itself, the ever-greater ground that does not have a 'beyond itself.' . . . The event, unexpectedly coming out from something other than itself, is that phenomenon in which being shows itself, gives itself, and speaks itself in order to call the human being into its own infinite beauty."[115] Seeking to prevent either a radical apophatic theology or the removal of the fundamental mysteriousness of God, López's window into the nature of God is the incarnation of Jesus Christ.[116] Christians who imagine God as an event argue that Jesus most often presents himself as an event—e.g., a gifting, a ransoming, a sending, etc.—rather than as a person.

The problem with understanding God as event is that it misconstrues the nature of divine and human agency. Whatever else a theist says, surely she wants to affirm that God has agency: the capacity to act in the world by self-determination in various ways under various conditions. God can choose to do X or Y, and God's choice is real, limited only by fundamental rules of thought.[117] A sense of agency requires an ability to weigh options

---

from the perspective of the Narrator are mitigated here. This is why I emphasize the equivalent of literary theory's "reader response" to divine revelation, its impact on the one who receives it.

113. Von Balthasar, *Last Act*, 67.

114. O'Hanlon, *Immutability of God*; Wallner, "Ein trinitarisches Strukurprinzip," 532–546; Mansini, "Balthasar," 499–519; Fields, "Singular as Event," 93–111; Scola, *Hans Urs von Balthasar*, 53–64. Passage taken from Lopez, "Eternal Happening," 214.

115. López, "Eternal Happening," 218.

116. Ibid., 221: "There can be no speech about God apart from what the person of Christ reveals of God."

117. This is not to suggest that we understand all of the ways in which seemingly incompatible options are compatible, but rather to repeat that nonsense remains nonsense even if we speak it about God (cf. Lewis, *Problem of Pain*, 25).

against values, make a decision, and act according to that decision.[118] One might say that agency requires a mind and will. Events, unlike persons, have no sense of agency; they are occurrences that happen between entities, only some of which may have agency. So in the Christian tradition, Jesus' "sending" and "gifting" and "ransoming" were actions that resulted from decisions God made, which implies agency (which an event does not have). Events cannot be agents since they possess no will or mind (as God and humans do). A second misunderstanding of "event" concerns their duration. Simply put, events are temporally finite: they come and go. This is *not* something theists wish to say of God, who has eternal permanence. So while the incarnation is an event in which the Word takes on flesh, the Word itself cannot be the event of "flesh-taking" since Christians want to affirm that the Word existed before the incarnation and after the ascension. The Word is not limited to Jesus' actions, and God is not limited to events.

We should also consider narrative symbolism's view of the God/world relationship. If God is a personal agent, then God decides to use symbols (most often narratives) in the event of revelation through an initiating sign. These signs can and do include obscure things like the kingdom of God and light, as Dulles suggested, and they can also include more tangible objects like a cross, a Bible, or Jesus Christ, God's very self incarnate. Although I will elaborate on the nature of divine self-revelation in chapter 5, it suffices to say here that at times the sign *is* God and at other times the sign is *not* God. In certain models of the God/world relationship, everything in the world is God (pantheism) or is interpenetrated by a greater God (panentheism). If what I am arguing is correct, then there are times when the sign is *not* God. To be clear: there are things in the world that are *neither* God nor *in* God, which rules out pantheism or panentheism as being acceptable God/world relationships for narrative symbolism. Rather, classical theism is the view that fits best with this model, according to which God is radically transcendent but also deeply immanent, because the former grounds the latter.[119]

Another facet of the God/world relationship concerns divine activity. Fortunately, narrative symbolism relates well to historically accepted positions on creation and providence. One can conceive of the aforementioned story/plot dynamic similar to how Aquinas (and Aristotle before him)

---

118. Here, "sense of agency" is different than a sense of ownership. In *How the Body*, Shaun Gallagher argues that agency requires self-determination whereas ownership requires self-involvement. For example, if someone lifts her own arm, she has both a sense of agency and a sense of ownership; however, if someone lifts her arm for her, she will have a sense of ownership—after all, it is *her* arm that is being lifted—but not a sense of agency since her will was not involved in the decision to lift her arm.

119. Kelsey, Warfield Lectures 2011. See also Tanner, *God and Creation*, 89 ff.

framed potentiality and actuality.[120] Each actual story is a potential plot, made so by adding awareness of causality through the meaningful ordering of events to the narratee. Yet each story cannot be the result of an infinitely long regress of efficient stories. Story requires contingent "actants," and actants must be ultimately traced back to a necessary being who created and sustains them. Implicit in Thomas is the notion of essential and accidental causes, *per se* and *per accidens* causes, "hierarchical" and "linear" causes.[121] Just as an infinite contingent being is an incoherent notion, so too is a series of stories without a creator/sustainer who gives life to them, the Narrator. All "substances have their existence of the prime agent: indeed their being created substances consists precisely in this, that they have their existence of another."[122] At the risk of belaboring the point, a narrative's "existence itself therefore is in these created substances as a sort of actualization."[123] Narrative symbolism as an event in which individual stories are situated in a larger narrative requires the existence and action of the larger narrative giver, the Narrator, "and this being we call God."[124]

Now this raises a question. If God is the being who reveals by connecting smaller stories to larger narratives, is God the only being who can perform such an action? The "narrative symbolism" view of revelation requires that this ability is one of the divinely communicable attributes. There are narrators, and there is a Narrator. Humans have the ability to connect smaller stories to larger narratives, and they do so often. This observation means that we are forced to posit criteria for adjudicating between competing narratives. It also means that we must elaborate on the incorrect use of this ability, missing the intended mark. Both of these subjects are addressed in the next chapter in an effort to help us discern whether one is truly hearing/seeing God's revelation or whether one has taken one's own perception—consciously or not—as God's revelation.

Let us also consider God's relationship to time in narrative symbolism. It is common for Christians to suggest that God is eternal, and various passages from Christianity's sacred texts are used in support of this notion of God's relationship to time: "Lord, you have been our dwelling place in all

---

120. Aristotle, *Basic Works*, 820–21. See also Aquinas, *Summa Contra Gentiles*, II, 53.
121. Davis, "Hierarchical Causes," 13–27.
122. Thomas, *Summa Contra Gentiles*, II, 53.
123. Ibid.
124. Aquinas, *Summa Theologica*. Cf. Pojman, *Philosophy of Religion*, 3

generations."[125] "You are the same and your years have no end."[126] "I am the Alpha and the Omega, the first and the last, the beginning and the end."[127] But what sort of eternity does the God of narrative symbolism possess? There are two options. In a "timelessly eternal" sense, God is thought to be "outside of time," and in a "temporally eternal" sense, God is thought to be "inside time," but still eternally past, present, and future. Narrative symbolism requires a Narrator to act at specific points in time, and from the perspective of humankind, one can say that God has acted "before" or "during" or "in the year 2015." I consider God to be temporally eternal and am inclined to think that such views are more compatible with my model of revelation. After all, it seems to me that only a God "inside" time can act in history to show a narratee her place in the larger narrative. In addition, it seems to me that we have never been shown in a satisfactory way what atemporal causation looks like.[128] However, if traditional believers in divine timeless eternity wish to appropriate my model then they are welcome to attempt it.

Let us also consider the nature of God as the greatest conceivable being. Three attributes in particular deserve attention: omnipotence, omniscience, and omnibenevolence. God's omnipotence means that God can do any possible action.[129] It is logically possible to change a person, and God is the infinitely skilled Narrator, who chooses the right combination of presentation method and content so as to create the best conditions for effectual narrative symbolism. In the Narrator's omniscience, God knows all that has gone before and all that will happen in the future and is able to construct the "now" moment of revelation in light of this knowledge. God's omnibenevolence ensures that God constructs revelations and situates narratives for the flourishing of the recipient of revelation.

Our final comments on God as the Narrator concern the nature of God as a Trinity.[130] Throughout our exploration of revelation we have seen several trinitarian configurations of divine revelation in which a specific

---

125. Psalms 90: 1–4.
126. Psalms 102: 25–27.
127. Rev. 22:13.
128. Cf. Davis, *Logic*, ch. 1.

129. I disagree with those who would suggest that God can do logically impossible feats, like create a married bachelor or draw a triangle with four sides.

130. The nature of God as Trinity is one of those topics that brings up the issue of authentication and adjudication. Here we risk circular reasoning unless we propose some way to authenticate the claim that God is a Trinity, which I will offer in chapter 5 under the headings "Revelation and Divine Self-Revelation" and "Authentication and Adjudication."

member of the Trinity is responsible for some aspect of divine revelation. For instance, in the introduction I showed how Barth and von Balthasar understand revelation to be a trinitarian unveiling: Barth's gulf was revealed and traversed by Christ who is the bridge between God and humankind whereas in von Balthasar the Spirit is the vehicle of revelation proceeding from the point of separation of Father and Son. Narrative symbolism, too, endorses a trinitarian model of God, but it is trinitarian in the sense that the God who reveals is a Trinity. It is *not* trinitarian in the sense that individual members of the Trinity act in different ways in the event of revelation. Narrative symbolism as a model of revelation is an action of God toward humans, and in line with Athanasius, Nyssa, and Augustine[131] I would suggest that all *ad extra* workings of the Godhead are workings of all three members of the Trinity.

Fifth, narrative symbolism requires a sign that initiates the event of revelation. There is a difference between the categories of symbol and sign. Signs are created to point to something else while narrative symbolism is the manner in which we interpret the action of pointing. Some signs have been common in the history of the Christian tradition, even while they have been grouped in different ways by different Christian thinkers: creation, morality, the incarnate Word, and Christian scriptures.[132] In terms of "revelation," some have situated these four into the categories of "general" revelation (creation and morality) and "special" revelation (Christ and the Bible). Each of these four is fully supported and embraced in narrative symbolism as a potential sign of divine revelation.[133]

---

131. See, e.g., Augustine, *De Trinitate* and "Sermon 52: The Trinity" in *Sermons*.

132. Which signs are used to initiate the event of revelation is not of great concern for this view to work, as I discuss below. Narrative Symbolism is equally amenable with the four "sources" which make up the so-called "Wesleyan Quadrilateral": scripture, tradition, reason, and experience. I will argue below that the sources themselves are virtually endless, which does not preclude the Christian from asserting the uniqueness of Christian scriptures.

133. The created world acts as a "stage" on which actants play their parts, and in a moment of revelation the actants see themselves in relation to a/the larger whole. One may sense one's imperfection and smallness in relation to beautiful natural scenery, for instance, and the event reminds one that there is something larger than what is normally seen operating in this world. One could see oneself as part of the creative process of God. This is similar to what Clifford Williams describes as an existential need to have "awe" of something larger than oneself. So too with morality, which enables value judgments of the actions of the actants. The moral code sets each action against larger notions of "good" or "right" as well as larger notions of "evil" or "wrong." Seeing one's place in the "big picture," one is reminded that one should be an agent for the good. In both creation and morality, an individual's story is positioned amidst a larger narrative backdrop, and as such both are initiators of revelatory narrative symbolism. This is also the case with initiators that have been traditionally considered "special" revelations.

But surely the potential signs of revelation are not limited to creation, morality, the incarnate Word, and Christianity's sacred texts. A view of revelation in which narratives figure heavily must take into account other potential signs. As narratologists remind us, narratives are everywhere and conveyed in many ways. Says Prince: "Narratives are found, and stories, told, in a variety of media: oral and written language (in prose or in verse, of course, but also sign languages, still or moving pictures (as in narrative paintings, stained-glass windows, or films), gestures, (programmatic) music, or a combination of vehicles.... Furthermore, a folktale can be transposed into a ballet, a comic strip into a pantomime, a novel brought to the screen, and vice versa."[134] There is great diversity in both the narrative media (oral, written, etc.) and the forms of narrative (novel, news report, ordinary conversation, etc.). The same story can be told in many different ways, and different stories can be told using the same forms of discourse. This was actually one of the contributing factors to the development of narratology as a discipline; it shows that narratives can be studied on their own without reference to the medium through which they are presented. Making the point using the written word, Prince argues that "within the medium—say, written language—a given set of events can be presented in different ways, in the order of their (supposed) occurrence, for example, or in a different order. The narratologist should therefore be able to examine the narrated,

---

Upon encountering Jesus Christ, one gets a glimpse of the Reality beyond him (e.g., the Father who sent him; John 14:8-9), one's existential predicament (e.g., the sinful life in which one lives vis-à-vis his sinlessness; 1 Cor. 5:21), and a model for living life as one's Creator intended (e.g., concern for the poor; Luke 12:44; 14:12-14; Matt 19:21). Each is a broader narrative into which the smaller story of the individual fits. This has implications for one's conduct. For instance, when victim to a crime, one can imagine Jesus literally turning the other cheek when stricken by a Roman soldier; one is then motivated to not retaliate. An encounter with Christ, even a mental replay of one of the gospel narratives, is sufficient to connect one's situation to the larger narrative. Very often one encounters Jesus in the Bible, which is host to many more narratives into which readers immerse themselves. On this view of revelation, the postconservative Evangelicals remind us, "the Bible is like a great nonfictional novel than like a book of philosophy. It contains philosophy (or something like it), but only within the framework of a grand narrative. It is an epic more than a textbook of information or ideas" (Olson, *Reformed*, 165). As an epic, the Bible presents a world into which the present-day reader is immersed: the narrative of God's relationship with humanity. The Bible, as Lindbeck said, "absorbs the world." One may read Ezekiel's story, for instance, and find that God can breathe new life into dry and desolate bones (Ezek 37:5-6). One can see oneself in the story, embodied in the characters, sharing their struggles, sharing their victories. So the traditional initiators of revelation are embraced—creation, morality, Jesus Christ, and Holy Scripture—but God's decision to use them as signs to initiate the revelation is their salient feature.

134. Prince, "Narratology," 524-25.

the story presented, independently not only of the medium used but also of the narrating, the discourse, the *way* in which the medium is used to present the *what*."[135] Our view of revelation—and our view of Christianity's sacred texts—needs to account for transmedia, multiplatform delivery.[136]

In consideration of the fact that narratives are ubiquitous and narrative discourse ranges a great deal, in narrative symbolism *any* object, *any* situation, *any* "thing" can be a sign that initiates the revelation event. The diversity of human experience requires such a broad field, and revelation is tailored to the unique person to whom it occurs.[137] With each initiating sign, potential exists for someone's story to connect to a narrative larger than his or her own; hence, each "thing" is a potential sign and each event is a potential moment of narrative symbolism, that is, a potential moment of revelation. It may happen through worship, the sacraments, a conversation, an unplanned insight, a sermon, a smile, etc. The signs that can initiate divine revelation are as diverse as the things God created. God may "speak to us through Russian communism, through a flute concerto, through a blossoming shrub or through a dead dog."[138] The key feature of divine revelation is God's action. God uses a sign to initiate an encounter in which an individual's smaller story is connected to the larger narrative of God's action.

Thus concludes the explanation of the explicit features of revelation when understood as an event of narrative symbolism. There are still features

---

135. Prince, *Dictionary of Narratology*, 59.

136. Both of these terms are borrowed from media studies, but they apply well to this model of revelation in which God can use any "thing" to interrupt and reform an individual's subjectivity by showing the ways in which her story is situated in a larger narrative. The earliest sustained treatment of the topic I could find was from 2006: Dinehart, "Transmedia Play." Since 2010, no fewer than a dozen dissertations and theses have been written on transmedia story delivery.

137. This explains the variety of perspectives one finds in the Bible regarding revelation. God reveals humanity's place in the larger narrative in a variety of ways: a still small voice, overturning Temple tables, reflecting on sacred texts, or speaking directly. To continue the discussion of the creation, morality, Christ, and Bible from before, those same insights can be reached in other ways. Whereas one might find it revelatory to reflect on creation/nature, someone else might sense her place in the created world by holding a newborn child. Whereas one person may connect to the moral code by seeing injustices by others, another may connect to right and wrong by telling a lie and feeling guilty about it later. Whereas imagining Jesus turning the other cheek gives some people motivation to do the right thing (or at least not the wrong thing), imagining a situation in which one is instructing one's child to do the right thing might do the same for another person. And whereas the Bible connects some people's stories with God's message of turning death into life, perhaps another person receives this message by looking at scientific explanations of the "natural" world's processes of decay, fertilization, growth, etc.

138. Barth, *CD*, I/1:60. Cf. Green, ed., *Karl Barth*, 24.

that, while not explicit (i.e., obvious), are implicitly required for narrative symbolism to work.

Implicit Features of Narrative Symbolism

The implicit features of narrative symbolism include some degree of self-awareness in the narratee, difference between the smaller and larger narratives, unity between the smaller and larger narratives, the linear passage of time, the narratee's willingness to participate, and a meaningful connection between the two narratives. Each deserves elaboration.

Sixth, the individual must possess some degree of self-awareness. Only by knowing oneself at some level is one able to have the requisite awareness of the contours of one's story. Only by knowing one's story is one positioned to contrast one's perception of the individual story with the larger narrative into which it is placed. This feature of narrative symbolism, like many of the others, raises the question of origin. But the self-awareness in the individual is not a product of some singular reflection or the human using natural capacities to understand. Instead, it is self-awareness of one's story ultimately traced back to God. God directs the process.

Seventh, if divine revelation is an event in which smaller stories are seen in the context of a larger narrative, there must be some degree of difference between the two narratives. If there were no differences between the smaller and larger narratives, the narratee would not be able to distinguish the two. The event would not be "revelatory" in any sense: nothing and no one *new* would be communicated to the self-aware person. The allegedly "new" thing offered by the event of revelation would merely be the continuation of the subject's own story perceived by the subject's self-awareness. An individual's story is the sum total of the events she has experienced along with her perception and understanding of them; it is her history.[139] If there were no difference, life would be predicable; however, unpredictability is required of narrative. It is one of the constitutive features of the narrative structure of human life.[140] When she encounters a sign that initiates revelation, she is presented with a larger narrative from which she can differentiate her own story; God uses the larger narrative to help her make meaning out

---

139. As noted by MacIntyre, *After Virtue*, 200.

140. Ibid. In narratives as in life, people cannot simply do as they please; they are constrained: "they do not begin where they please, they cannot go on exactly as they please either; each character is constrained by the actions of others and by the social settings presupposed in his and their actions. . . . [I]t is crucial that at any given point in an exacted dramatic narrative we do not know what will happen next. . . . [This] is required by the narrative structure of human life."

of her smaller story, i.e., the past. The future at that moment is potentially different than it would have otherwise been. And this difference between the "already" and the "not yet" is vital to the subject's ability to understand. That which is conveyed in narrative symbolism contrasts at some level with the experience of the narratee such that she is able to distinguish the two.

Eighth, however, there must also be unity between the smaller story and the larger narrative. The narratee must recognize and accept that the larger narrative is related at some level to her experience. Otherwise, it would be an irrelevant detail, easily dismissed without significance. The subject must understand that the revelation answers some existential question that concerns her on an ultimate or proximate level.[141] If there is no unity between the smaller and larger narratives, there is no connection made between the Narrator's revelation and the narratee. The "unity" feature of revelation is supported by recent research in literary theory. Researchers found that readers are "influenced to agree with the causes the stories implicated when the stories 'evoked memories of similar characters and causal circumstances in the minds of the readers.'"[142] Revelation requires that there must be some degree of unity between the smaller story and the larger such that the person sees in the revelation the development of *her* story, the unfolding of *her* life. If a narratee's predicament could be formulated as a question, there must be some degree of unity there for the person to recognize that the revelation is the answer.[143]

---

141. See, e.g., Tillich, *Systematic Theology*, vol. 1.

142. Strange and Leung, "How anecdotal accounts," in *Personality*, 444. Cf. Schank and Berman, "Pervasive Role," 302.

143. Explanation of the difference/unity dynamic is aided by attending briefly to deconstructionist and post-deconstructionist thought. In *The Other Heading*, Derrida writes that history "presupposes that the heading not be *given*, that it not be identifiable in advance and once and for all. The irruption of the new, the unicity of the other *today* should be awaited *as such* . . . it should be anticipated as the unforeseeable, the *unanticipatable*, the non-identifiable, in short, as that of which one does not yet have a memory" (Derrida, *The Other Heading*, 18). Literary theorist Daniel Punday suggests that Derrida anticipates the question of narrative after deconstruction in asking how Europe can be both part of a cultural tradition and "unanticipatable." (Punday, *Narrative After Deconstruction*, viii.) Derrida elsewhere writes that, like a "pledge," what is "no longer archived in the same way is no longer lived in the same way" (Derrida, *Archive Fever*, 18). The point is this: moving into a new direction necessarily involves looking back into the past for a sense of origin; once one has seen the origin, one departs from it. In Pundays' view, narrative is still relevant because it both departs and takes its cue from deconstruction: "To understand this 'new' writing, this narrative after deconstruction, we need both to appreciate its continuities with deconstruction and to recognize the effort that it exerts to create the discontinuities that constitute it as a mode of thinking in its own right" (Punday, *Narrative After Deconstruction*, ix). The same framework with which Punday understands "narrative after deconstruction" may

Ninth, if divine revelation is an event in which the story of an individual is meaningfully connected to a larger narrative, then narrative symbolism—like the concept of God—requires a linear passage of time. As Gary Saul Morson suggests, "Time is of the essence. Intellectual models—whether pertaining to the natural or the social world, to history or psychology, to ethics or politics—implicitly or explicitly depend on a specific sense of time."[144] As our subject is "narrative," the specific sense of time required is linear. Simply put, stories require time to pass; so does plot (which shows causality).[145] The only way to demarcate where one event begins and another ends is to locate them in relation to each other in terms of time in the same way one would locate where one object begins and another ends in relation to space. If not located along a linear continuum of time there is no meaning made by locating one's story in a larger narrative; indeed, there would be no "larger" narrative at all as all events would be one. Without the linear passage of time, one can still have a literary work which is meaningful to some on many levels, but it is not a "story" or "narrative." Stories require time: A, *then* B. So do plots: A, *then* B, because C.

Incorporating the idea of linear time requires clarification. It does *not* mean two things. On one hand, linear time does not necessarily remove *sjužet*. Surely, each narratee does not know all of the manifold events that bear on her situation, and nor does she know all of the causes for events of which she *is* aware, the causal links for each aspect of each story in her life. So while this view of revelation requires the linear passage of time for events to happen, it does not require that the narratee know what has happened elsewhere or at another time until the revelation itself occurs. She

---

be applied to this theory of divine revelation. The narratee to whom revelation comes is shown how the chronology of past events is causally linked, and what emerges is a new thing, both distinct from and similar to what has gone before. It replaces the past by offering a new mode of being, a fresh and new perspective, and divine insight. However, the event of revelation also continues some of the features of the old life such that the recipient of revelation is able to identify the revelation as the answer to her existential question. The larger narrative that is opened up to the narratee in the event of revelation must include both continuities and differences with the smaller story of the individual or community.

144. Morson, *Narrative and Freedom*, 1.

145. Obviously here I am referring to issues related to causality, which brings up the controversy surrounding Hume and Kant, to which I will devote little attention. Hume thought that we can not directly apprehend causality: a billiard ball strikes another one, yet all we witness is the movement of the first ball and the movement of the second. Intuitively and experientially, however, we recognize the causal links between them. Kant responded by suggesting that the "Humean problem" is much larger and only solved by positing a priori concepts and principles of the understanding (and his concept of synthetic a priori judgments). See Hume's *Enquiry* and Kant's response in the *Prolegomena*.

is presented with some information only after the fact or before the fact. This view of revelation does not require that information comes to her as it happens, but as the Revealer/Narrator deems appropriate for the greatest potential for revelation to occur, for the greatest chance that she will correctly locate her story in the larger narrative.[146] To make the point explicit: the ordering of the material in the presentation to the narratee is not the same as the ordering of the material in the *fabula* or "story proper." Nor does linear time mean that narrative symbolism illuminates only what has occurred in the past. The linear passage of time is adopted to allow for causality, and revelation makes meaning by showing these connections to the narratee. It does not require that she experience the events as they happened chronologically. Hope in a future event—the eschaton, to cite a Christian example—can be meaningfully revelatory to the narratee. In the present, the narratee may happen upon a sign that the Narrator uses to bring her into the larger story, even if some aspects of that story have not yet occurred. It gives her hope for the future, which changes her in the present.

Tenth, when revelation is understood as an event in which a sign initiates the situation of the narratee's smaller story into a larger narrative, the narratee must be, at some level, willing to participate in the revelation. She must give herself over to the sign's power to initiate the revelation. Dulles and Lindbeck are correct on this point. For "if we surrender to their power they carry us away, enabling us to integrate a wider range of impressions, memories, and affections. . . . To enter the world of meaning opened up . . . we must give ourselves; we must be not detached observers but engaged participants."[147]

The origins of a subject's willingness to give oneself over to the sign's power to initiate is another matter. When that which is revealed is God and God's activity in the world, this view claims with Barth that God is known

---

146. This is a point noted by literary theorist Paul Cobley: "Even if its ultimate reference might be thought to be the movement of the clock, time in narrative does not necessarily unfold linearly. . . . Narration can move backwards in time to depict events which have taken place before those that have most recently been narrated [known as *analepsis* or *retroversion*], and . . . events in the future can be narrated [known as *prolepsis*]. Both phenomena involve the narrative opting to choose some things or events (in the past or the future) rather than others. The same can be said of a similarly prominent feature of narrative usually called "summary and scene." Summary is a form of prose in a narrative that tells about events or people without directly presenting their speech: a narrative might move, by way of summary, to a later point in time, passing over quickly what happens in between; alternatively, by the same means it can move from one place to another, more distant one. Scene, conversely, bears affinities with dramatic narrative: it shows the events, and, more often than not, such events will contain speech that scene is able to imitate . . . ." (Cobley, "Narratology" in Groden, Kreiswirth, and Szeman, eds., *Hopkins Guide*).

147. Dulles, *Models of Revelation*, 132-33.

by God. Humans merely participate in God's self-knowledge.[148] At each stage in the process, God directs the action: the human story, the location of the sign, the moment of awakening in which the narratives are connected (narrative symbolism), and the movement from one revelation until the next event of revelation. That which is revealed is one's place in the larger narrative of God's work in the world, and the willingness to give oneself over to the sign's power also comes from God, who does the disrupting and reforming of an individual's subjectivity through divine revelation.

Very often when philosophers of religion and theologians claim God's intervention in or direction of the world's affairs, two thorny and related issues rear their heads. (a) If an omnibenevolent God is unfolding the plot, whence comes evil? (b) What is the relationship between the divine and human will? This book is not primarily on the subject of competing wills, and much less on the problem of evil. So my remarks on the matter are admittedly terse. In this model of revelation, I adopt two solutions, one for each of the problems with the second depending on the first. For the problem of competing wills, Kathryn Tanner's *God and Creation in Christian Theology* provides an acceptable if not entirely satisfactory way for theologians to claim that divine and human causality both exist. She insists that there are two different planes of causality, "a 'horizontal' plane, an order of created causes and effects; [and] a 'vertical' plane, the order whereby God founds the former."[149] To pose some competition between the wills is to confuse the

---

148. Barth, *CD* II/1, 40: "But in order to consider the necessary determination and limit which is here set us in the fact that the known object is God while we are only the knowing men. If we know Him in consequence of His giving Himself to be known by us in His revelation, then indeed we know Him in His mystery.

'In His mystery.' In these words we are saying only that we know Him as He gives Himself to be known by us. But in these words we also make the important declaration: thus and only thus, in this clarity and certainty and in no other. The fact that we know God is His work and not ours. And the clarity and certainty in which we know Him are His and not ours. The possibility on the basis of which this occurrence is realized is His divine power. The actuality in which it happens is the actuality of His will and decision. The order in which it happens is the free disposition of His wisdom.... We cannot understand anything at all in this matter except as deriving from God—neither the possibility nor the actuality in which we know God, neither the order in which it happens nor the fact that it happens in that indisputable clarity and certainty. Bound to the Word of God in regard to our knowledge of God we have to give the glory to God Himself and indeed to God alone."

149. Tanner, *God and Creation*, 89–90. She continues: "Predicates applied to created beings may concern what happens within the created order; they can be understood to hold simply within the horizontal plane of relations among created beings. Predicates of that sort say nothing about the vertical relation of a creature's dependence upon God. Ascribing them to created beings cannot run contrary, then, to our rules for talk of God's agency and the creature.... There need be no contradiction in saying relations

planes of causality; rather, God exists in a relationship of "non-competition" with humanity.[150] If Tanner has successfully defended human agency, then the problem of evil has a solution as well. One can sidestep the challenge that evil raises by appealing to the Free Will Defense, a theodicy that assumes a greater good "in the end" that was "obtainable by God in no other way."[151] One reconciles evil with omnipotence and omnibenevolence by suggesting, "all the evil that exists in the world is due to the choices of free moral agents whom God created, and no other world which God could have created would have had a better balance of good over evil than the actual world will have."[152] Taken together, these conclusions allow for narrative symbolism to maintain on the one hand that God directs events and on the other hand that the narratee's agency is uncompromised. (In the next chapter I will illustrate this principle at work using the human creative process.) If the agency of the narratee is uncompromised, then this allows us to posit the willingness-to-participate feature of narrative symbolism at the same time as we affirm that willingness is ultimately God-given.[153]

If revelation is centered on God's activity from start to finish, how might it work when the subject—in her freedom—resists? Wolterstorff suggests that revelation is still revelation if "something is done which *would* dispel ignorance if attention and interpretive skills were adequate."[154] If attention is directed elsewhere and/or interpretive skills are inadequate, how does divine revelation fare? Here narratologist Gerald Prince proves helpful. Narratology, as we noted above, is methodologically approached by examining "story" or "narrative discourse." Narrative discourse takes into account the Narrator's practices and the narratee's response, and it emphasizes narrative's "process" more than narrative's "product." As a process, narratives are vehicles for all sorts of communication like "informing, diverting attention, entertaining, persuading, etc."[155] The process of communication is an exchange between the two parties in which one figure basically says

---

that are free or contingent along the horizontal axis of a created order are determined to be so in a vertical relation of absolute dependence upon divine agency."

150. See also Tanner, *Jesus*, 1–6, for an overview of this view of non-competition.

151. Davis, *Encountering Evil*, 71. To me, this seems like a "greater good" theodicy wrapped in a Free Will defense.

152. Davis, "Free Will and Evil," 72.

153. Many, will find this so-called "solution" ultimately unsatisfying. However, to delve into such issues would distract from the view of revelation being advanced. One is tempted to agree with Volf when he concedes in *Exclusion and Embrace* that "no theodicy can succeed" (135).

154. Wolterstorff, *Divine Discourse*, 23.

155. Prince, *Dictionary of Narratology*, 59.

"I will tell you a story if you promise to be good, [or] I will listen to you if you make it valuable."[156] Prince describes this as a "contract" between the narrator and narratee in which the narrative is communicated for a reason. However, Prince also discusses "unsolicited narratives" for which there is no prior contract. In these situations, the narrator solicits attention by conveying a narrative of the highest quality. The narrator

> must awaken and maintain desire in the audience by relying on the dynamics of surprise and suspense.... Narrators try to make it clear that their narrative has a point; and [narrators show] why the very shape of a narrative is affected by the situation in which it occurs and the goal which it seeks to attain, with the sender of the message giving certain kinds of information, disposing it in a certain way, adopting one kind of focalization as opposed to another, underscoring the importance or strangeness of certain details, so that the receiver can better process the information in terms of certain imperatives and ends.[157]

Clearly this circles back to the *sjužet*: the information is presented in such a way so as to be compelling to the narratee, intentionally highlighting specific aspects of the narratee's story by answering her existential questions.

One can easily apply Prince's comments on the "unsolicited narrative" to revelation, and it ties in directly with the "willingness" feature of narrative symbolism. In a situation with a narratee who is unwilling to be affected by the sign, the Narrator purposefully surprises (i.e., interrupts) her by showing how she fits within the larger narrative of God's work. The event of revelation is such that she is shown what God desires her to be shown in the context of her temporal realities, and events that may have seemed insignificant are shown to be significant. The Narrator shows the narratee that her story has a point, a reason for existing in the larger narrative. The Narrator shows her that the shape of her story is affected by the situation in which it occurs and that there is a goal the Narrator seeks to attain for her. This is key: the Narrator is infinitely skilled at selecting and emphasizing certain pieces of information to use in the event of revelation. The Narrator is also infinitely skilled at conveying the content in a certain way, focusing on certain aspects of her story, and underscoring the importance or strangeness of certain details such that the receiver can process this information in terms of the Narrator's imperatives and ends.[158] The Narrator, in short, is infinitely skilled at creating narratives of the highest quality. The narratee

156. Ibid.
157. Prince, *Dictionary of Narratology*, 60.
158. Ibid.

becomes willing after the Narrator creates in her the willingness by tailoring the method of presentation to her unique circumstances.

Eleventh and finally, the connection of the smaller story to and in the larger narrative must be a meaningful one. Otherwise, the larger narrative holds no potential for the bearer of the smaller story; the larger narrative would have neither appeal nor significance for the narratee. However, like "story" and "narrative," the term "meaning" is a relative concept that depends on a context to provide what sort of meaning the connection contains. The meaningful connection between the two narratives may, to borrow a Tillichian phrase, be a matter of "ultimate concern."[159] Or, it may be a matter of proximate concern. The Narrator may reveal the purpose, causal links, and/or significance of events in the story of the narratee irrespective of the type of meaning.

One can think of the "meaning" feature by considering one of the purposes of storytelling: to teach. Schank and Berman say, "in some sense, all stories can be considered to be didactic in nature, in that they are intended to teach, or convey something to a listener."[160] One of the reasons an author may tell a story—one of the things taught in the storytelling—concerns the self-disclosure of the storyteller. At the very least, in telling a story the Narrator reveals to the narratee that s/he is a storyteller. The disclosure is meaningful to the narratee for many reasons, one of which may be that she is given notice about the ways in which revelation works, and she may expect it in the future. The connection of the smaller and larger narratives that happens in revelation requires that the events do not just happen: they have to *matter* by showing the narratee their *meaning*, which is to say, the causality and reason why things are the way they are. A simple recollection of events (story) is not the same as showing why those events happened (plot) and what they mean.

---

159. Tillich, *Systematic Theology*, vol. 1, 14, 27–28.

160. Schank and Berman, "Pervasive Role," 288–89. The authors continue: "This is true even when our stories are intended to entertain. To understand this perspective, we have to ask why we are telling the story. We can assume we are motivated to do so to achieve a goal of some sort. If we tell the story for entertainment purposes, we are also telling our listeners something about ourselves as persons and our current purposes. Every story has at least one point and has at least one reason for being told. The point and the reason suggest what is intended to be taught. Sometimes the point is not direct, like a moral of a story, but is instead intended indirect, as in when we mean to convey to our listener that we are funny, worldly, or interested in similar topics. We may simply mean to convey that we enjoy what we are conversing about with our listener, so we tell stories to continue the conversation. Whether or not the listeners understand or receive the lesson we mean to teach, the utterance is meant to inform. So we consider stories to be didactic when we choose to relay them."

This point is made well by Wolterstorff in *Divine Discourse*. When showing the differences between speaking and revealing, Wolterstorff says that "revelation is not dispelling just any sort of ignorance. Telling you I left the keys on the counter is not, in normal circumstances, *revealing* to you the location of the keys—even though it does dispel your ignorance. Dispelling ignorance becomes *revelation* when it has, to some degree and in some way, the character of unveiling the veiled, of uncovering the covered, of exposing the obscured to view."[161] Just as "story" had two meanings above—one in relation to the other linguistic subsystem and the other in relation to plot—so too does the term "discourse." As we mentioned above, "narrative discourse" is the second branch of narratology that examines the author's methods and the reader's response. However, the word "discourse" also simply means "speaking," even though this is not a move that Gerald Prince makes. In Wolterstorff's view, for revelation to be set apart from "discourse" or "speaking" it has to have an element of the hidden-made-unhidden, or the concealed-made-unconcealed. Since I argued above that revelation adds causality to chronology, reasons to events, why to what, it follows that revelation is a *meaningful* connection between the smaller and larger narrative. Prince adequately sums up this feature of divine revelation when discussing how narrative makes meaning:

> Narrative can thus shed light on individual fate or group destiny, the unity of a self or the nature of a collectivity. Through showing that apparently heterogeneous situations and events can make up one signifying structure (or vice versa) and, more particularly, through providing its own brand of order and coherence to (a possible) reality, it furnishes examples for its transformation or redefinition and effects a mediation between the law of what is and the desire for what may be. Most crucially, perhaps, by marking off distinct moments in time and setting up relations among them, by discovering meaningful designs in temporal series, by establishing an end already partly contained in the beginning and a beginning already partly contained in the end, by exhibiting the meaning of time and/or providing it with meaning, narrative deciphers time and indicates how to decipher it. In sum, narrative illuminates temporality and humans as temporal beings.[162]

---

161. Wolterstorff, *Divine Discourse*, 23.
162. Prince, *Dictionary of Narratology*, 60.

UNIQUENESS OF SACRED TEXTS

Thus far in this chapter I have discussed a method for integrating some central revelational themes that emerged from three great twentieth- and twenty-first-century philosophers of religion and theologians. Symbol stands at the top of our model, but does so as a variable. I argued that meaning-making and interpretation happens primarily—though not exclusively—through narrative, which therefore deserves to be considered the primary—but not only—symbol as opposed to "scripture," which acts more as a sign that initiates revelation.

Some elaboration on the nature of "scripture" and its place in narrative symbolism is warranted. Readers of the conservative evangelical persuasion will no doubt reply to this view fails to preserve the uniqueness of their sacred texts. Historically Christianity's sacred texts have been seen *as* revelation, and many conservative thinkers list the "doctrine of the Bible" first in their systematic theologies.[163] Not only evangelicals, but also *all* thinkers who work within the Christian tradition must explain how their view of revelation relates to their sacred texts.

My claim that God can choose any sign to initiate divine revelation may be taken to mean that I do not take these writings to be unique in any strong sense. Nothing could be further from the truth. So here I offer some further comments show some ways in which scripture qualifies as revelation.

What does it mean to say that the Bible is uniquely revelatory? There seem to be four replies to this question. In this section I discuss the revelatory uniqueness of Christianity's texts by presenting them along continuum of uniqueness (figure 4.3) on which narrative symbolism can be found. Explication of this continuum involves reflection on the nature of God vis-à-vis all that is not God and the notion of the Bible as an origins story, as "our" story, and as God's story.[164]

Figure 4.3: Continuum of Biblical Uniqueness

On the far right side of the continuum, the Bible is considered ontologically (or intrinsically, inherently) unique. According to this view, God purposefully authored the specific texts of Christian canonical Holy

---

163. See, e.g., Grudem, *Systematic Theology*, who conceives the "Word of God" solely in biblical terms.

164. Jenson, "Scripture's Authority," 27–37.

Scripture, even to the point of choosing specific words. The *text itself* has value, whether or not a reader is present. J. Barton Payne is as good an example of this view as one will find. Thinking he speaks for all evangelicals, he asserts that the evangelical "believes that the Bible is a human book, but it is also, and more fundamentally, a divine book and is to be so treated."[165] The Bible itself is divine in Payne's view, the implication of which is that the Bible deserves worship.

What are we to make of this position? Is this the best way to contend that the Bible is unique? As a Christian philosopher of religion and theologian, one of my goals in this book is to elevate God far above anything God created. In my discussion of revelation, I seek primarily to preserve the majesty and unparalleled perfection of the triune God Almighty. *God* is without error, perfect, and absolutely unique in perfection—inherently, intrinsically, and ontologically. Christians praise God not for what God can do for us—be it salvation, liberation, or a sense of purpose—but rather because of who God is. In short, we praise the "uselessness"[166] of God.

God's revelation, when it occurs as intended without corruption or frustration, is likewise perfect as an extension of God's perfection. The perfection of revelation lies not in a specific medium of transmission but rather a dynamic encounter between divine intention and human reception in which the event happens without frustration and the revelation is received without error. To be clear: the key is not in the medium of transmission. Various media are created things. And lest this turn into some form of pantheism or panentheism, both of which were eliminated as viable options, I assume that there are real distinctions between God and all else that is not-God. Humans, for example, are not God and are therefore imperfect in comparison. So too with reason, or books, or cars, or scenery, or relationships. Even while all of them can be the sign that initiates the event of divine revelation, they are imperfect—i.e., errant—at some level. The point is this: *God* is singularly and uniquely without error.

Kierkegaard tells us that, "the fundamental error of modern times lies in the fact that the yawning abyss of quality in the difference between God and man has been removed. The result in dogmatic theology is a mockery

---

165. Payne, "Higher Criticism," 96.

166. The statements made in this paragraph are in basic agreement with David Kelsey's praise of the "uselessness" of God. According to Kelsey, we should praise God not for what God can offer to us, not for God's use to us, but rather whether or not God is useful to us. God deserves praise simply because of God's perfection. See Kelsey, "In Praise of the Uselessness of God," as part of his Warfield Lectures at Princeton Theological Seminary, 2010.

of God...."[167] I take seriously and support Kierkegaard's view, namely, that all that is not-God is imperfect at some level. To act as if something created could be perfect in effect mocks God. Although well intentioned, unfortunately much of conservative evangelical thinking about revelation has inadvertently removed this distinction. To remove the distinction is tantamount to idolatry. John Collins says, "One of the most persistent themes in the Hebrew Bible is the critique of idolatry. This applies not only to carved or molten statues, but to the human tendency to absolutize things that are merely part of the created order. Perhaps the greatest irony in the history of the Bible is that it itself has so often been treated as an idol and venerated with a reverential attitude while its message is ignored."[168]

A theist's focus should be on the inerrancy of *God*, who should be elevated far above potential signs or symbols of divine revelation. Removing the distinction between Messenger and medium not only leads to idolatry of some created thing, but also a confused and potentially *impossible* hermeneutic,[169] a mediated presence of God instead of an immediate "personal relationship," confusion of the origins of power, academic irrelevance, and disservice to sacred texts. Christian theists should be reluctant to say *anything* is divine except God. As N. T. Wright says, "the God of the Bible refuses to be fitted into our blanks. We have to reshape our lives around him."[170]

Revelation requires an encounter between Revealer and receiver. Toward the end of his career, Ramm recognized this truth; he suggested that the "internal witness of the Spirit can be operative in situations where there is no written word, such as through sermon, song or Christian literature."[171] If the model of revelation I have outlined is correct, then we can extend the list of signs to include quite anything because the focus is on the operation of God, and God may choose to use anything to interrupt and reform one's subjectivity by showing people their place in the larger narrative. Any initiating sign—on its own without a narratee—is not individualized. Texts without a revealing God are merely black ink on white pages. However, signs of revelation's initiation *become* individualized by the action of God to reveal one's place in the larger narrative of God's work. The emphasis is

167. Kierkegaard, *Journals* (November 20, 1847).
168. Collins, *Introduction*, 604.
169. Smith, *Bible Made Impossible*, ch. 1.
170. Wright, *Small Faith*, 76.
171. Ramm, *Witness*, 62–65; 98–99. Cf. Grenz and Olson, *20th Century Theology*, 368. Ramm obviously bought into the theology of the early Barth, who said, "the Word of God still happens today in the Bible; and apart from this happening the Bible is not the World of God, but a book like other books." Barth, *Die Lehre vom Worte Gottes*, 63.

rightly put on God's action on our behalf rather than a sign with no power in and of itself to birth insight or effect change. Language of inerrancy is appropriately used in reference to God, the unsurpassable, to which all else is secondary. Inerrancy language is useful insofar as it reminds Christians that God's communication and God's purposes are achievable by God.

In terms of our continuum of biblical uniqueness, narrative symbolism is *not* found in any view in which something other than God can be thought of as divine. Therefore, the Bible does *not* have ontological perfection or uniqueness. That space should be saved for God alone.

On the other side of the continuum, the far left, is the position that the biblical texts are not theologically unique at all. They tell us nothing of the nature of ultimately reality, of God, or our relationship to God. They are merely documents of ancient peoples, and as such they have historical and sociological significance, but not more. Concepts of "biblical revelation" and "scriptural inspiration" are vacuous terms to people with this view. This position rests on a particular historical consciousness and political awareness that was unavailable to pre-Enlightenment thinkers. Post-Enlightenment history is different; it suggests that our methods of historical inquiry prohibit us from positing any supernatural influence in history. The same is true with critical readings of texts: they convey theological statements that are actually motivated by political gain.[172] While there are surely different methods of inquiry that limit what we can say when doing history and political motivations that infiltrate our theological views, in my estimation one is hard-pressed to find a Christian theist who advocates this extreme position. For those who take seriously the idea of revelation in philosophy of religion and theology, this position is unhelpful at best.

In the middle are two positions that fall under the heading of "instrumental uniqueness."[173] The Bible is not ontologically unique and divine, but neither does it lack all uniqueness. It is unique to the extent that it has been

---

172. In *Misquoting Jesus*, Ehrman describes the process of writing, collecting, and canonization of the New Testament documents in such a way that one gets the impression he views the whole endeavor as politically motivated. Even if it was *not* politically motivated in Ehrman's view, he certainly does *not* concede that an actual divine Reality might be behind these texts.

173. The poles of the continuum are obviously unacceptable, especially in an evangelical Christian context. One could argue that this central position I am describing is actually a number of positions that claim the Bible increases in uniqueness the further right one goes. Fair enough, but they are gradations of instrumental uniqueness, which is all that is required to locate this view vis-à-vis other views (e.g., a hyper-conservative view of inherent, intrinsic, and ontological uniqueness on the one hand, and the liberal position that the Bible is not at all unique).

chosen, and the two "instrumentally unique" positions are separated by who is credited with the choosing.

One version of "instrumental uniqueness" says that people have chosen these texts to function authoritatively in religious communities. We have *given* them a certain authority, but they are not thought to have this authority on their own and their authority is not derived from God's free decision. The texts are instrumentally unique as a self-imposed mirror. We draw conclusions about our present reality based on them. Despite their lack of ontological uniqueness, they are still instructive, so much so that we can conceive of them as "inspired," even when they lack historical accuracy or portray God in a bad light. Apologist for higher criticism, John Collins, represents this position. He talks about inspiration in a text like Joshua, which speaks of war in the name of God: "Joshua is not an exercise in historiography in the modern sense of the term. There is no reason, in principle, why a work of fiction should not be inspired as easily as a historical chronicle. . . . There is [also] no reason in principle why a text that is shocking might not be inspired. Such a text can raise our moral consciousness by forcing us to confront the fact that immoral actions are often carried out in the name of religion."[174] According to this view, Christianity's texts are instrumentally unique for us because through them we see our world, our conflicts, and ourselves in a new light. They present images of human nature against which we choose to judge our present day actions.

When the choice is attributed to humankind, that is, when the Bible is instrumentally unique only as a mirror for present-day *human* behavior in a reflectively *human* endeavor from start to finish, we face some problems. One wonders whether a purely human-chosen instrumental uniqueness is sufficient to render the Bible *theologically* unique. This "mirroring" can occur through any story or narrative, can it not? Why specifically the *biblical* narratives? Collins himself admits "Claims of inspiration and revelation can scarcely be discussed profitably in an academic context" and "rather than impose principles of uniformity on this literature, we should recognize it for what it is: the literature of a people that reflects the ever-changing circumstances of that people's history."[175] No distinctively *theological* uniqueness can be preserved if one maintains that humanity has chosen these texts to be Christian canonical holy scripture.

The other version of "instrumental uniqueness" credits *God* with deciding that the Bible would be used the life of the Christian Church throughout her history and today. Claiming instrumental uniqueness in this sense

---

174. Collins, *Introduction*, 601.
175. Ibid., 599–600.

concedes that there is nothing in the text itself that is unique. Rather, the texts *become* unique in *God's* decision to use them. The integrative model of narrative symbolism I am outlining here fits most naturally in this portion of the biblical uniqueness continuum for several reasons: it is how God shows Christians their origins, it is the story in which Christians presently participate, and it is God's story. All of these deserve elaboration.

The Bible, unlike any other medium, is a narrative of origins.[176] Now an "origins story" is but one of many literary genres. The Bible itself is obviously a diverse collection composed of texts of many genres, and it is crystal clear that not all of these texts are in the genre of narratives of origin. However, I am proposing that we might think of the Bible as having what I'll call a "metagenre." By this term I am trying to find a way of getting at the idea that the Bible as a whole, when read as a canonical unity, is greater than the sum of its parts. When read as Holy Scripture all of it can be read as a story of origins, irrespective of the literary genres of the individual parts. In other words, I am suggesting that we might think of the Bible considered as a whole as something *akin to* a genre—a metagenre. Although it is most closely related to the "coming of age" story, the origins story can be incorporated into other genres as well.[177] Its purpose, not surprisingly, is to narrate a thing's beginnings, and in this way, the narrative of origins can be seen as a "myth."[178] Robert Segal argues that there are no direct studies of myth *per se*,[179] a phenomenon that may change as it did with narrative, but he says myths are grouped together to the extent that they all ask three questions: origin, function, and subject matter.[180] Mircea Eliade, a Romanian-born historian of religions, proposed a version of this view. For Eliade, "myth is an explanation . . . of the origin of a phenomenon and not just of its recurrence."[181] The criterion for a myth is simple: the story requires a feat of

---

176. See Segal, *Myth*.

177. This will be crucial in showing how the various genres in the Bible all serve to show the origins of the Christian church.

178. The concept of "myth" is unfortunately distorted to mean "fictitious" nowadays. This is not the meaning I attach to the term.

179. Segal, *Myth*, 2: "Each discipline harbors multiple theories of myth. Strictly, theories of myth are theories of some much larger domain, with myth a mere subset. For example, anthropological theories of myth are theories of culture *applied* to the case of myth. Psychological theories of myth are theories of the mind. Sociological theories of myth are theories of society. There are no theories of myth itself, for there is no discipline of myth in itself. Myth is not like literature, which, so it has or had traditionally been claimed, must be studied as *literature* rather than as history, sociology, or something else nonliterary. There is no study of myth as myth."

180. Ibid.

181. Ibid., 54.

exceptional proportions, so its subject turns into a superhuman figure. The idea of "myth tells how, through the deeds of Supernatural Beings, a reality came into existence, be it the whole of reality, the Cosmos, or only a fragment of reality—an island, a species of plant, a particular kind of human behavior, an institution."[182] The feat of a mythic superhero is creation. And for Eliade, myths do more than explain; they also—more importantly—foster regeneration (recall Olson's view that "speech acts" make things happen). Eliade says, "To hear, to read, and especially to re-enact a myth is magically to return to the time when the myth took place, the time of the origin of whatever phenomenon it explains."[183]

Because "ritual recitation of the cosmogonic myth implies reactualization of that primordial event, it follows that he for whom it is recited is magically projected *in illo tempore*, into the 'beginning of the World'; he becomes contemporary with the cosmogony."[184] He continues: "What is involved is, in short, a return to the original time, the therapeutic purpose of which is to begin life once again, a symbolic rebirth."[185] To the critic who thinks that modernity moved beyond the need for myths, Eliade shows how this is an illusion;[186] myths are part of who we are, in pre-modern, modern, and postmodern times. If the Bible can be considered an origins story, a "myth," then it squares nicely with a "narrative symbolism" view of revelation, as smaller stories/histories are connected to a larger narrative that transports and transforms the narratee:

> Even reading includes a mythological function . . . because, through reading, the modern man succeeds in obtaining an "escape from time" comparable to the "emergence from time" effected by myths. . . . Reading projects him out of his personal duration and incorporates him into other rhythms, makes him live in another "history."[187]

---

182. Eliade, *Myth and Reality*, 5–6.
183. Segal, *Myth*, 55.
184. Eliade, *Sacred and Profane*, 82.
185. Ibid.
186. Ibid., 205. He notes some examples of "modern man's" myths: "A whole volume could well be written on the myths of modern man, on the mythologies camouflaged in the plays that he enjoys, in the books that he reads. The cinema, that 'dream factory,' takes over and employs countless mythical motifs—the fight between the hero and monster, initiatory combats and ordeals, paradigmatic figures and images (the maiden, the hero, the paradisal landscape, hell, and so on.)"
187. Ibid.

The Bible's instrumental uniqueness is preserved as God uses it in the capacity of an origins story, an etiological or founding "myth," an *aition*.[188]

But of whose origins does the Bible testify? Many Christians are inclined to suggest that the Hebrew Bible points to Jesus Christ and the New Testament reflects upon him; indeed, some popular introductory textbooks to the Bible suggest this very thing (e.g., Michael Harbin's *The Promise and the Blessing*). The whole Bible, according to this view, is an origins story of Jesus. However, limiting the scope of Christian canonical holy scripture in this way creates some difficulties, not the least of which is the relevance of non-christological material to *today*. There is more in the Bible than the expectation of and reflection on the incarnate Word.

Rather, the Bible is an origins story of the Christian Church. When the Bible is understood as an origins story of the Christian Church—whose story includes and is founded upon the life, death, and resurrection of Jesus Christ and its salvific import, but is not limited to it—the *full* Bible's uniqueness is preserved. On this view, we have a present-day phenomenon we call the Church, which is a group of people who have decided to engage in certain practices and believe certain things about their existential situation, their goal, and the mode of transformation. This is a more appropriate hermeneutical lens through which to view the Bible, as it encompasses not only the biblical material that has to do with the Word's incarnation, but also the material that does not have to do with him. Moreover, viewing the Bible as an origins story of the Christian Church includes how it functions today in the life of the Church. If a person wants to know what she should do today, the Bible shows her by giving stories of people who tried, some successfully, to commune with God. If one wants a picture of the origins of Christian faith and practice, including its founder's life and mission, they will go to the Bible. The Bible is instrumentally unique in that through it God shows the Church her beginnings.[189]

---

188. The Merriam Webster's Dictionary defines "aition" as "a tale devised to explain the origin of a religious observance." Passage taken from their online dictionary at: http://www.merriam-webster.com/dictionary/aition

189. To be sure, there is a certain christocentrism in the Bible, but not an overt one. Without the life, death, and resurrection of Jesus Christ, understood as God's salvific self-revelation, as the savior of all who have turned away from God, then there would be no *Christian* scriptures. To understand the Bible in this way (as a testimony to the testimony of Jesus concerning God's love for those who do not love God) is not merely an individual affair, but profoundly a communal one. So it is conceded that without reference to Jesus Christ at some level, and God's salvific presence in human life, there would be no serious reason at all to speak of revelation with respect to scripture. This approach to preserving the Bible's uniqueness includes, but is not limited to such observations.

The Bible is not only an origins story, but it is also uniquely instrumental in showing the Christian who she is today. Knowing where we came from helps us know who we are. If the Bible is the origins story of the Christian Church, then it is also a story in which the present-day Church still participates. As such, it is "our" story. This is yet another area in which Dulles and Lindbeck are helpful, as they emphasized the participatory nature of divine revelation. Robert Jenson agrees. When discussing scripture's authority in the Church, Jenson argues that "not only is Scripture within the Church, but we, the church, are within Scripture—that is, our common life is located *inside* the story Scripture tells."[190] The present-day Church is the same Church that existed at the time of the writing of the biblical documents, and it is the same Church that existed at their compilation. For example, "the church to which Paul belonged is the very same, diachronically continuous church to which we belong."[191] And "the canon itself establishes the continuation of its story to include us. . . . The church republished [documents] for a future group of readers, her own future self."[192] Apart from use in the Church, the Bible has no reason to exist, says Jenson, and there is no correct interpretation outside the Church: "The question, after all, is not whether churchly reading of Scripture is justified; the question is, what could possibly justify any other?"[193] Christians participate in the story that Scripture tells. In chapter 2, we also saw this view in Ronald Thiemann, who said that Jesus' gaze in Matthew's Gospel moves off of the characters to whom he speaks and brings in the reader. These observations obviously mesh well with narrative symbolism, because the Bible tells a narrative of God's work into which the smaller story of an individual is placed today. Our smaller story is easily seen in the larger context of the biblical narratives.

Gerard Loughlin agrees with Jenson that the reader is part of the story the Bible tells, because in "postmodern scripture" text and reader work together. He states, "it is no longer possible to think that there is an absolute divide between the knower and the known, subject and object, because both exist only as they are mediated within a reality that is, as postmoderns like to say, always-already textual, always-already given over to the 'word.'"[194] The relationship between the text, events the text narrates, and reader is likewise intertwined:

---

190. Jenson, "Scripture's Authority," 30.
191. Ibid., 31.
192. Ibid., 30.
193. Ibid., 27, 29.
194. Loughlin, "Postmodern Scripture," 306.

> The Bible is in part constitutive of the events it discloses, just as the events are constitutive of the Bible. The relation between situation and imagination, event and text, is interconstitutive of both. Describing the events of revelation and the testimony of the Bible as interconstitutive reminds us that the Church is at least in part a sociotextual reality, shaping the texts by which it is shaped. Thus it has always been. There never was a non-textual event of which the text is but the record or to which it is but response. All events within the life of the people of God are textualized events. They are always-already interpreted; always-already a reading of what has gone before, in part constituted by a preceding textual reality.[195]

This point is perhaps best illustrated by analogy. Daniel Gordis provides this sort of illustration when discussing a family diary: "Were any of us to find the diary of our great-great grandparents, we would not only save it but would savor it. We would read it carefully and repeatedly for what it could tell us about the places and people from which we come. Why? We would relish that diary because as we uncover our past, we discover parts of ourselves. We come to understand better the shadows and images that seem to pervade our parents, our siblings, our own psyches. We learn that no matter how hard we struggle to become unique, there are ways in which we are chillingly similar to those who came before us. In learning about our ancestors, we learn about ourselves."[196] Each person who accepts the diary from a parent can read about her family history and understand herself better as a result. Moreover, she contributes to the story, not by adding to the diary—for it is already full—but by living out the hopes and aspirations of its early authors, the original writers of the story. This is how it works with the Christian canonical scriptures: Christians participate in the story it tells; they are its unfolding. Since God uses the Bible to illuminate present-day reality in relationship to a reader, the Bible is instrumentally unique.

If the Bible is something in which present-day Christians participate, then their posture toward God as revealed to them through the texts is one of recognition, acknowledgement, and submission.[197] Christians should give themselves over to God in the moment of revelation, personally and

---

195. Ibid., 307.

196. Gordis, *God Was Not in the Fire*, 40–41.

197. It is recognition of one's place in the larger narrative of God's work in the world, acknowledgement of God's action on one's behalf, and submission to the overarching principles one finds therein, especially those derived from the stories and speeches of Jesus.

theologically. Dulles, Lindbeck, and Ramm, as well as Jenson and Stephen Davis all make this point. Jenson says,

> If we are in and not out of the story Scripture tells, certain ways of construing scriptural authority cannot be right.... Scripture constrains our lives and thinking the way a play or novel constrains the lives and thinking of its characters.... Scripture is authoritative for us, as characters in the story that it tells, somewhat as the existing transcript of an unfinished play is determinative of what can be true and right for its characters in the part that remains to be written.[198]

The Bible is uniquely authoritative in the life of the Church because it is a collection of reflections of ancient believers whose story is their own. Reading how God dealt with them shows us how God has worked in the past, which provides clues on how to practice faith today. Davis says "those who hold the Bible to be true . . . trust it, listen to it, look to it, submit to it, consider it normative. . . . [They] believe the Bible to be true with a great deal of firmness or certainty. Their belief in it is not tentative; their submission to it is not halting. The Bible is allowed to guide their lives, influence their behavior, and form them as persons."[199] This is obviously related to the "willingness" feature of divine revelation mentioned above. The revelation event requires that the narratee give herself over to the sign's power to initiate the divine revelation. And the Bible is precisely this sort of thing: it is the tried and true sign that has very often in the history of the Christian Church initiated the situating of an individual's smaller story into the larger narrative of God's work in the world. When it happens, God interrupts and reforms individual subjectivity.

Finally, if the Bible is an origins story in which present-day Christians participate by—among other things—giving themselves over to it, the Bible should be seen as a powerful tool that God often uses. The Bible is the story into which subjective readers immerse themselves. It is the narrative of God's dealings with the world, and present day readers are a part of that story. But let us be clear about whose story it is, ultimately. In short, the Bible is "God's story."[200] It is God's larger narrative into which the smaller stories are placed, and it is God's action that situates these smaller stories into the larger narrative in the event of revelation. God directs and superintends the process to orient the subject from self to God or others. The Bible becomes the "word

---

198. Jenson, "Scripture's Authority," 34.

199. Davis, "What Do We Mean," 90.

200. Cf. Ford, *Barth and God's Story*. For a different perspective, see Murphy, *God is Not a Story*, 7.

of God" for those people who God has destined to encounter God in that way. And historically, it seems as if God has chosen to use the Bible more than any other sign save Christ himself to show narratees their place in the larger story, God's story. Says Jenson: "Scripture's story is not a part of some larger narrative; it is itself the larger narrative of which all other true narratives are parts. Biblical exegesis is reading sides and prop lists and so forth for the drama that God and his universe are now living together."[201] Jenson beckons readers of Scripture not to figure out how the biblical material fits into a larger story—in one's life, in science, in history, etc.—but rather to see all of those things fitting into the story scripture tells.[202]

At the start of this book I described two audiences, one of whom was the conservative who would isolate herself from uncomfortable truths that conflict with her understanding of reality by burying her head in the sand on the issue of the relationship between text and revelation. This lengthy justification of the instrumentally unique character of Christian canonical holy scripture has been primarily directed toward her, the one who maintains the ontological uniqueness of the Bible. If what I have said is correct, ontological uniqueness is an idolatrous practice with disastrous results for both conservative scholars and the parishioners in the pews. Rather, the Bible is instrumentally unique insofar as God has decided (and continues to decide) to use it to show Christians their history (origins story), their present situation ("our" story), and how both relate to divine activity in the world (God's story).

LINGERING QUESTIONS

The reader will notice that this view of revelation—narrative symbolism—raises some important questions. For one, what in this model prevents *every* event from being revelatory, and if every event is revelatory might it also be the case that no event is revelatory? With this model of revelation, therefore, one is forced to posit some criteria for adjudicating between competing claims to revelation to discern which putative revelations have their source in God and which most likely have their source elsewhere. Perhaps chief among the questions this view raises concerns how this view of revelation relates to some self-consciously Christian understandings of the human person, sin, and salvation. Posing and answering these questions is the task of the next chapter.

201. Jenson, "Scripture's Authority," 34.
202. Ibid.

At the close of this chapter, however, it is worth reiterating the challenge that bibliolatry poses to a God-honoring bibliology. As one may expect, a story illustrates the principle at work.

When I recently visited my grandmother for July 4th weekend, she and I went to an Independence Day parade. The Marine Marching Band led the charge with a mixture of brass and percussion, playing inspirational and national pride-inducing tunes. The crowd stood and applauded, shouted and whistled. Children and adults alike sang along; they knew the words. Some danced. Most waved. One of the songs struck me as interesting:

> *You're a grand old flag; you're a highflying flag*
> *And forever in peace may you wave*
> *You're the emblem of the land I love*
> *The home of the free and the brave*
> *Every heart beats true 'neath the red, white and blue*
> *Where there's never a boast or brag*
> *But should auld acquaintance be forgot*
> *Keep your eye on the grand old flag*

I was impressed by the exceptionally timed movements and sharply pressed uniforms of the band and its conductor, but this is not what struck me as most interesting. And I was impressed by the song's powerful ability to solicit national pride, yet this is not what was most interesting to me.

I was struck by the song's subject: the flag. The flag gets most of the attention: its colors (*Red, white and blue*), its action (*Forever in peace may you wave*), its impact (*Every heart beats true*), and the resulting imperative (*Keep your eye on the grand old flag*). The song is powerful, and it does excite its listeners. But amidst all the red, white, and blue, we forgot a simple and timeless truism: the flag is simply a symbol for a much larger, richer, and more meaningful idea. The "Grand Old Flag" is about stars and stripes, to be sure, but that is not what the song is *really* about, is it? If the flag became the subject of our attention, the object of our veneration, then we have lost something precious, haven't we? So far as I can tell, the flag has no power in and of itself. Seeing it merely initiates an encounter in which the stories of individuals are located in the broader narrative of the origins, ongoing struggles, and victories of their country.

As I sat there and watched the parade, as I viewed the flags affixed to each Corvette, Army Hummer, fire truck, high school float, and miniature Shriner vehicle whizzing by jumping children, I was taken back to my childhood. Once a week during "Sunday School," and every day during "Vacation Bible School" week, we sang a similar melody:

The B-I-B-L-E.
Yes, that's the book for me.
I stand alone on the Word of God
The B-I-B-L-E.

And we forgot the same types of things as the parade goers, chief among them that the Bible is a tool rather than an end in itself. We mistook the Bible for the Reality behind it, Who uses it as a sign to point humans to their place in the ongoing narratives of God's work in the world. The Bible, like anything else in the hands of an omnipotent Revealer, is used by God to initiate an encounter and launch an event, rather than having any power on its own or ontological status *as* the event. The Word of God cannot be contained in black ink on white pages.

CHAPTER 5

Making Connections
Narrative Symbolism and Traditional Systematic Loci

CONSTRUCTIVE AND SYSTEMATIC THEOLOGY

In the previous chapter I argued that recent advances in literary theory—i.e., the emergence of narratology, which studies the components of stories irrespective of the media of transmission—provide a framework within which one can imagine revelation today. I showed how the concept of narrative aids in understanding the symbolic character of revelation and how revelation works. I proposed an integrative model of divine revelation in which narrative acts as the primary symbol through which people make sense of their world, a process initiated by signs that point to a larger vision of reality than their own.

The line between "constructive" and "systematic" theology is permeable. The proposal outlined in the previous chapter would remain incomplete without also showing the ways in which this view relates to other Christian concepts. That is the task of this chapter. Although I argue that in narrative symbolism revelation is an event in which God interrupts and reforms an individual's subjectivity by situating their smaller story into a larger narrative of God's work in the world, I have not yet shown in any concrete way how this view relates to some standard systematic theological loci—the human person, sin, and salvation—the last of which raises what is potentially the greatest problem for this view, how to tell whether a putative revelation has its origins in God or elsewhere. As I show revelation's relationship to these areas I will also demonstrate how this view solves some peripheral conceptual and theoretical problems.

Philosophy of religion and theology are collaborative enterprises, not competitive. Therefore, the reader is encouraged to view this chapter as an invitation to dialogue. With respect to each locus, I offer some ways they relate to narrative symbolism. Not all observations blend equally well with the others, but are rather paths along which one can imagine the relationship between narrative symbolism and these loci. They are not meant to be grouped together, even though I will argue that some of them do work very well together. In each case I will show what I believe to be the best relationship between this narrative symbolism and the issue under consideration but this does not mean that other interpretations are defective. Flexibility is one of the attractive features of this model.

ANTHROPOLOGY: REVELATION'S RELATIONSHIP TO THE HUMAN PERSON

How does narrative symbolism relate to Christian understandings of the human person, that is, to theological anthropology? There are three ways to explore this question: first, with reference to Rahner's "supernatural existential"; second, with reference to the divine communicable attribute of communication; and third, with reference to the communicable attribute of creativity.

First, Karl Rahner's theological anthropology relates to narrative symbolism insofar as his "starting point" was the human being. Recall from chapter 1 that in Rahner's view humans have a capacity to receive God's revelation; it is part and parcel of who they are, the central feature constitutive of their very identity. They are "hearers of the word." God does two things: God pulls humanity toward the ultimate or infinite horizon or mystery, but God also comes close toward humanity and gives Godself to humanity. Rahner terms this process the "supernatural existential."[1] The supernatural existential is differentiated from supernatural grace in that the capacity to receive revelation is a part of the human whereas grace is something that comes from without. Rahner's supernatural existential relates to revelation insofar as the human—her story, her history—is part of the revelation event. To be sure, the human ability to be a part of the revelation event is itself given by God. Revelation requires the God-directed activity of a smaller

1. Rahner, *Foundations*, 126–33.

story to be placed into a larger narrative, so the smaller story is part of the revelation event. God's revelation depends on the existence of a receiver, and the story of the receiver is part of the content of revelation.

Recall from the last chapter that the significance of an event is conveyed in two ways, one of which is the ordering of the events in a specific way to a particular individual. This adds the unique story of the individual to the revelation event. Until the narratee's story is situated in the larger narrative, it is not a revelation event; they are simply two narratives that differ in shape, size or significance. They are connected in no meaningful ways. Only when the larger narrative includes the smaller story (the metaphysical reality) and only when the narratee is made aware of it (the epistemological reality) does revelation take place. Otherwise expressed, human experience figures into that which "counts" as revelatory. This is one way a distinctively Christian theological anthropology relates to narrative symbolism.

In addition to the relationship between revelation and anthropology shown in the supernatural existential, there are two others I will mention, both of which involve attributes of God that are communicable to humanity. Anthropology in the Christian tradition has often been normed by appealing to the creation narratives in the Hebrew Bible. In Genesis 1:26, the so-called Priestly source narrates God creating the human creature "in our image and likeness." The point is reiterated in v. 27: "In the image of God he made him." Traditionally the addition of *imago dei* language in the biblical witness and the fact that humans are part of the created order (all that is not-God), notes David Kelsey, has occasioned "creation" as the doctrinal home of anthropology.[2] But this doctrinal home migrated during the modern period from creation to others like the doctrine of incarnate grace (Rahner; Barth),[3] eschatology (Pannenberg),[4] and even the Trinity (Zizioulas).[5]

These modern understandings notwithstanding, if anthropology's home is creation, the Genesis narrative and its traditional interpretations are important. On the plain reading, humans are unique among all that is not-God insofar as they are "in" the *imago dei*. What precisely "images" God in the human has been a matter of dispute among theologians, although human reason has been a top contender. For our purposes, being in the image of God means at some level that humans share some similarities with God; they have the potential to share or mirror God's "communicable" attributes. Of course, any attribute humanity shares with God will be

---

2. Kelsey, "The Human Creature," 122–24.
3. Rahner, *Foundations*; Barth, *CD*, III/2.
4. Pannenberg, *What Is Man?*
5. Zizioulas, *Being as Communion*, 27–65.

derivative, incomplete, and imperfect. Nonetheless, an exploration of the human and her capacities, therefore, may show the human something of her maker. Knowledge of God is impossible without knowledge of humanity, and knowledge of humanity is impossible without knowledge of God. Anthropology aids theology. Two issues in particular link them—human communication and the creative process—both of which help us understand divine revelation.

Therefore, second, narrative symbolism relates to theological anthropology in light of the fact that one of the divine communicable attributes is communication. Simply put, God communicates and so do humans. Human communication is grounded in God's ability to communicate, as is the case with love or agency. Revelation, we noted in chapter 4, is, among other things, an event in the form of communication between the Narrator and narratee. And conveying a narrative is a form of communication. Not only in narratology, narrative theory, literary theory, semiotics, and theology, but also in philosophy, history, and several other fields, one hears echoes of MacIntyre's assertion that whatever else we are, "human beings are storytellers."[6] Humans create, imagine, and convey narratives of all sorts. These narratives in turn tell us something of God.

Some scholars have gone so far as to suggest that narrative is the appropriate rubric under which all forms of human communication can be placed. Beginning with the publication of two articles[7] and then incorporated into his landmark study, *Human Communication as Narration*, Walter Fisher intends to replace the "rational world" and "dramatist" paradigms with a "narrative paradigm," and his proposal has generated a substantial following. In the rational world paradigm humans are seen as primarily arguing agents (i.e., rhetoricians), but Fisher subsumes argument and persuasion "under the dominant metaphor of narrative. People are not essentially arguers, but rather storytellers, and sometimes those narratives merely take the form of argument."[8] Fisher says, "the ideas of the [narrative] paradigm hang together and ring true with humans: storytelling is, after all, a universal phenomenon."[9] For Fisher, narratives unite the self; in narratives, "the whole mind [is] in concert with itself."[10] Says Fisher: "I suggest that

---

6. MacIntyre, *After Virtue*, 216: "Man is in his actions and practice, as well as in his fictions, essentially a story-telling animal."

7. The first is "The Narrative Paradigm: In the Beginning," 74–89, and second, "The Narrative Paradigm: An Elaboration," 347–66.

8. Roberts, "Texturing the Narrative Paradigm," 130–31.

9. Ibid., 132.

10. Fisher, "The Narrative Paradigm: In the Beginning," 299. Passage taken from Roberts, "Texturing the Narrative Paradigm," 132.

we experience and comprehend life as a series of ongoing narratives, as conflicts, characters, beginnings, middles, and ends. The various modes of communication—all forms of symbolic action—then may be seen as stories, interpretations of things in sequences. Viewed in this way, all kinds of discourse are reflective of logos in one degree or another."[11]

Fisher's "narrative paradigm" is related to, yet distinct from, insights generated in the discipline of narratology. Most narratologists operate in the field of literary theory whereas most of Fisher's converts work in communication studies. Both Fisher and narratologists explore narratives, but they do so for different reasons. Narratologists examine narratives to uncover a their internal workings, structure, power, etc. Fisher and others who endorse his narrative paradigm explore narrative in an attempt to uncover universal insights about all human communication. The narrative paradigm has a larger agenda than narratology; its conclusions are more far-reaching and, if true, subsume insights from narratology into their all-encompassing vision of human communication.

Yet just as narratology helps explicate a narrative understanding of divine revelation, Fisher's narrative paradigm opens up possibilities for theology as well. If one accepts that humans are essentially storytellers and human communication is essentially a series of ongoing narratives conveyed, then the ramifications for theology are straightforward. The anthropological observation that humans are essentially storytellers authorizes the use of narrative in a contemporary view of revelation because it means that God also communicates via narratives. To be sure, just because a certain feature is observed in humanity does not mean that it is also applicable to God. The attribute said to correspond to a divine attribute must be consistent with God's character. This is why in the Western Christian tradition, sin is considered a basic feature of humanity, at once an existential state and a series of wayward decisions. But it would be a mistake to suggest that because sin is a feature of humanity that it is a feature of the Divine; omnibenevolence is a basic divine attribute, universally accepted among Christians. Unlike the sin example, imagining God as a storyteller—at least insofar as God communicates/reveals to humanity—does not conflict with one of the divine attributes.

This corresponds well with the Christian tradition in which the Bible is seen as the collection of narrative(s) of God's relationship with humanity. Conversions happen because someone has seen their life vis-à-vis God's activity, seen their smaller story placed in the context of God's larger narrative. It is not only because narrative is a feature of human communication that it

---

11. Fisher, *Human Communication as Narration*, 24.

is useful, but also because it aligns with the manner in which the traditional Christian sources are understood: as narratives. This is the great insight of Hans Frei for this book. So anthropological consideration of the narrative paradigm authorizes narrative as a useful tool for theology.

Third, narrative symbolism relates to theological anthropology in light of another communicable attribute of God, creativity. God is creative, and so are we. Like communication, human creativity is derivative. God's creativity grounds human creativity. Attending to the human creative process, therefore, may generate insights into the ways in which God is creative, both of which relate to the ways God reveals. Consider the creative process of an artist. Great artists are often said to "create," but not predetermine, their works of art. The work of art is already there to be discovered by the artist. Insofar as the artist is the "creator," she is responsible for making the pre-existing work of art plain to its viewers.

A few examples will suffice: one from a sculptor, one from a playwright, and one from a literary figure. It is said that when Michelangelo viewed a large slab of marble, he did not see the actuality of the slab. Rather, he saw its potentiality: "Some have eyes that see not: but in every block of marble I see a statue—see it as distinctly as if it stood before me shaped and perfect in attitude and action. I have only to hew away the stone walls that imprison the lovely apparition, and reveal it to other eyes as mine already see it."[12] Referring to a specific statue, Michelangelo is reported to have said "I saw the angel in the marble, and I carved until I set him free."[13] Or consider a similar analogy from playwright William Nicholson. Into the mouth of his main character, Nicholson puts the following:

> God loves us, so He makes us the gift of suffering. Through suffering, we release our hold on the toys of this world, and know our true good lies in another world. We're like blocks of stone, out of which the sculptor carves the forms of men. The blows of His chisel, which hurt us so much, are what make us perfect. The suffering in the world is not the failure of God's love for us; it is that love in action.[14]

And finally, a popular American novelist describes his process of finding his material:

> Stories are relics, part of an undiscovered pre-existing world. The writer's job is to use the tools in his or her toolbox to get as much

---

12. Longfellow, *Poetical Works*, 329
13. Blech and Doliner, *Sistine Secrets*, 63.
14. Nicholson, *Shadowlands*, 9.

of each one out of the ground intact as possible. Sometimes the fossil you uncover is small. . . . Sometimes it's enormous [but] the techniques of excavation remain basically the same. . . . I want to put a group of characters (perhaps a pair; perhaps even just one) in some sort of predicament and then watch them try to work themselves free. My job isn't to *help* them work their way free, or manipulate them to safety. . . . [Instead, I] watch what happens and then write it down.[15]

This idea of the creative/artistic process illustrates the problem of competition between human and divine wills in revelation. For many artists, the creative process is such that the work of art is already there. The artist's job is simply to capture, display, and use the materials at her disposal to reveal it. The artist shows the world what is already there. On this reading, the characters "created" by the artists are created and sustained, but also free. The artist is simply responsible for sustaining the creative process by which the characters take on lives of their own, make their own decisions, and deal with their own consequences. If the creative process of image-bearers mirrors that of what they image, then we can conclude that God creates and sustains, but also endows the characters in the narrative with agency to make their own decisions. This is consistent with the traditional concept of the free will, whereby humans are given options and ultimately "choose whom they will serve."[16] If God stops creating or ceases to be in a causal relation with the world, then humans cease to be. A narrative reading of revelation, therefore, supplies the conceptual tools to maintain on the one hand that human agency is real and a "free will" exists and, on the other hand, that God is the absolute author and sustainer of the narrative, the ultimate Narrator.[17]

There is one more way that humans share attributes with God that I will mention here, but the issue will be given fuller treatment in the following section. The communicable attribute is the ability to connect smaller stories to larger narratives. God has this ability, and humans do too. The human ability to connect smaller stories to larger narratives is derivative, and when used properly results in confirmation that what one is experiencing is

---

15. King, *On Writing*, 160–61.
16. Josh 24:15.
17. In narratology, one should perhaps refer to God as the "Implied Author" and "Real Author" as well. Since this view of revelation argues that God communicates to people how/why their smaller stories fit into the larger narrative, the narration is most important rather than the authoring of the story (which is involved in discussions of who the real and implied author of a story are).

indeed divine revelation. The improper use of this ability takes us into the topic of human sin, to which we now turn.

HAMARTIOLOGY: REVELATION'S RELATIONSHIP TO ORIGINAL AND ONGOING SIN

How do Christian understandings of original and ongoing sin relate to narrative symbolism? Sin is as unpopular today as it was when H. R. Niebuhr was active ("A God without wrath brought men without sin to a kingdom without judgment through the ministrations of a Christ without a cross"[18]). Nonetheless, it is a central—if unpopular—tenet of Christian faith, perhaps the only empirically verifiable doctrine in the whole lot.[19] The concept of sin can fit into this model of divine revelation in three ways: (a) as antagonistic forces in the narrative, (b) as the refusal to give oneself over to the sign's power to initiate, and (c) most tragic, misreading the revelation. All three require elaboration.

First, one way sin relates to this concept of revelation involves how narratives work and how actants behave in them. The term "actant" was introduced into the field of narratology by French semiotician A. J. Greimas as a reworking of prior attempts to designate the functions served by each character in a narrative.[20] Greimas eventually arrived at six actants in narratives, although one character could play more than one part. One of Greimas' actants is the "subject," who is the main focus of the narrative. It is the subject's "quest" that puts him in motion to achieve the sought-for "object." This quest is frustrated by the "opponent," an actant discussed by other narratologists as the false hero, villain, mars, etc. In Greimas' first taxonomy of actants, the opponent represented the sum total of antagonistic forces in a narrative. However, since his first "actantial model," Greimas developed his view further, and in its more recent version the forces of opposition were differentiated.[21] An "opponent" is now seen as a distinct actant from the "anti-subject." In the newer model, the opponent is a momentary obstacle in the subject's quest for the object, and the opponent may encounter the subject incidentally. The anti-subject, however, is an actant on a quest of

---

18. H. R. Niebuhr, *Kingdom of God*, 193.

19. Paraphrase of R. Niebuhr, *Man's Nature* from the *Times Literary Supplement* in Finstuen, *Everyday Protestants*, 69: "the doctrine of original sin is the only empirically verifiable doctrine of the Christian faith."

20. Greimas, *Du sens* in Prince, *Dictionary of Narratology*, 1.

21. Greimas and Courtes, *Semiotics and Language*.

his own, yet his quest and aims "are at cross purposes with those of the Subject."[22]

When revelation is understood as narrative symbolism, viz., a smaller story being meaningfully situated amidst a larger narrative, one can make use of all of these categories. The narratee is the subject in her own story. She is on a quest for the object of her desire, which we understand to be a life lived in communion with her creator. Her quest is not without its complications, however, and this is where "sin" enters the picture. When "sin" refers to the discrete actions of individuals and not the existential state under which all humanity finds itself (i.e., "original" sin), it is equivalent to the work of the opponent. Sin in this sense momentarily frustrates the efforts of the subject to achieve her sought-for object. Its entrance into the subject's narrative may be incidental; it need not have been present for a long time and it need not be overwhelming. Sin can be understood in this way as any obstacle to seeking or following the will of God for one's life. This is sin with a lower case "s."

When "sin" refers to the existential state under which humanity finds itself and not discrete actions, it corresponds to the anti-subject. The anti-subject is evil itself. This is the unavoidable human tendency to desire the wrong thing. Evil itself and original Sin are at cross-purposes with the subject's quest for the object, communion with the holy God. Sin is a problematic reality of the human condition, and one of the marks of a narrative is "a causal sequence of events pertinent to a character or characters seeking to solve a problem or reach a goal."[23] The goal to be reached is communion with God and the problem to be solved is how to achieve this communion despite the presence of an existential condition and individual temptations. Within the narrative itself, this is one way that sin figures into this model of revelation.

A second approach to exploring the relationship between narrative symbolism and hamartiology suggests that sin is present when the narratee refuses to give herself over to the sign's power to initiate the revelation. Recall that above we asserted that the narratee must be willing to give herself up to the sign's power, and when the narratee is unable or unwilling to do this, the expert Narrator creates in her the ability and/or willingness. Upon being invited into the revelation of God, sin in this case would be the continued refusal to adjust one's life according to that which one has been shown. This person sees the Narrator as the Narrator, and she sees her part as a part, yet she continues to refuse to give herself up to what she has been shown. She

---

22. Prince, *Dictionary of Narratology*, 68.
23. Ibid., 91.

shares God's ability to connect her smaller story to a larger narrative; her ability to do this has been given by God. Yet after the connection is made, she refuses to accept the consequences of that connection. She refuses to live with the ramifications of what she has been shown in the event of revelation.

Third, sin relates to narrative symbolism by impacting the interpretation of the revelation event. In this case, the subject/narratee has a sincere desire to understand her situation in light of the larger narrative and adjust accordingly. But as Wolterstorff suggests, the full impact of the revelation is limited because the subject does not possess adequate "attention and interpretive skills."[24] Unlike the refusal to give herself over to the ramifications of the divine revelation, this third way is more tragic because she sincerely desires revelation but is unable to recognize it. Despite the sincerity of the subject, despite her willingness to be transformed by the sign's power to initiate the revelation, what might have been ultimately revealed is misconstrued. In situations like this, "sin" is found in the actions of others that have prevented her from receiving the revelation in full, understanding its import, and acting according to what she has been shown. Here "sin" is most akin to its etymological origins: one "misses the mark" by "misreading the revelation." However, when an individual is willing, the misinterpretation of the would-be revelation cannot be counted against her. It is simply the unfortunate consequences of the sin of others (e.g., the visitation of "the iniquity of the fathers on the children to the third and the fourth generation"[25]).

In such cases, Christians appeal to God's inscrutability: we do not (and can not) know why God allows the actions of some to negatively impact those who are (more) innocent, and we must trust that in each case "the works of God might be displayed in him."[26] Here again humans use their ability to connect their smaller story to a larger narrative, yet the larger narrative to which they connect it is not of God. They err when they take one larger narrative to be God's when, in point of fact, a different path were God's. In this situation, the subject mistakes a mere narrator for the Narrator. She is unable to see her situation objectively; she is too entrenched, too hurt by the actions of others, to get God's point of view on the matter. Even though she is unable to accurately find God's larger narrative, she wants to. Therefore, sometimes in narrative symbolism divine revelation contends with the sin of others whose actions have prevented her from seeing the situation accurately.

---

24. Wolterstorff, *Divine Discourse*, 23.
25. Exod 20:5.
26. John 9:1–3.

Sin affects people in all sorts of nefarious ways, subtle and obvious. To summarize the ways in which this view of revelation incorporates a self-consciously Christian understanding of sin, we proposed three avenues, all of which can work together.[27] On the first account, sin is like the forces of antagonism in a subject's narrative, limiting her ability to achieve her object of desire incidentally or ultimately. The second and third accounts show how this plays out. Sin can be understood as the narratee's refusal to be affected by the revelation she has seen, in which case she refuses to accept the consequences of the revelation and refuses to make the changes the revelation event showed her she needed to make. Or, sin can be a misreading of the revelation, missing the mark and failing to make the appropriate changes, but this is due to the sin of others in a world created and sustained by an inscrutable God who granted free will to humans. In such cases, the revelation does not even occur, despite the narratee's willingness to be changed.

SOTERIOLOGY: REVELATION'S RELATIONSHIP TO CHRISTIAN RELIGIOUS ENDS

Much has been said thus far about the "how" of divine revelation. Much less has been said about the "what" question. What *specifically* is conveyed in the event of divine revelation? God's very self as the incarnate Word in Jesus Christ, as neo-orthodox thinkers assert? The specific epistemic requirements for one to be "saved," as many conservative evangelicals propose? The truth on any matter into which one investigates? Something else entirely? By addressing the relationship between narrative symbolism and soteriology, we will address the "what" of divine revelation, which includes a set of criteria to distinguish authentic revelations from those that have their origin elsewhere.

Many of the world's religions posit some religious end to which their tradition is the pathway. In Christianity, the religious end is "salvation." The issue of salvation is unlike the aforementioned doctrines of humanity and sin for conservative exclusivists because soteriological views are thought to have eternal consequences. Since various religious worldviews are, in essence, different narrative understandings of God and the world, they are relevant to this project. But while many philosophers of religion and

---

27. They are not inconsistent with one another; rather, they represent different types of questions. The "opposition" and "anti-subject" versions of sin/Sin are more theoretical, and the second and third are ways in which the first is lived out.

theologians would normally use language of "exclusivism,"[28] "inclusivism,"[29] and "pluralism"[30] in conversations about salvation and other religious worldviews, I would rather show "empathetic interest" whenever possible.[31] If Lindbeck is correct about untranslatability then this sort of empathetic interest is impossible. But on the chance that he is mistaken, every attempt should be made to keep dialogue open. The full implications of this view of revelation for the discipline of comparative theology are more fully addressed in chapter 6, but empathetic interest conveys the spirit with which the relation of revelation and salvation is assessed.

Before unpacking a further distinction between revelations with soteriological and non-soteriological content, consider a distinctively Christian narrative of salvation into which any individual's story can fit: An individual is a created being loved by the triune God and granted freedom to love God back. The individual inexorably falls out of relationship with God through sin. Salvation happens when God reunites the fallen individual with Godself.[32] The requisite concept of revelation here is one in which the receiver sees the larger soteriological picture of which her story is a part. She recognizes that only through the work of the triune God on her behalf is she saved from the consequences of sin. God welcomes her with open arms and she is moved to live a life of holiness in appreciation for God's action. In a nutshell, this is how the narrative approach to revelation I have outlined in the previous chapter relates to traditional Christian ideas about salvation. But this raises many questions, chief among them how it is that she comes to see her story in relation to God's larger narrative.

---

28. See, e.g., Netland, *Encountering Religious Pluralism*.

29. See, e.g., Pinnock's inclusivist approach in Okholm and Phillips, eds., *Four Views*.

30. Hick, *God Has Many Names*.

31. According to Neusner, empathetic interest "concerns not whether religions are true (which in the end is for God to decide) but how all religions are interesting and important. We maintain here that every religion has something to teach us about what it means to be a human being. Here we take a different path from the one that leads us to questions about religious truth. It is a path that carries us to a position of empathy for our fellow [religionists], in all their rich diversity. We are trying to understand others and to explain ourselves in terms others can understand." Neusner, ed., *World Religions*, 6.

32. The best model of atonement is subject to debate, but which method one prefers does not matter for my argument.

Soteric and Non-Soteric Revelation

In chapter 4 I agreed with Bernard Ramm that there are a number of ways to talk about revelation, most of which involve dividing the concept in one way or another. I argued that we should think less in terms of dualistic binaries and more in terms of various continua. I then argued that along the content/event continuum, the event sense of revelation deserves primacy since receiving information is itself an event. At this point another distinction is important, and it involves the impact of revelation. Ramm says that one can divide revelation according to *when* it happens. If it was before the "fall" Ramm calls it "prelapsarian" or "preredemptive" revelation and after the fall "postlapsarian," "soteric," or "remedial" revelation. What is of interest to us is the distinction between "soteric" revelation and "non-soteric" revelation, which is a different distinction than Ramm's. Whereas Ramm differentiates soteric and other forms of revelation chronologically and according to its recipient,[33] I would differentiate them primarily by their content and impact.

In short, some revelations concern salvation, but not all. That is, there are some revelations with content that has a soteriological impact; they are geared toward a person's salvation in response to the person, work, life, death, and resurrection of Jesus Christ and its *soteric*, or saving significance for us today. But there are also revelations that are *non-soteric*, revelations with content that does not have a soteriological impact.[34] The decision to recycle, for example, is a good decision in line with something God cares about: responsible stewardship of natural resources. God would want us to recycle, I think, and most likely God has put it upon some Christians' hearts to take as good care of the environment as they can. One can say that the motivation to recycle comes from a "revelation" in which humankind sees their role in taking care of the larger world. However, whether one recycles has no impact on one's salvation.[35]

---

33. Ramm suggests a connection between "soteric" revelation and "special" revelation. I am leaving out the "general/special" distinction rather than redefining it since I argued that each divine revelation is tailored to its specific recipient, i.e., there is no general revelation: all is special.

34. It may be argued that both soteric and non-soteric divine revelations depend on a certain sense of God and recognition of God as God. Further, it may be argued that this is precisely what is "soteric" about revelation: knowing God as God. If what I am saying is correct, however, there are divine revelations that do *not* depend on knowing God as God. These are important revelations, and they align with the things God values, but one need not recognize God as the source of the revelation.

35. As with most theological claims, there is always someone to disagree. For an example of someone who ties care of the environment to salvation, see Jenkins, *Ecologies of Grace*.

In non-soteric revelation, one is given a glimpse of the things God *values*—creation, beauty, relationships, forgiveness, excellence, and fulfillment of promises, to note just a few of the manifold examples. But the extent to which these things have an impact on salvation is determined not by their chronology (as Ramm had opined) but by the impact of their content, the extent to which they effect salvation. Some ideas that may come from a revelation—that I should forgive someone, for instance—are closer to soteric revelations than others. And along this continuum there is a point at which revelations become soteric.

Making explicit a division of this type—between soteric and non-soteric revelations—is helpful for two main reasons: (1) it impacts the revelation/self-revelation question, and (2) it provides a solution to the authentication and adjudication circularity problem. Both of these are addressed below.

Revelation and Divine Self-Revelation

Many thinkers in the twentieth-century understood and configured revelation in terms of divine *self*-revelation. Karl Barth, for example, writes that the "content of the Word of God addressed to man . . . will always be an authentic and definitive encounter with the Lord of man, a revelation which man cannot achieve himself, the revelation of something new which can only be told him."[36] In Barth and many others, one does not primarily encounter information *about* God, but rather encounters *God's very self* in the moment of revelation. A version of this point of view is found in several of the theologies of revelation I have already discussed; von Balthasar and Rahner supported it, as did Dulles, Ramm, Pannenberg, and Grenz.

But why should we limit the content of revelation to only ever be God? Might God have intentions in the world that do not impact the salvation of souls? To prioritize divine self-revelation is to indicate that salvation is the only thing God cares about, but surely this is not the case. When we make the soteric/non-soteric distinction, we open up a space for revelations that have little or no impact on salvation.

And this is how narrative symbolism relates to the revelation/self-revelation question. If one experiences a soteric revelation, it is precisely God who is revealed, not merely something God values. God *is* the sign, pointing to God's self. In a gracious and kenotic act of condescension, God encounters a person directly in the event of revelation. Confronted with the reality of God, one is confronted with the reality of one's relationship with God. In this type of revelation, one is forced to make a decision about

---

36. Barth, *CD* I/1, 191, 193–194, 196. Cf. Hodgson and King, *Readings*, 99.

one's status before God, a decision that has a certain soteriological impact. Divine self-revelation, in other words, is soteric revelation. God's very self is revealed, and when a person encounters the God she is confronted with the reality of her relationship to God.

The category of divine self-revelation is useful because without it we would have no ability to speak meaningfully about God. And it is the key to knowing the things God cares about; knowledge of God allows us to know the things God values. This makes divine self-revelation the preeminent, logically prior form of revelation, but certainly not the only form of revelation.

Given the overwhelming efforts among twentieth-century theologians to defend divine *self*-revelation as the only form of revelation, we must also carve out a space for revelations with very little impact on salvation. Some revelations, for instance, have to do with making this world a better place to live (stewardship; compassion), or reuniting estranged people (forgiveness), or any other issue on which God is not value-neutral. But these are non-soteric revelations because they have no impact on salvation and the initiating sign is something other than God. These are not unimportant revelations because they are still things God values, which we know from the prior act of divine self-revelation. But the recipient of non-soteric, non-divine self-revelation need not know of their source in order to experience the event of non-soteric revelation.

Authentication and Adjudication

When the revelation/self-revelation debate is framed in this way, the circularity problem in adjudicating and authenticating revelation finds a solution. The circularity problem states that any attempt to judge between competing claims to revelation, that is, the effort to authenticate which one comes from God and which one does not, will inevitably rely on some understanding of God. And that prior understanding of God will, according to the critic, inevitably rest on some view of what God has revealed about Godself. Presumably one is unable to judge which is most likely to have come from God unless one already has some notion of God and the things God values, which will come from revelation.

A second order question concerns whether this type of inquiry is even appropriate given the subject matter of divine revelation. Is revelation the type of thing that humankind can authenticate? John Locke would argue it *is* our job to discern using reason what revelation discloses and guard against "enthusiasm." Locke is a foundationalist and evidentialist who argues that our level of belief should be proportionate to the evidence we have.[37] Locke is quite clear about this point with respect to revelation: "No proposition can be received for Divine Revelation . . . if it be contradictory to our clear intuitive Knowledge."[38] For Locke, reason is the instrument of authentication and the tool of adjudication between competing claims to revelation. He avoids the circularity problem by claiming that reason is conceptually prior to revelation; no revelation can overturn something we absolutely know by reason. He mitigates the force of this claim, however, by suggesting "a well-attested revelation might overturn a belief that is merely probable for reason."[39] Locke also redefines the idea of revelation by saying that "reason is natural revelation,"[40] in accordance with this reason-centered view. To summarize his position in the *Essay Concerning Human Understanding*, Locke says "natural *Reason* [is] enlarged by a new set of Discoveries communicated by God immediately, which *Reason* vouches the truth of."[41] In answer to the question of whether it is our place to authenticate divine revelations, therefore, Locke answers in the affirmative.

Karl Barth disagrees with Locke on the self-authentication point. Whereas Locke says reason authenticates divine revelation, Barth suggests that divine revelation is *self*-authenticating. In the first volume of the *Church Dogmatics*, Barth is quite clear about this point. He treats the Word of God as a "fact" that "does not receive its dignity and validity in any respect or even to the slightest degree from a presupposition that we bring to it."[42] The truth of the Word of God "is grounded absolutely in itself."[43] He continues to describe his task based on this understanding of revelation:

> The procedure in theology, then, is to establish the self-certainty on the certainty of God, to measure it by the certainty of God, and thus to begin with the certainty of God without waiting for the validating of this beginning by self-certainty. . . . Men can know the Word of God because and insofar as God wills that they know it.[44]

---

37. Locke, *Essay* (Oxford), 697.
38. Ibid., 692 (emphasis removed).
39. Evans, "Faith and Revelation," 332. Summary of Locke, *Essay*, 694–96.
40. Locke, *Essay* (Dent), 339.
41. Locke, *Essay* (Oxford), 698.
42. Barth, *CD*, I/1, 196. Cf. Hodgson and King, *Readings*, 100.
43. Ibid.
44. Ibid.

This sentiment is continued in the second volume of the *Dogmatics*.[45] We cannot find the truth on our own, according to Barth. Our reasoning is always limited by our finitude and impaired by our sin. Divine revelation, however, is self-authenticating, self-interpreting, and received in faith.[46]

The view of revelation I have sketched here attempts to bridge these two options. It stands to reason that when God reveals Godself in soteric, divine self-revelation, it is self-authenticating. God reveals Godself, which cannot be untrue. With non-soteric revelation, however, one encounters a created thing as opposed to the uncreated Revealer, and created things are more susceptible to misreading and misinterpretation. In non-soteric revelation it is not God authenticating the revelation by God's very presence as the sign. So criteria are needed to authenticate it and adjudicate between competing claims to revelation in non-soteric contexts. Below I lay out some of these criteria. But to be clear, we need no authenticating criteria in divine soteric self-revelation like we do in non-soteric revelation.

There is an order here: divine self-revelation tells us something of who God is, from which we learn about the things God values. This then is the basis on which we test other revelations to see if they are from God. In terms of logical priority, this makes the self-revelation of God the primary category since what is learned about God and experienced through divine self-revelation are the necessary preconditions for the possibility of evaluating non-soteric revelations. Without some self-revelation of God, which offers some knowledge of God and knowledge of what God values, there is nothing on which to base any further judgments. Or still otherwise expressed, the self-revelation of God shows us the things God values, which are used as criteria for non-soteric revelations. But non-soteric revelation is no less divine revelation than soteric revelation.

---

45. Says Barth: "The truth that God is God and our Lord, and the further truth that we could know him as God and Lord, can only come to us through the truth itself. This 'coming to us' of the truth is revelation. . . . We need to see that in the view of God all our activity is in vain . . . that of ourselves we are not in a position to apprehend the truth, to let God be God and our Lord. . . . We need to be ready and resolved simply to let the truth be told to us, and therefore to be approached by it. . . . The man to whom the truth has really come will concede that he was not at all ready and resolved to let it speak to him. . . . For in faith, Man's religion as such is shown by revelation to be resistance to it. From the standpoint of revelation religion is clearly seen to be a human attempt to anticipate what God in his revelation wills to do and does so."

46. Not all theologians were equally satisfied with this view of revelation. Bonhoeffer went so far as to accuse Barth of a "positivism of revelation" in his *Letters*, 140.

IMPLICATIONS OF THE SOTERIC/NON-SOTERIC DISTINCTION

Now that the difference is made explicit between (a) soteric, self-authenticating, divine *self*-revelation and (b) non-soteric revelation, a number of other issues fall into place. First, properly speaking, divine *self*-revelation would be incongruous with narrative symbolism only if narrative symbolism asserted that narrative is the *only* symbol of divine revelation. But this is not what narrative symbolism suggests. Rather, narrative symbolism suggests that narrative is the primary symbol, but there are other types of symbols. Surely there is a narrative component to divine self-revelation, even if not primary. By stating that narrative is the primary symbol, space is left for divine self-revelation in which God is that which is revealed.

Second, a proper understanding of divine self-revelation affirms that it has only ever been manifest in two ways: in the incarnation of the second member of the Trinity, the Word of God; and in the soul of the individual who realizes her existential situation vis-à-vis the reality of God. With respect to the incarnation, one can get glimpses of divine self-revelation by reading scripture or hearing preaching, but the glimpse one gets is not itself divine self-revelation. Rather, it is merely a witness to it (*à la* Barth). The only access present-day Christians have to divine self-revelation comes in the deepest part of their being, the place in which God confronts them directly, speaks to their souls, and takes up residence in their lives.

Third, the soteric and non-soteric distinction has implications for the idea I argued against in chapter 4, namely that God is best understood *as* the event of divine revelation, namely. In divine self-revelation "event" language is only appropriately applied to revelation, not to God. The Word of God, while signifying an event of divine condescension and kenosis, is not the event itself because the Word possesses agency and eternality whereas events do not.

Fourth, drawing the distinction between soteric and non-soteric revelations means that a person need not recognize God as the source of revelation. In non-soteric revelations, a person is confronted with certain values, not necessarily the God who gives those things value. The claim "God values X" is not the same claim as "X has value." Insofar as the former presupposes the reality of God, it is only available in divine self-revelation whereas the latter is a type of non-soteric revelation if, in fact, God does value X.

Fifth, the soteric and non-soteric distinction offers a solution to the access question: Does revelation provide mediated or unmediated access to God? A similar question is found in discussions of Christian canonical scripture and the extent to which access to God is mediated through it. Does the Bible, or any other non-soteric/non-divine sign provide access to *God* or merely access to the *narrative* of God? Dulles and Lindbeck suggested that access to God is mediated, and Dulles says it is mediated by the symbol. However, Ramm indicates that the encounter is *immediate*.[47]

Dulles differentiates his "symbolic mediation" view from the "experiential model" by appealing to this very point: "The difference between the two seems obvious. The symbolic theory holds that there is no revelation apart from the created signs by which it is mediated. The mystical approach, on the contrary, affirms the possibility of an unmediated perception of God or of the transcendent through interior, spiritual union. If symbols are important for this school of thinkers, it could only be because they prepare for, or express, an ecstatic peak experience that has no context except the ineffable Presence."[48] Dulles lauds the experimental model for "insisting that revelation necessarily involves a real union between the human spirit and the God who bestows himself in grace."[49] When faced with the necessity of defending "symbolic mediation" against an unmediated encounter, Dulles concedes part of the point. Instead of merely mediation, as his terminology inappropriately suggests, Dulles says revelation is some mysterious combination of mediated and unmediated access to God. The mediation/immediacy of God through revelation can also be approached from a distinctively Lutheran angle. In particular, Luther described divine revelation in terms of the cross in which "God is revealed through self-veiling."[50] This creates the need for faith and illumination from the Spirit to recognize revelation as concealed in historical events. Revelation conceals what it reveals to create dependence on the Revealer.

Another relevant figure here is Karl Rahner. In Rahner's view, there is a "mediated immediacy" which shows the dualism of revelation. There is a sign in the event of revelation, but that sign is neither the content nor main purpose of the revelation. For Rahner, the immediate thing is "the self-communication of the divine, the experience of grace." However, "the inner presence of God cannot be known and cannot achieve itself except insofar

---

47. Says Grenz and Olson of Ramm in *20th Century Theology*, 306: "The primary principle of authority—God in the divine self-disclosure—produces the *immediate* principle of authority—the Spirit speaking in the Scriptures. As a result, final authority lies neither in the book itself nor in the Spirit, but in the revelation (Jesus Christ) to which the Bible witnesses as the Spirit effects illumination. Consequently, the New Testament is authoritative in the church, because it is the witness of the apostles (and those associated with them) to the revelation of God in Christ" (emphasis added).

48. Dulles, *Models of Revelation*, 148.

49. Ibid., 149.

50. Lohse, *Martin Luther*, 194.

as it becomes mediated, or mediates itself, in created symbols. The symbols, however, do arouse a genuine awareness of the divine itself—an awareness that always surpasses all that we can say about it."[51] For Rahner, and for Dulles (notwithstanding his perhaps inappropriately titled "symbolic mediation" approach), revelation is a mysterious combination of mediated and unmediated access to God.

This question can be taken as a central dividing issue that separates conservative thinkers from mainline theologians and Catholics like Dulles. Can a person truly encounter God without a mediator? Ironically, the notion of "personal relationship" so popular in evangelicalism seems to preclude such mediation, yet evangelicals are wont to elevate the Bible in discussions of divine revelation, which stands between them and God. Also ironically, if God's revelation is defined solely in terms of God's *self*-revelation, as Barth was trying to do, then presumably there is no mediating presence.

The distinction between soteric and non-soteric revelation suggests a solution to this debate. In fact, it bridges both perspectives by suggesting that divine self-revelation is unmediated (in agreement with Barth) and non-soteric revelation is mediated (in agreement with Dulles). If God is revealed, the "thing" a person encounters, then the encounter is unmediated. However, if the symbol or sign merely points to something God values (as in non-soteric revelation), then access to God is mediated through that sign. On this account, therefore, it is inappropriate to speak univocally about whether revelation provides mediated or immediate access to God. Different types of revelations provide different sorts of access.

The sixth and final implication of the soteric and non-soteric distinction is that we need criteria for judging non-soteric revelations since the signs it uses are susceptible to misinterpretation. Essentially the problem here is one of competing narratives: almost any smaller story can be situated in almost any larger narrative and this is one of the communicable divine attributes. So how can we know which larger narrative is of God and which is not? How do we sort out all the putative revelations?

Here I will give four sets of criteria, and in the end discuss the way they work together. They can be grouped under the following rubrics: (a) human flourishing, (b) correspondence to the ways in which God relates to humanity, and methods of judging that arise from our two conversation partners—(c) literary theory and (d) communication studies. Different approaches will resonate with different people, but one can cull from this list a set of helpful criteria to judge whether a putative divine revelation is of God or whether it originated elsewhere.

51. Dulles, *Models of Revelation*, 148–49.

One method for judging between competing narratives has to do with human flourishing. In the sacrificial act of condescension and kenosis, we learn through divine self-revelation that God values human flourishing. The larger narrative that best promotes human flourishing, individually or collective, is the one most likely to have originated with God. God is interested in humans living an abundant life, one lived in accordance with their intended purpose. (Recall "intentionality" in MacIntyre's explication of the narrative self.) Insofar as living according to God's purposes will eventuate in an abundant life oriented around goodness, truth, and beauty, it will not primarily be a life of meaninglessness or unintelligible suffering.[52] This criterion proscribes actions or beliefs that clearly do not contribute to human flourishing. For example, it strongly opposes any claim to divine revelation that authorizes unprovoked and unjustified violence, sees people as a means to an end rather than an end in themselves, or supplies information, goods or services that harm others. Further, it sanctions claims to divine revelation in which God thought to have motivated an act of love or compassion for another person.[53]

Part of the "flourishing" criterion has to do with the complexity/simplicity dynamic. People flourish when they understand what is before them, what has transpired in the past, and what their current role is in that larger narrative. Confusion about one's place is antithetical to any revelation that comes from an omnibenevolent God, whose "yoke is easy and burden is light."[54] Therefore, according to this model of revelation, any putative revelation that complicates one's situation or perception of a situation is not of God. Stated as a criterion, the complexity/simplicity observation goes something like this: one can adjudicate between competing narratives by asking whether the putative revelation complicates or simplifies one's predicament (knowing that complication and interruption are different ideas).

---

52. There is a difference here between "suffering" and "sin." It is true that sin does not equal suffering; often quite the opposite is true insofar as suffering can be purposeful and meaningful, in which case it is included in the "abundant life" I am describing which is also synonymous with "human flourishing." A life lived in sin, while it might make us seemingly happy, is always ultimately unfulfilling since it does not reflect our Creator's intentions for us.

53. In this criterion there is nothing distinctively "Christian" in the reception of revelation; the important aspect of this criterion is not whether a *Christian* is promoting human flourishing, but rather anyone is promoting human flourishing. Anyone who willingly participates in a narrative of liberation, for instance, has received divine revelation, irrespective of the tradition from which it comes. Liberation is, after all, a concept with enormous power and it is found in many religious traditions.

54. Matt 11:30.

If it simplifies, it is more likely to have originated from God, but if it complicates, it is more likely to have originated elsewhere.[55]

Even though divine self-revelation does not require external authentication, this criterion could act as such if it did. The "flourishing" criterion relates to authorial intention and what sort of Narrator is conveyed in or conveying the narratives. A revelation in which the intentions of the author are seen as benevolent and presented in interesting or creative ways is more likely to have originated with God. If a narrative does not display any authorial intention, or displays bad/treacherous authorial intentions, then it is likely to have originated elsewhere. The best stories are ones in which the reader/narratee trusts the author/Narrator. Without this trust the reader is unable to give herself fully over to the event of revelation. But when it is done well, the event solicits the reader's attention and piques her interest. This is related to the "flourishing" criterion in obvious ways: if the author of the narrative is good-willed and that good will is creatively presented to the narratee, that divine revelation is more likely to have originated from God.

A second set of criteria for adjudicating between competing claims to divine revelation involves the ways in which God relates to humanity. Here we take our cue from David Kelsey, whose argument is unavoidably simplified in this chapter for the sake of space. Many theologians have understood God's relationship with the world to fall under one meta-narrative, one grand story with three (or more) parts: creation, redemption, and

---

55. Simplification and ease are different concepts. A sinner may believe that what she hears in the revelation seems more complicated than how she experiences her life now, because sin feels very good and a divine revelation in which the receiver is told to resist sin is going to seem overwhelming. But in a non-soteric "interruption" a person is shown the need to change the way she thinks, her basic orientation from "self" to "other." This interruption is part of the revelation event and is ultimately intended for the subject's good. One might interpret a revelation as complicated if it requires a response that is difficult. A new Christian reading the Sermon on the Mount, for instance, might ask "Do I really have to do all this?" But what might seem complicated to the new convert is in fact a simplification. In difficult discipleship scenarios like this I would suggest this image: God is peeling away layers of sin so that a person can live as she was intended to live, unhindered by those distractions. This is an act of simplification, not complication. Greater complexity is not necessarily intended for the subject's good and does not necessarily show connections between seemingly disparate phenomena whereas a simpler revelation has greater potential to do so, even if the revelation includes a practical or behavioral change that is difficult to carry out. Complexity is to be attributed to one of the three ways that sin affects the divine revelation. Note, too, that this criterion plays a part in the argument I make in the chapter 5, namely, that this view of divine revelation is remarkably egalitarian. If only those with the intellectual capacity for detangling complicated arguments can receive revelation, God is not entirely good. Stated quite plainly, God's revelation needs to be as simple as possible for as many people as possible to grasp it. So revelations that complicate matters are not revelation at all.

eschatological consummation. In his magnum opus, *Eccentric Existence*, Kelsey argues that God relates to humanity in three ways, not just one. Kelsey finds these three narratives to have irreducible narrative logics; none can be subsumed under another, and the three cannot be conflated to form a larger narrative. Creation, fall/redemption, and consummation are not, using narratology's tools, smaller "stories" in a larger narrative. They are top-level narratives in their own right, according to Kelsey. They all occur simultaneously in the history of the world: God created, still creates, and will continue to create; God redeemed, redeems, and will continue redemptive activity; and finally, God has drawn humanity to Godself, is drawing humanity today, and will continue to draw humanity in the future. They are displays of God's "intentions" toward humanity.[56] They act as "genres" in which God's action to humanity can be made intelligible, where genres help give us "ability to grasp the thread of the conversation . . . to bring it under some one out of a set of descriptions in which the degree and kind of coherence in the conversation is brought out."[57] Of course, a single event can be a part of more than one "genre" at a time; conversion, for instance, is at once God's creative activity of making a person new as well as God's redemptive activity of forgiving sins. Some events "are both endings and beginnings" or "embedded in another."[58]

Through God's self-revelation we learn that God values creation, redemption, and consummation, and therefore they act as three sub-criteria for evaluating a non-soteric putative revelation's veracity. Used as a criterion for adjudicating between competing narratives, Kelsey's perspective goes something like this: if one narrative promotes destruction and another promotes creation, the latter most likely originated with God and the former somewhere else; if one narrative promotes redemption and another does not, the former likely originated with God; and if one narrative promotes consummation while another fractures or blunts it, the former is of God and the latter is not.[59]

---

56. This is similar to what MacIntyre is talking about in *After Virtue*, 92ff. God intends to relate to us creatively, redemptively, and eschatologically.

57. MacIntyre, *After Virtue*, 196.

58. Ibid., 198.

59. MacIntyre actually goes so far as to suggest that all lived narratives have a teleological character. "We live out our lives, both individually and in our relationships with each other, in the light of certain conceptions of a possible shared future, a future in which certain possibilities beckon us forward and others repel us, some seem already foreclosed and others perhaps inevitable." Ibid., 200. More could be said about redemption as a sub-criterion. Redemption makes good out of evil. Where there once were negative consequences of sin, redemption reduces their stronghold on an individual. Basically, therefore, one can adjudicate between competing narratives by

Literary theory and narratology offer another set of criteria for adjudicating between narratives. Schank and Berman ask a simple question: "what makes the best stories?"[60] Their answers line up with several of the themes I argued above. The best stories concern their listeners personally, not abstractly, and the effectiveness of the story is at least in part dependent on the unique location—personally, theologically, emotionally, spiritually, mentally, etc.—of the listener: "The stories with the most impact are those that apply to listeners' goals and that are relevant to their personal frames of reference. Any story can be good or bad depending on who is hearing it, and what they are thinking about or caring about at the time."[61] With respect to revelation, if God is the ultimate Narrator, God knows the hearts of people and chooses which precise combination of events and experiences to use in the revelation. God builds upon the experiences and interests of the person to whom revelation comes: "The most powerful storytellers and speakers address the topics and questions about which the audience is most curious. . . . Storytellers can make their stories more appealing to listeners, more interesting to them, if they add appropriate details to bring the story within listeners' frames of reference."[62] This of course corresponds to what I argued above, namely, that the Narrator is infinitely skilled at assessing a narratee's situation to craft the best revelation possible, and the most effective stories are the ones so carefully crafted that they reach a narratee at the precise time and in the precise way so as to be most effective given that narratee's unique situation. When framed as criteria for adjudicating between competing revelations, the literary and narratological observations go something like this: the revelations that most clearly concern and resonate with the narratee are more likely to be divine revelation whereas the ones that do not concern the narratee are less likely to have originated with God.

---

asking whether the larger narrative accepts and promotes the triumph of good over evil. If one can locate one's story among a larger narrative in which good is triumphant, that larger narrative is more likely to have originated with God than elsewhere. But this raises a question about the utility of the genre of "tragedy." In this model of revelation, an omnibenevolent God will reveal using tragedies only when it is clear that they are tragedies. According to this model, revelation is unlikely to be found in life situations which imitate the theater of the absurd and postmodern, anti-plot narratives in which good and evil are indistinguishable. Divine revelation clarifies and simplifies what is good and what is evil, and divine revelation teaches that the forces of good ultimately triumph over evil, and it is tragic when they do not. Robert Jenson says, "If there were not God . . . our situation would be precisely that of characters in a sequence with no outcome and therefore no plot. But the drama we inhabit is not absurd: it has an author with intentions." Jenson, "Scripture's Authority," 32.

60. Schank and Berman, "Pervasive Role," 307.
61. Ibid., 307–8.
62. Ibid., 308.

There are other insights from literary theory which are more problematic as methods for judging between competing narratives, specifically if the one inquiring is Christian. Schank and Berman argue that the strongest stories are those in which the narratee sympathizes with the hero; indeed, she or he can see her/himself in the role of the hero:

> The closer we can come to relating to the hero, the more personally relevant the story becomes, and the more likely we are to learn from it. That means that if the storyteller can get us to really sympathize with the hero, it also implies that we can imagine being in the same circumstances, and we begin to think about what we might do, or how we might feel if we were in the hero's shoes. Adding to a story rich details that touch on references the broader public understands assists this effect.[63]

However, the strongest and most Christian narratives are those in which a narratee sees herself in *need* of the hero, not *as* the hero.[64] So on this score, literary theory fails to account for the categorical difference between humanity and the Word incarnate.

A second area in which literary theory posits a method of evaluation that is antithetical to a distinctively Christian understanding of revelation concerns plasticity. Kathryn Tanner argues that for most created things, the highest level of existence is for X or Y to be the best X or Y it can be, depending on the thing it is. However, the best humans are notable for their plasticity, their ability to be molded into something new and different in the image of God.[65] If humans are essentially plastic creatures, then they are noteworthy due to their ability to be changed. Some literary theorists, however, suggest that the most effective stories are those in which a narratee is confirmed in what s/he already believes. "When we listen to stories we attempt to find evidence that confirms what we already believe. Changing our beliefs requires expectation failures powerful enough to convince us there is actually something wrong with our existing beliefs, our representations of the domain."[66] In revelation, God interrupts and reforms our subjectivity instead of confirming what we already believe and take to be true. When stated as a criterion for adjudicating between competing narratives, one could ask a question like this: does this putative revelation correspond to what one already believes or does it challenge one in new ways? Whereas

---

63. Ibid., 308.

64. For an excellent discussion of how Jesus came to occupy "hero" status for a number of different communities in different ways, see Riley, *One Jesus, Many Christs*.

65. Tanner, *Christ the Key*, 1–57.

66. Schank and Berman, "Pervasive Role," 309.

in literary circles the best narrative corresponds to what one already thinks (according to Schank and Berman), in a distinctively *Christian* view the revelation that challenges a person to think in a new and/or different way is most likely of God, but within parameters (those of the historic creeds). This is the interruption and reformation of the individual's subjectivity. The key difference is not necessarily thinking differently about timeless truths, but rather thinking differently about one's own place in a broader narrative: it's *practical* theology at work. In the Christian narrative, one is looking to be transformed from old to new, again and again, not to confirm what one already knew or believed. As Roger Olson and other postconservative theologians remind us, the event is about *transformation* more than *information*. And transformation assumes an old state changed into a new state.

Another potential avenue for adjudicating between competing narratives is found in communication studies. In Walter Fisher's narrative paradigm, he discusses "what makes one story better than another."[67] His answer is simple—"good reasons"—yet this requires some elucidation. Kathleen Roberts summarizes nicely: "Good reasons vary in form (depending on the context) but may be tested by two qualities of the narrative: its coherence (probability) and its fidelity. Coherence describes how well a narrative hangs together or makes sense internally and structurally, while fidelity assesses whether or not a narrative rings true with its participants."[68] Coherence is similar to Lindbeck's intrasystematic test for truth in which the internal structure of a narrative hangs together well. In *Human Communication as Narration*, Fisher explains the criteria that separate one story from another. When asking what makes one story better than another,

> Two features come to mind: formal and substantive. Formal features are attributes of narrative probability: the consistency of the characters and actions, the accommodation to auditors, and so on. In epistemological terms, the question would be whether or not a narrative satisfied the demands of a coherence theory of truth. The most compelling, persuasive stories are mythic in form, stories reflective of "public dreams" that give meaning and significance to life. Substantive features relate to narrative fidelity. While there is work to be done on the problem, I think the logic of good reasons is the most viable scheme presently available by which narratives can be tested. Its application requires an examination of reasoning and an inspection of facts, values, self and society. In epistemological terms, narrative fidelity is

---

67. Fisher, *Human Communication as Narration*, 75.

68. Roberts, "Texturing the Narrative Paradigm," 131. Cf. Fisher, "The Narrative Paradigm: In the Beginning," 297.

a matter of truth according to the doctrine of correspondence. The most engaging stories are mythic, the most helpful and uplifting stories are moral.[69]

Two tests are deployed, then: coherence and fidelity. Coherence is a way of discussing a narrative's probability, how well it hangs together internally and structurally, while fidelity—the more relevant concept for an origins story—"assesses whether or not a narrative rings true with its participants."[70] In Fisher's view, the Christian story has both coherence *and* fidelity, and thus passes the test for narrative privilege. Fisher says the cosmological myths of Christ satisfy "both narrative probability and narrative fidelity for those cultures for whom they were intended—and many others across time and place. Far from denying the humanity of persons, they elevate it to the profoundest moral and metaphysical level the world has known."[71] To be sure, the Christian story is not the only narrative with narrative coherence and fidelity for Fisher,[72] but it is helpful to note that it at least does not fail Fisher's tests. When phrased as a criterion for adjudicating between competing narratives, insights from Fisher and communication studies go something like this: the narrative that makes sense and hangs together internally, as well as the narrative that rings true with its participants is most likely of God and the narrative that does not make sense and does not ring true with its participants is more likely to have originated elsewhere.

In sum, we can say a few things about judging non-soteric revelations, that is, adjudicating between competing narratives when seeking which larger narrative should be privileged. Claims to divine revelation are mistaken if they (a) foster violence, (b) complicate one's situation, (c) betray God as ill-willed or harmful, (d) do not correspond to God's creative, redemptive, or eschatological activity, (e) do not concern the person to whom they come proximately or ultimately, and (f) make little sense to members of that story-community. Conversely, claims to divine revelation are likely to have originated with God if they (a) foster peace, (b) simplify one's situation, (c) demonstrate God's omnibenevolence, (d) correspond to God's creative, redemptive, or eschatological activity, (e) concern the person to whom they come proximately or ultimately, and (f) make sense to members of that story-community. The list presents a cumulative case: the more

---

69. Fisher, *Human Communication as Narration*, 76.
70. Roberts, "Texturing the Narrative Paradigm," 131.
71. Fisher, *Human Communication as Narration*, 76.
72. Fisher also admits other religious narratives that pass his test: Lao-Tzu, Buddha, Zoroaster, Muhammad, and some fictional narratives, e.g., the works of Homer, Dante, Shakespeare, and Tolstoy.

criteria are present, the more likely a putative revelation is to have come from God; the fewer criteria are present, the less likely the putative revelation is to have originated with God.

There are two questions raised by these criteria: first, is this view Christian, or at least Christian enough? And second, is this view helpful, or at least helpful enough to aid someone attempting to determine which direction God intends? To the first question, we respond in the affirmative. It does not matter whether the person who participates in the good realizes that it is about/from God. As Augustine claimed, all good will comes from God,[73] and the good that results from the good will is likewise attributable to God whether or not its recipient recognizes it. So without hesitation this book claims that narrative symbolism is undoubtedly Christian. The "good" and the "Christian" do not differ.

To the second question, we also respond in the affirmative. Many putative revelations are proscribed if these are our criteria, and many of the things considered secular charity can be considered religiously authorized and motivated by revelation (e.g., feeding the poor, clothing the naked, housing the homeless, etc.). One need not recognize that God is the author of the revelation one receives, or that the revelation is a revelation from God to receive it. The willingness to forgive, for instance, is God-given and God honoring, whether or not a person realizes its source.

---

73. Augustine, *On the Merits*, 2.30.

Chapter 6

Leveling the Field
The Implications of Revelation

A SUMMARY OF THE MODEL

Thus far, this book has explored the idea of revelation in some major twentieth-century thinkers, and it presented an integrative model of divine revelation that is conversant with recent advances in a number of disciplines. In this chapter, I will (a) summarize the constructive and systematic portions, material from chapters 4 and 5, (b) discuss how this model reframes previous views of divine revelation, and (c) show some of the implications of this model.

I began chapter 4 by describing flexibility in the concept of "revelation" such that one can map all sorts of continua onto it, one of which was the content/event continuum. I then proceeded to integrate the three central revelational themes that emerged from our three thinkers: I situated symbol at the "top," but noted that it stood for a variable. I then defended *narrative* as the primary symbol, the primary means by which we make sense of the world and its created signs. I argued that a move like this makes sense since theology as a discipline has changed in three important ways: away from methodology, towards praxis, and into other disciplines. The model I outlined in chapter 4 took its cue from the last of these shifts. I argued that humans are storytellers. We have an innate, God-given need to seek patterns and see ourselves as part of something larger, and what we are learning about humankind through various disciplines supports it. Literary theory provided the conceptual tools to understand what precisely happens in a revelatory event of narrative symbolism: God, the infinitely skilled Narrator, chooses the best content and form of delivery to show a subject her place in the larger narrative. Narrative symbolism adds purpose to seemingly purposeless events, why to the what. It includes several obvious features: individuals, their smaller stories, the larger narrative, the Narrator, and a sign that initiates the encounter. Moreover, narrative symbolism also requires some less obvious features: a degree of self-awareness, difference between the smaller story and larger narrative, unity between the smaller story and the larger narrative, the linear passage of time, a willingness to give oneself over to a sign's power to initiate, and finally a meaningful connection between the two narratives. The model, I argued at the close of chapter 4, fully endorses the Christian scriptures as instrumentally unique, chosen by God to play a part in the event of revelation.

In chapter 5 I described how this integrative model of revelation relates to some of the central issues in a systematic theological framework: humanity, sin, and salvation. With respect to theological anthropology, the inclusion of the smaller story of the individual means that the human is part of the revelation event. Furthermore, humans share some of God's attributes, three of which shed light on the ways a narrative account of revelation relates to anthropology: all human communication can be subsumed under the metaphor of narrative, human creativity illustrates a solution to the agency problem in revelation, and humanity shares God's ability to connect smaller stories to larger narratives. This opened the door to the discussion of ways in which "sin" figures into this model. Literary theorists posit several "actants" in a narrative, two of which show how sin works: opponents momentarily disrupt an actant's quest for the sought-for-object, unity with God (lower case "sin") while the anti-subject is at cross-purposes with the subject and is more like the existential condition of (capital "S") Sin, or Evil itself. In the narratives of our lives, we can reject revelation in two ways: first, by refusing to give ourselves over to that which as been revealed and comprehended, and second by misreading the revelation as a result of the unique and tragic circumstances in which we find ourselves. With respect to the Christian religious end of "salvation," I distinguished soteric revelations from non-soteric ones, a distinction that generates proposals for the revelation/self-revelation debate, mediated/unmediated access debate, and the authentication and adjudication circularity problem. I suggested that divine self-revelation is self-authenticating soteric revelation but that revelation is a broader category and should not be limited to divine self-revelations. The other revelations—non-soteric in nature—require some criteria to judge whether the putative revelation is of God. Non-soteric revelations that promote flourishing, correspond to God's relational activity, concern their receivers ultimately, and make sense in their context are more likely to have originated with God than elsewhere.

THE IMPLICATIONS OF DIVINE REVELATION

In 2005 a book was released by a conservative evangelical scholar called *The Benefits of Providence*. In it, James Spiegel enters the "open theism" discussion not by defending an Augustinian perspective on providence, but rather by showing that if one assumes the truth of an Augustinian perspective, a number of other issues fall into place. This chapter is similar in that I will not be defending the view of revelation I proposed; that is what chapters 4 and 5 were for. Rather, I will show some of its implications in other areas, beyond those of the theological concepts of the human, sin, and salvation. Implications of narrative symbolism that were only hinted at throughout the text are now made more explicit.

Implications for the Challenges to Revelation

The first set of implications concerns the challenges to the concept of revelation mentioned in the introduction: (a) the philosophical charge of question begging, (b) increased awareness of advances in higher criticism, (c) cultural, ethical, and religious relativism, (d) the resurgence of naturalism, (e) the nature of God, and (f) the complicated nature of the revelation question. If what I have argued is correct, then each of these challenges is met with an answer.

In response to the challenge of question begging, the difference between soteric, self-authenticating divine self-revelation and non-soteric revelation provides a solution to this problem. One does not beg the question if, in agreement with Barth, one claims that self-revelation is logically prior to other types of revelation, and it gives us criteria by which we can judge those other revelations. To the challenge that higher criticism mounts against revelation, narrative symbolism suggests that Christianity's sacred texts are not ontologically unique but instrumentally unique in the hands of an inerrant God, who uses them as an origins story for the Church, who participate in the narrative and worship the God to whom scripture attests. The Christian can, therefore, like Ramm and Barth before him, be unafraid to open any door in search of God's truth. To the challenge of relativism, I proposed universally acceptable criteria to measure the authenticity of non-soteric revelations such that a person of nearly any worldview would accept them. Things like creation, charity, generosity, redemption, and flourishing cannot be relativized; they are absolute goods in this world. To the challenge of naturalism, I argued that humanity is such that it looks for higher purpose and meaning. As Clifford Williams suggests, the satisfaction of existential needs provides not proofs for the existence of a divine reality but rather sufficient justification for our looking. We are meaning-seekers, and meaning cannot come from this world alone. Fifth, I discussed the nature of God that relates to this model of revelation: temporally eternal,[1] existing in a relationship of non-competition with the world, *not* pantheistic or panentheistic, the greatest conceivable being, and triune. Finally, to the challenge of the complicated nature of the revelation question, narrative symbolism can be simply summarized in this way: smaller stories are connected to the larger narrative of God's work in the world. Of course, this requires quite a lot of explanation, a book-length treatment, in fact. But explanation is not complication. If I am right about these issues, then an integrative model of revelation in which (a) narrative acts as the primary symbol and (b) a distinction is made between soteric and non-soteric revelation successfully answers challenges to divine revelation.

Implications for the Models of Revelation

A second set of implications concerns Dulles' typology presented in chapter 1. There were five models of revelation to which he devoted attention: (a) revelation as doctrine, (b) revelation as history, (c) revelation as inner experience, (d) revelation as dialectical presence, and finally (d) revelation as new awareness.

Narrative symbolism does not fit well with the "revelation as doctrine" model because whatever else revelation is, it is *not* primarily propositional. It is, rather, primarily an event. Propositional awareness/knowledge emerges from the encounter, to be sure; otherwise the event would be unintelligible. But propositions are not the point or focus of divine revelation. Whereas "revelation as doctrine" argues that natural revelation is given in deeds and supernatural in words, narrative symbolism suggests that this dichotomy is false and that all revelations are tailored to a specific person and encountered in an event (not words). In this much, narrative symbolism is in agreement with "revelation as history." But it part ways with the "revelation as history"

---

1 Though, as mentioned previously, if believers in divine atemporality wish to attempt to show how my model of revelation is compatible with their views then I will not stand in their way.

perspective as advocated by Cullmann when he argues for the necessity of a prophet. In divine self-revelation no mediating presence is needed, as Pannenberg says. But Pannenberg does not, in my estimation, draw enough attention to the soteric/non-soteric distinction. The dynamics of "revelation as inner experience" are very similar as those in narrative symbolism: the support of mediated immediacy (depending on whether the revelation is soteric or non-soteric), God as transcendent and immanent, rejection of the general/special distinction, and communication from Spirit (God) to spirit (humankind). But narrative symbolism disagrees when proponents of "inner experience" fail to leave room for non-soteric revelations. If revelation were only ever about God's self-communication, then people without a relationship with God would never be moved to do a positive action in line with something God values (e.g., recycling, forgiveness). Similarly, "revelation as dialectical presence" adequately captures God's self-revelation but fails to recognize non-soteric divine revelation, which *can* be known by human reason on the basis of knowledge of things God values identified through a prior divine self-revelation. Finally, narrative symbolism does create some level of "new awareness," which is a deeper and more mysterious familiarity than propositional knowledge. But whereas the "new awareness" model is not strongly anchored to tradition, narrative symbolism is anchored to the Christian story as expressed in the historic Christian creeds and as attested to by scripture and many of the greatest thinkers in the history of Christianity thought.

In sum, narrative symbolism is a combination of the history, inner experience, and new awareness models of divine revelation, with inner experience the one with which it has most similarities. Not surprisingly, narrative symbolism coupled with the soteric/non-soteric distinction takes the best of all of the approaches and builds upon them in beneficial ways.

Implications for Revelation's Receivers

A third set of implications concerns those who are recipients of revelation. God, according to this model, tailors each revelation to each receiver for the greatest potential for the revelation to occur without frustration. So who has access to it? If it is a basic feature of humanity that we are storytellers, *everyone* has access to revelation. Therefore, to make the this implication of this view explicit, we affirm that revelation is remarkably egalitarian: it allows for varying levels of mental and/or intellectual ability, variations in language, variations in context, etc. There is no special knowledge or ability needed to receive this type of revelation. This radical egalitarianism counters any view of revelation or ecclesiology in which special or specially trained individuals are the authoritative messengers of God. Divine revelation requires no familiarity with ancient Hebrew or Greek, no knowledge of church history, no command of symbolic logic, and no mastery of arguments for God's existence. If only those with the intellectual capacity for translating ancient languages or untangling complicated arguments can receive revelation, God is not entirely good. Not everyone shares those abilities.

To state the point as plainly as possible: God's revelation is remarkable egalitarian since it is tailored to the unique recipients, some of whom communicate and understand in ways as far removed from academia as one can imagine. There is no elitism in this model of revelation. It is radically inclusive, open to everyone, including the powerless and lowly as well as the powerful and mighty. Stories are common to the powerless and powerful alike. One interpreter of Walter Fisher had this to say: "The narrative paradigm is less elitist than the rational world paradigm, since narratives and opportunities to 'live' them are universally accessible. The narrative paradigm offers a model for community life by proposing a progression from story to narrative: when a story has enough coherence and fidelity that it can be agreed up by a people, it becomes public and is therefore a narrative."[2] As Walter Fisher himself has said, storytelling is a ubiquitous practice found in contexts that range from folk religion to high church: "The narrative use of language is not a property of subordinate cultures, whether folk, or working class, or the like, but a *universal* function."[3] An empowered laity, moreover, carries with them great potential to impact the kingdom for the good. So this model of revelation plays a part in "transforming Christian theology"[4] from exclusive to inclusive, bringing others into the conversation about what God is up to in the world and the ways in which their smaller stories participate in it.

---

2. Roberts, "Texturing the Narrative Paradigm," 131. See also Arnett and Arneson, *Dialogic Civility*.

3. Hymes, "A Narrative View," 132 (emphasis added).

4. According to Clayton in *Transforming Christian Theology* (2–3), "We need to stop delegating theology to specialists and return it to the people who need it, the people whose right (and responsibility) is to 'just do it.' . . . Actually, taking this step is more than a democratic move; it's a revolutionary move. Who knows what ordinary Christians might do if given permission to think deeply about what their faith implies for themselves, for their local churches, and for all the other roles they play in society?"

Implications for Revelational Concepts

A fourth set of implications has to do with two concepts related to revelation. When revelation is conceived as specialized communication from God to specific individuals, this has implications for the general/special distinction and progressive revelation.

Simply put, as I have said before, the distinction between general and special revelation falls apart in this model. Each revelation is a "special" revelation because the event of revelation includes the stories of the individuals. This is similar to Barth's approach, or at least Barth's approach as interpreted by Ramm (who disagrees with it): "According to Barth . . . there is no such thing as general revelation or common grace."[5] My proposal agrees with Barth insofar as God's revelation cannot be spoken about using "general" or "common" terms. The difference between my proposal and Barth's, however, is that I am arguing for a concept of revelation in which that which is revealed is at times soteriological in character, but not always. God also reveals for different—and lesser—purposes than to bring one into the fold of Christianity. God is up to more than just saving souls, and so divine revelation speaks to more than just salvation.

Moreover, this model endorses the notion of progressive revelation. This deserves some explanation. It is *not* the case that the ancient communities were too stupid or primitive to understand God's plans for them. Rather, revelation is progressive because individuals and communities progress and change from one state to another. God's revelation meets them where they are and shows them their place in the larger narrative of God's work in the world, but the process of revelation is ongoing. Individuals and communities change, so their stories change. If their stories are part of the larger narrative of God's work, revelation itself will be progressive in character. Revelation adds new information and changes the perception of the receiver; it is the new added to the old, spoken in a language the present day individual understands.

Implications for Christian Practice

A fifth set of implications of narrative symbolism has to do with Christian practice, specifically a "personal" relationship with God, preaching, evangelism and missions, and liturgy and prayer. Since revelation is tailored to specific individuals, there is a greater sense of "personal" relationship between God and humanity. The encounter with the divine in the event of

---

5. Ramm, *Special Revelation*, 18.

revelation may have a number of consequences, each "personal" in its own way: the personalized attention may make the receiver more at peace in the world, perhaps less bothered by the world's problems. The receiver may see beauty in places she did not see it before. Or the receiver may feel humbled and terribly ashamed. The receiver of revelation may even have the sense of descending from a mountaintop experience during which the world has continued to function; the Lover and beloved shared a secret encounter in revelation. This is the essence of a personal relationship with God. Most personally, God personally met humanity in a gracious, condescending, kenotic act of incarnation.

Another Christian practice with an interesting relationship to narrative symbolism is preaching. Revelation tells a story and puts it into God's larger narrative. One finds this practice in the use of the lectionary. Priests and pastors look for a theme in the lectionary readings; they try to tie these stories together to form a larger narrative that has potential to change their parishioners.

This model of revelation also impacts evangelism and missions. Evangelism becomes in this model less about converting others and more about showing the meaning of stories and narratives, providing hope to those who need it, and seriously entertaining what a member of another faith tradition has to offer. It is "empathetic interest" at its best. Evangelism gives others a purpose in the larger narrative, a role to play. The negative perception of evangelism—i.e., its colonial mindset—is mitigated in this model. If the narrative paradigm is complemented by the "performance paradigm," the results are the absolute democratization of revelation with less intent to deceive others: "One criticism of rhetoric . . . is that it can be deceptive to its audience, . . . it is dependent on a group of elite speakers whose role in society is to move the masses to a generalized way of thinking. . . . While only some speakers are arguers, even they—along with everyone else—are storytellers."[6] Again, one sees the egalitarian nature of this model of revelation in evangelism and missions.

One final implication of divine revelation for Christian practice (of which there are more) involves liturgy and prayer, which play a large role in providing regularity and stability. In this model, God convicts individuals and changes their hearts and minds. Perhaps the chief settings for this type of encounter are liturgy and prayer, in which God reforms a person's sense of self in order to transform her into the person God desires. "Prayer doesn't change God," the Lewis character says in *Shadowlands*, "rather it changes *me*." Through prayer, our selves have the potential to become interrupted and

---

6. Roberts, "Texturing the Narrative Paradigm," 139.

reformed when God uses the activity in the event of revelation. Moreover, liturgy and prayer provide stability and haven from a volatile world. Liturgy and prayer offer worshipping communities—which are simply groups of individuals who have gathered around a similar story—the chance to retell the narratives into which their smaller stories fit. In a postmodern culture, a narrative-based revelation provides stability. These days "public narratives are marginal and few" so "storytelling (rather than arguing or acting) as a mode of human behavior is more significant now than ever."[7] In prayer, in the act of seeing oneself as a character in the larger drama of one's life and God's larger narrative, one becomes "a person rather than an individual."[8] And personhood has profound implications for one's behavior.[9] Revelation defined as narrative symbolism "provides direction, where one would instead be gullible to ever-changing rhetoric."[10] In sum, an implication of this model is that the retelling of one's story in the context of God's larger narrative through prayer and liturgy provides stability in uncertain times.

Implications for the Academy

A sixth set of implications of narrative symbolism concerns the academic study of philosophy and religion. Most obvious, revelation is an integral category in many religious traditions. One wonders, therefore, why it has been so infrequently explored in the past twenty-five years, especially considering the events that have transpired on the global stage in the past decade and a half. As I said in the introduction, religious beliefs often motivate public actions, and one's religious beliefs are informed primarily through the ways in which one believes God has revealed Godself and God's intentions in the world. Given the criteria I laid out in chapter 5 for adjudicating between competing narratives, one is better positioned to prioritize those views of revelation that build bridges with others. Revelation, on this account, is an ethical and socio-political issue insofar as conflicts are based, at least in part, on putative revelations that have come between whole people groups and nations. All of this is to say that divine revelation deserves much more attention from scholars of religion, ethicists, political scientists, etc.

---

7. Ibid., 131.

8. Ibid.

9. Ibid: It "binds one in a moral duty to other persons in the narrative," namely God. Further, "narrative frames one's actions consistent with a shared mission and common center, where the negative would be to base those actions on the selfish whims of emotivism."

10. Ibid.

In particular, revelation deserves exploration by those doing comparative theology or comparative religion, and there is plenty of grist for that mill. One potential bridge between this model and others involves the fitting of smaller parts into larger wholes. This idea is found in a number of non-Christian traditions, even Eastern ones. In Hinduism, for instance, the central feature of liberation is the recognition that one's inner *atman* is actually a part of the much larger, comprehensive *Brahman*. Some Buddhists go so far as to suggest that the self itself is a fiction (*anatta*); we are *all* part of a larger reality from which our desires lead us astray. Confucius faced widespread social disharmony, and in response he created order by suggesting the cultivation of deliberate tradition, a move that shows people their place in relation to the larger family and the vastly larger society as a whole. Lao Tzu extended the Confucian principle even further, as *wu wei* or "creative quietude" attains balance by removing preoccupation with self, removing one's will and being subject to the larger cosmos.

In the non-Christian Abrahamic faiths this is also true. One follows the Torah to remember the covenants made between God and God's people, and covenants involve people oriented toward a larger Reality, their God. Each of the Islam's five pillars, in their own way, guards against *shirk*, the elevation of anything to the level at which only Allah belongs. The word itself means "submission" to the highest power, which is a relationship between the small and Large.

But the interesting areas of overlap do not end there. One can also point to tribal or indigenous religions as powerfully demonstrating the diversity of revelation's signs. Huston Smith says that anything can be "transparent to transcendence" in primal faiths.[11] Smith actually goes so far as to suggest that something is lost when experiential revelations are written down.[12] A Christian conception of divine revelation is entirely amenable to primal religions' tendency to see the world as a work of art that removes distinctions between categories (e.g., general/special revelation).[13] And in more recent religions the dynamic is present as well. For instance, the Baha'i faith has an ambitious agenda of showing how anything and everything, all of the world's seemingly disparate parts, are actually one, the whole. This is why they work so diligently against racism, sexism, and division among people based on religion. They see their stories as part of a larger narrative.

Now these comments on other religions are certainly not intended to suggest that soteric revelation happens in these traditions or, if it does, that

---

11. Smith, *World's Religions*, ch. IX.
12. Ibid., 368–70.
13. Ibid., 376.

one can remain a part of that tradition. Some of these traditions do not even recognize a supernatural deity (e.g., some forms of Buddhist thought assert that belief in the supernatural gets in the way of enlightenment). Whether soteric revelation happens in these traditions (or even needs to) are questions for other scholars and practitioners to debate. My mention of these other traditions is to suggest that narrative symbolism is flexible enough to be applied to other traditions (modifying, of course, some of the criteria for adjudicating). With the exception of Buddhism (and possibly Confucianism) this often happens through the influence of the divine, a set of practices, and a sign that initiates divine revelation.

Conclusion
Old Wine, New Wineskins

At the close of this book, it is worth reiterating that the view outlined here, while unique in the way its concepts and conclusions are reached, is not new. In fact, it is what one might call "old wine in new wineskins."

Although narratology in literary theory and the narrative paradigm in communication studies are still hotly debated and relatively new as disciplines in their own right, using narrative as a conversation partner for theology is well-trodden territory for mainline scholars in the past four decades. In *The Doctrine of Revelation: A Narrative Interpretation*, Gabriel Fackre undertakes a similar project as the one I attempted here. In many respects his project and mine have similar aims. We both believe

> Narrative is more faithful to the engaged, affect-drenched push and pull of human existence than the abstractions and manipulations of the failed culture of technocracy. Narrative reflects the drama of the times, the century of magnified horror and hope. Narrative is an attempt to find coherence in apparent incoherences, personal and social, staying close to the temporal givens rather than choosing flight to the atemporal or irrational.[1]

---

1. Fackre, *Doctrine of Revelation*, 2. I mentioned in chapter 4 that my approach differs from Fackre's in three important respects that are worth mentioning. First, Fackre uses some terminology with which I have taken issue, e.g., the general/special distinction in revelation. Whereas he supports the distinction (see, e.g., ibid, 50–54), I argued in chapters 4 and 5 each revelation in narrative symbolism is tailored to the person who receives it. Second, Fackre suggests that the Bible is the only significant revealer of doctrine (ibid, 162 and *Christian Story*, 20–29) whereas I extend revelation to any medium God decides to use to convey anything God decides to convey, which leads to the third major difference between Fackre and my approach: salvific revelation. Fackre says that revelation is the Trinity's self-disclosure (*Doctrine of Revelation*, 226), an understanding that, to my mind at least, suggests a revelation with soteric implications. However, I argued that the content of revelation is only sometimes Godself. Not all revelation is divine self-revelation, and not all revelation has salvific intentions in narrative

Moreover, the view advocated here is not dissimilar from the view advocated decades before Fackre by H. R. Niebuhr. Revelation comes through history, and "story is a well-known pedagogical device."[2] Important in Niebuhr's view is the difference between "inner" and "outer" history, "history as lived" and "history as seen."[3] Revelation is "not the succession of events which an uninterested spectator can see from the outside but our own history. . . . When we speak of revelation in the Christian church we refer to *our* history, to the history of selves or to history as it is lived and apprehended from within."[4] This distinction is crucial for Niebuhr's view of revelation, which sounds *very* similar to the view I have presented in chapter 4 with the help of narratology and the narrative paradigm: "Revelation means for us that part of our inner history which illuminates the rest of it and which is itself intelligible."[5] Niebuhr gives an example:

> Sometimes when we read a difficult book, seeking to follow a complicated argument, we come across a luminous sentence from which we can go forward and backward and so attain some understanding of the whole. Revelation is like that. . . . Revelation means this intelligible event which makes all other events intelligible.[6]

Similar to the view I have proposed, Niebuhr also says "the revelation of God is not a possession but an event, which happens over and over again when we remember the illuminating center of our history,"[7] which he takes to be Christ and I am describing as the triune God (not simply one person of/in it). Essentially, revelation is the event in which, as Whitehead suggested, "rational religion appeals to the direct intuition of special occasions, and to the elucidatory power of its concepts for all occasions."[8]

In fact, the ability of a particular revealing moment to show the larger narrative of which one is a part goes back further than Niebuhr and

---

symbolism. Unlike Fackre, who says that Christ is the interpretive tool to understand a revelation that exists in the Bible, I'm arguing that the Bible contains material with little to no bearing on the Christ. In his narrative interpretation of the doctrine of revelation, moreover, Fackre does not delve into what narratologists are actually saying these days. This, of course, is likely due to the fact that his book was written before many of the narratologists published the material we mentioned in chapter 4.

2. Niebuhr, *Meaning of Revelation*, 46.
3. Ibid., 59.
4. Ibid., 60.
5. Ibid., 93.
6. Ibid.
7. Ibid., 177.
8. Whitehead, *Religion in the Making*, 26.

Whitehead. In his *Symposium,* Plato talks about humans as fractured selves trying to become whole.[9] In narrative symbolism, we become more whole and less fractured in the event of revelation as we see our smaller story as part of a larger narrative. God's interruption of our subjectivity fractures it, but God's reformation of it begins to make it whole again, better. Bracketing out the sexual context of Aristophanes' remarks, one can appreciate the notion that when one's smaller story is connected to a larger narrative, holistic growth happens. It is "the very expression of his ancient need. And the reason is that human nature was originally one and we were a whole"[10] but fell away from oneness with the creator. Again, the idea is old wine in new wineskins.

AVENUES FOR FURTHER INQUIRY

What I have done in these pages is, admittedly, a Tillichian move, as the existential questions this generation raises are answered using the resources from the Christian tradition. After all, the business of Christian theology is to cast new light on old themes and new insights on old topics. Obviously more could be said on how revelation relates to other theological topics. Space precludes such explorations. These are hopefully features of future work, of my own and others.

Narrative symbolism does not solve every problem, and some lingering questions remain. First, although it is amenable with a wide range of conservative and liberal philosophical and theological viewpoints, and it overlaps with non-Christian religions in interesting ways, it is still an integration of the perspectives of our three primary interlocutors. Avery Dulles, George Lindbeck, and Bernard Ramm were white, male, and middle class theologians operating in a specific time (end of the twentieth-century) in a specific place (United States). So the first avenue for further inquiry is to ask the question about the origins of this model. To what extent would the

---

9. Plato, *Symposium* (online). Aristophanes conveys the myth that because we were a threat to Zeus, he decided to "humble their pride and improve their manners; men shall continue to exist, but I will cut them in two and then they will be diminished in strength and increased in numbers.... If they continue insolence and will not be quiet, I will split them again.... So ancient is the desire of one another which is implanted in us, reuniting our original nature, making one of two, and healing the state of man. Each of us when separated, having only one side only, like a flat fish, is but the indenture of a man, and he is always looking for his other half." The yearning is of something "which the soul of either evidently desires and cannot tell, and of which she has only a dark and doubtful presentiment."

10. Plato, *Symposium* (online).

model change if it accounted for or was informed by non-white, non-male, or non-middle class theological concerns? Would starting from three different thinkers change the model that is an integration of their work? Or what if the starting point were non-American yet European? There are certainly a host of German thinkers whose work is worth considering on revelation.

My hunch is that the model is flexible enough to handle the experience of *any* individual; this is due to the fact that any individual story is part of the revelation event. The clearest example of this is perhaps James Cone. In his view, theology's sources and norms were at some level drawing on the black experience, and revelation is incomprehensible without a prior understanding of the concrete manifestation of revelation in the black experience and in black history.[11] For Cone, revelation is always an event in human history. On this much the model I have provided is in full agreement. Where Cone takes it next, and where other contextual theologies take it, is resisted by narrative symbolism. Cone says divine revelation is God's self-revelation to humans *through the act of liberation*. For blacks, revelation must also correlate with black historical experience. Cone says, therefore, "revelation is a black event—it is what blacks are doing about their liberation." Cone criticized American theologians for being silent with respect to this fact. Insofar as revelation is an event in which the story of an individual is seen in the context of God's work in the world, Cone's view is compatible with narrative symbolism. But where his view is limited to liberation, narrative symbolism is not. Narrative symbolism includes liberation (as falling under the criteria of flourishing and redemption, among others), but it is not limited to it. When phrased as a question for further inquiry, this issue goes something like this: how can revelation so broadly construed be meaningfully applicable to any one person?

A potential answer worth investigating says that flourishing, creation, redemption, and consummation are profoundly *human* concerns irrespective of race, gender, and socioeconomic status. So while this is indeed worth pursuing further, this question may pose no threat to the model of divine revelation in which God interrupts and reforms a person's subjectivity by showing the ways in which their story relates to the larger narrative of God's work in the world.

Another lingering question concerns the disciplines with which this book has interacted. I have shown how literary theory and communication studies, as well as positive psychology and neurobiology shed light on what happens in the event of revelation. These other disciplines impact what philosophers of religion and theologians say and how they describe a religious

---

11. Livingston, *Twentieth-Century*, 357.

phenomenon. But might philosophy and theology impact those areas as well? Might the idea of narrative symbolism add depth and a new aesthetic dimension to the conversations happening in those fields? This is a question for further inquiry by specialists in those fields, but my hunch is that interdisciplinarity cuts both ways.

THE BRIDGE AND THE BRIDGE BUILDER

In the introduction I discussed divine revelation using the metaphor of a bridge, an approach that was reiterated in several of the thinkers I have discussed throughout. One further use of the "bridge" metaphor is needed, and it relates to conservative evangelicalism. Kathryn Tanner has recently said that "Critical assessment of a claim to knowledge requires consideration of who makes the claim, in what context and for what purpose."[12] It is only fair to the reader that I mention the concerns that motivated a study like this and the spirit in which it was undertaken.

In my own case, I am concerned with divine revelation due to the tendency in some conservative circles to mistake a created sign for the Revealer, usually subconsciously. A rigid, overly "objective" account of revelation takes the focus off of God and puts it on some created thing. Perhaps due to our finitude or sin, we crave to put that which is infinite into finite categories, to speak *ad nauseum* about that which is ultimately ineffable. We search for ways to put our world into little boxes we can understand and/or control. Perhaps the model here has unknowingly done the same.

Nevertheless, so long as evangelicals keep a "point and shoot" hermeneutic, irrespective of the place of a particular passage in context or in ways that ensure their academic irrelevance, this book has tried to correct them. These problems have enabled me to find a model that, I believe, elevates God beyond that of any of the other models operating today. It also does justice to concerns of higher criticism, as the text is a tool rather than an end in itself. This model is also remarkably egalitarian since everyone tells stories and many worldviews share the act of situating those stories amidst larger narratives. My hope is that this book plays a part in building bridges between conservative evangelicalism and those on the moderate-to-liberal side of things. To that extent, this has been an exercise in "postconservative" thinking about revelation.

People like me worry that if the Word of God is only written, then those without eyes to see are doomed. If the Word of God is only preached, those without the ability to hear are as well. Sight and hearing are also

---

12. Tanner, "Shifts in Theology," 41.

metaphors, of course, for if the Word of God is limited to any created thing or any single action a human performs, it is limited.

When narrative symbolism is coupled with the soteric/non-soteric distinction, the Word is unleashed. This happens when one prizes and prioritizes the Author rather than the medium through which the Author or Author's values are communicated. In the process, the Author will speak in all sorts of ways, some expected and some unexpected. The Author speaks directly to human souls desperately in need of good news, assuring them in soteric revelation that he exists, cares about them, and has good plans in store for their future. Soteric and non-soteric revelations alike involve *everyone's* story. The lesson here is that the content of *our* story matters to God; *we* matter to God. However small, anything and any event can be "transparent to transcendence."

When we wonder if there is a way into the Author's country from our individual worlds, the Author responds "There is a way into my country from *all* the worlds." When we ask for directions on how to get from here to there, the Author says he has been and will continue to show us: "I will be telling you all the time." When we ask how long until we get there, the Author responds, "I will not tell you how long or short the way will be; only that it lies across a river." And as we make our way there, when the river's waters are rising fast, at the moment of our breaking when we cannot muster the fortitude to move on, when good news seems like fiction, then the Author meets us directly, momentarily silencing the water's roar, and whispers into the chaos, "Do not fear . . . for I am the great Bridge Builder."[13]

---

13. Lewis, *Dawn Treader*, 215.

Bibliography

Abbott, S.J., Walter M., ed. *The Documents of Vatican II*. Translated by J. Gallagher. New York: Herder and Herder, 1966.
Abdul-Masih, Marguerite. *Edward Schillebeeckx and Hans Frei: A Conversation on Method and Christology*. Waterloo, Ontario: Wilfrid Laurier University Press, 2001.
Adam, Karl. "Die Theologie der Krisis." In *Hochland: Monatschrift fur alle Gebiete des Wissens, der Literatur und Kunst, 23*, 271–86. Munchen: Kempten, 1926.
Aquinas, Thomas. *Summa Contra Gentiles*. Translated by A. C. Pegis. Notre Dame: University of Notre Dame Press, 1955.
Aristotle. *The Basic Works of Aristotle*. Edited by R. McKeon. New York: Random House, 1941.
Arnett, R. C., and P. Arneson. *Dialogic Civility in a Cynical Age*. Albany, NY: State University of New York Press, 1999.
Augustine. *De Trinitate*. Translated by E. Hill. Hyde Park, NY: New City, 1991.
———. "Sermon 52: The Trinity." In *Sermons*. Translated by E. Hill. Edited by J. Rotelle. Brooklyn, NY: New City Press, 1997.
Balmer, Randall. *The Making of Evangelicalism: From Revivalism to Politics and Beyond*. Waco, TX: Baylor University Press, 2010.
———. *Thy Kingdom Come: How the Religious Right Distorts the Faith and Threatens America: An Evangelical's Lament*. New York: Basic, 2006.
Balthasar, Hans Urs von. *The Glory of the Lord: A Theological Aesthetics: Seeing the Form*. Translated by E. Leiva-Merikakis. San Francisco: Ignatius, 1982.
———. *Heart of the World*. Translated by E. Leiva. San Francisco: Ignatius, 1979.
———. *Theo-Drama: Theological Dramatic Theory*, vol. 4: *The Action*. Translated by G. Harrison. San Francisco: Ignatius, 1994.
———. *Theo-Drama: Theological Dramatic Theory*, vol. 5: *The Last Act*. Translated by G. Harrison. San Francisco: Ignatius, 1983.
———. *The Theology of Karl Barth*. New York: Hold, Rinehart and Winston, 1971.
———. *You Crown the Year with your Goodness: Radio Sermons*. Translated by G. Harrison. San Francisco: Ignatius, 1989.
Barth, Karl. *Church Dogmatics*. Edited by G. W. Bromiley and T. F. Torrance. 4 vols. Edinburgh, T. & T. Clark, 1932–67.
———. *The Epistle to the Romans*. Translated by E. Hoskyns. New York: Oxford University Press, 1968.

———. *Die Lehre vom Worte Gottes. Prolegomena zur christlichen Dogmatik.* Munich: Kaiser, 1927.

Bateson, Gregory. *Mind and Nature: A Necessary Unity.* Toronto: Bantam, 1979.

Bebbington, David. *Evangelicalism in Modern Britain.* New York: Routledge, 1989.

Benveniste, Emile. *Problems in General Linguistics.* Translated by M. E. Meek. Coral Gables, FL: University of Miami Press, 1971.

Blech, Benjamin, and Roy Doliner. *The Sistine Secrets: Michelangelo's Forbidden Messages in the Heart of the Vatican.* San Francisco: HarperCollins, 2009.

Bonhoeffer, Dietrich. *Letters and Papers from Prison.* Edited by E. Bethge. New York: Macmillan, 1967.

Boys, Mary C. *Biblical Interpretation in Religious Education.* Birmingham: Religious Education Press, 1980.

Bracken, Joseph. *The One and the Many: A Contemporary Reconstruction of the God-World Relationship.* Grand Rapids: Eerdmans, 2001.

Brown, David. *Transformational Preaching: Theory and Practice.* College Station, TX: Virtual Book Worm, 2003.

Bultmann, R., and A. Weiser. *Faith.* London: Black, 1961.

Calvin, John. *Institutes of the Christian Religion.* Translated by F. L. Battles. Edited by J. T. McNeill. Philadelphia: Westminster, 1977.

Caputo, John. *Radical Hermeneutics.* Bloomington, IN: Indiana University Press, 1987.

Castle, Gregory. *The Blackwell Guide to Literary Theory.* Malden, MA: Blackwell, 2007.

Clayton, Philip. *Transforming Christian Theology: For Church and World.* Minneapolis: Fortress, 2010.

Cleage, Albert. *The Black Messiah.* New York: Sheed and Ward, 1968.

Collins, John J. *Introduction to the Hebrew Bible.* Minneapolis: Fortress, 2004.

Comstock, Gary. "Two Types of Narrative Theology." In *Journal of the American Academy of Religion* 55.4 (1987) 687–717.

Cone, James. *A Black Theology of Liberation.* Philadelphia: Lippencot, 1970.

———. *Black Theology, Black Power.* Maryknoll, NY: Orbis, 1997.

Craigo-Snell, Shannon, and Shawnthea Monroe, *Living Christianity: A Pastoral Theology for Today.* Minneapolis: Fortress, 2009.

Craigo-Snell, Shannon. *The Empty Church: Theater, Theology, and Bodily Hope.* New York: Oxford University Press, 2014.

Crenshaw, James. *Samson: A Secret Betrayed, A Vow Ignored.* Atlanta: John Knox, 1978.

Cross, F. L., ed. *The Oxford Dictionary of the Christian Church.* New York: Oxford University Press, 2005.

Cullmann, Oscar. *Salvation in History.* New York: Harper & Row, 1967.

Dalferth, Ingolf. *Philosophy and Theology.* Eugene, OR: Wipf and Stock, 2001.

Dalferth, Ingolf, and Michael Ch. Rodgers. *Revelation: Claremont Studies in the Philosophy of Religion, Conference 2012.* Tübingen: Mohr Siebeck, 2012.

Davies, Brian. *The Thought of Thomas Aquinas.* Oxford: Clarendon, 1993.

Davis, E., and R. Hays, eds. *The Art of Reading Scripture.* Grand Rapids: Eerdmans, 2003.

Davis, Stephen T. *The Debate about the Bible: Inerrancy versus Infallibility.* Philadelphia: Westminster, 1977.

———. *Encountering Evil: Live Options in Theodicy.* Atlanta: John Knox, 1981.

———. "Hierarchical Causes in the Cosmological Argument." *International Journal for Philosophy of Religion*, 31.1 (1992) 13–27.

———. *Logic and the Nature of God*. Grand Rapids: Eerdmans, 1983.
Flint, Thomas P., and Michael Rae, eds. *The Oxford Handbook of Philosophical Theology*. New York: Oxford University Press, 2009.
Derrida, Jacques. *Archive Fever: A Freudian Impression*. Translated by E. Prenowitz. Chicago: University of Chicago Press, 1996.
———. *Margins of Philosophy*. Translated by A. Bass. Chicago: University of Chicago Press, 1982.
———. *The Other Heading: Reflections on Today's Europe*. Translated by P. Brault and M. Naas. Bloomington, IN: Indiana University Press, 1992.
Dinehart, Stephen. "Transmedia Play." PhD diss., University of Southern California, 2006.
Dulles, Avery. *The Assurance of Things Hoped For: A Theology of Christian Faith*. New York: Oxford University Press, 1994.
———. *Church and Society: The Lawrence J. McGinley Lectures, 1988–2007*. Bronx, NY: Fordham University Press, 2008.
———. *A Church to Believe in Discipleship and the Dynamics of Freedom*. New York: Crossroad, 1982.
———. *The Craft of Theology: From Symbol to System*. New York: Crossroad, 1992.
———. *Magisterium: Teacher and Guardian of the Faith*. Naples, FL: Ave Maria Press of Sapientia University, 2007.
———. *Models of Revelation*. Maryknoll, NY: Orbis, 1992.
———. *Models of the Church*. Garden City, NY: Double Day, 2002.
———. "The Orthodox Imperative." *First Things* (August/September 2006). No pages. Online: http://www.firstthings.com/article/2006/08/002-the-orthodox-imperative
———. *Revelation and the Quest for Unity*. Washington, DC: Corpus, 1968.
———. *Revelation Theology: A History*. New York: Herder and Herder, 1969.
———. *The Survival of Dogma: Faith, Authority, and Dogma in a Changing World*. New York: Crossroad, 1982.
Ehrman, Bart. *Misquoting Jesus: The Story of Who Changed the Bible and Why*. San Francisco: Harper Collins, 2005.
Eliade, Mircea. *Myth and Reality*. Translated by W. Trask. New York: Harper Torchbooks, 1963.
———. *The Sacred and the Profane*. Translated by W. Trask. New York: Harvest, 1959.
Erickson, Millard. *The Evangelical Left: Encountering Postconservative Evangelical Theology*. Grand Rapids: Baker Academic, 1997.
Estep, Alison, and Anthony, *A Theology for Christian Education*. Grand Rapids: B. & H., 2008.
Fackre, Gabriel. *The Christian Story: A Narrative Interpretation of Basic Christian Doctrine*. Grand Rapids: Eerdmans, 1978.
———. *The Doctrine of Revelation: A Narrative Interpretation*. Grand Rapids: Eerdmans, 1997.
Feuerbach, Ludwig. *The Essence of Christianity*. Translated by G. Elliot; New York: Prometheus, 1989.
Fields, Stephen, S.J. "The Singular as Event: Postmodernism, Rahner, and Balthasar." *American Catholic Philosophical Quarterly* 77.1 (2003) 93–111.

Finstuen, Andrew S. *Everyday Protestants and Original Sin: The Theology of Reinhold Niebuhr, Billy Graham, and Paul Tillich in an Age of Anxiety*. Chapel Hill, NC: University of North Carolina Press, 2009.

Fishbane, Michael. *Text and Texture: Close Readings of Selected Biblical Texts*. New York: Schocken Books, 1979.

Fisher, Walter R. *Human Communication as Narration: Toward a Philosophy of Reason, Value, and Action*. Columbia, SC: University of South Carolina Press, 1987.

———. "The Narrative Paradigm: An Elaboration." *Communication Monographs* 52.4 (1985) 347–67.

———. "The Narrative Paradigm: In the Beginning." *Journal of Communication* 35.4 (1985) 74–89.

Fletcher, Jeanine Hill. *Monopoly on Salvation: A Feminist Approach to Religious Pluralism*. London: Continuum, 2005.

Ford, David. *Barth and God's Story: Biblical Narrative and the Theological Method of Karl Barth in the Church Dogmatics*. Frankfurt: Lang, 1985.

———. *The Modern Theologians: An Introduction to Christian Theology Since 1918*. Malden, MA: Blackwell, 2005.

Forster, E. M. *Aspects of the Novel*. London: Methuen, 1927.

Fraassen, Bas van. *The Empirical Stance*. New Haven, CT: Yale University Press, 2002.

Franke, John. *The Character of Theology: A Postconservative Evangelical Approach*. Grand Rapids: Baker Academic, 2005.

Frei, Hans. "The Doctrine of Revelation in the Thought of Karl Barth, 1909–1922: The Nature of Barth's Break with Liberalism." PhD diss., Yale University, 1956.

———. *The Eclipse of Biblical Narrative: A Study in Eighteenth and Nineteenth Century Hermeneutics*. New Haven, CT: Yale University Press, 1974.

———. *The Identity of Jesus Christ: The Hermeneutical Bases of Dogmatic Theology*. Philadelphia: Fortress, 1975.

———. *Types of Christian Theology*. Edited by G. Hunsinger and W. Placher. New Haven, CT: Yale University Press, 1992.

———. Unpublished lecture notes from the series "Contemporary Issues in Theology." Delivered January-March 1975. In Frances M. Henderson. "The Logic of Belief and the Content of God: Hans Frei's Theological Grammar." PhD diss., University of Edinburgh, 2010.

Frodeman, R., J. T. Klein, and C. Mitcham, eds., *The Oxford Handbook of Interdisciplinarity*. New York: Oxford University Press, 2010.

Gallagher, Shaun. *How the Body Shapes the Mind*. New York: Oxford University Press, 2006.

Geisler, Norman, ed. *Inerrancy*. Grand Rapids: Zondervan, 1980.

Gordis, Daniel. *God Was Not in the Fire: The Search for a Spiritual Judaism*. New York: Simon and Schuster, 1997.

Graham, Billy. "Biblical Authority in Evangelicalism." *Christianity Today* 1.1 (1956) 5–7, 17.

Green, Clifford, ed. *Karl Barth: Theologian of Freedom*. Minneapolis: Fortress, 1991.

Green, M., J. Strange, and T. Brock, eds. *Narrative Impact: Social and Cognitive Foundations*. Mahwah, NJ: Erlbaum, 2002.

Greene-McCreight, Kathryn. *Feminist Reconstructions of Christian Doctrine*. New York: Oxford University Press, 2000.

Greimas, A. J. *Du sens: essais semiotiques*. Paris: Seuil, 1970.

Greimas, A. J., and Joseph Courtes, *Semiotics and Language: An Analytical Dictionary.* Translated by L. Crist et al. Bloomington, IN: University of Indiana Press, 1982.

Grenz, Stanley, and John R. Franke. *Beyond Foundationalism: Shaping Theology in a Postmodern Context.* Louisville: Westminster John Knox, 2001.

Grenz, Stanley, and Roger Olson. *20th Century Theology: God and the World in a Transitional Age.* Downers Grove, IL: IVP, 1992.

———. *Who Needs Theology? An Invitation to the Study of God.* Downers Grove, IL: IVP, 1996.

Grenz, Stanley J. *Rediscovering the Triune God: The Trinity in Contemporary Theology.* Minneapolis: Fortress, 2004.

———. *Renewing the Center: Evangelical Theology in a Post-Theological Era.* Grand Rapids: Baker, 2000.

———. *The Social God and the Relational Self: A Trinitarian Theology of the Imago Dei.* Louisville: Westminster John Knox, 2001.

———. *Theology for the Community of God.* Grand Rapids: Eerdmans, 2000.

Groden, M., and M. Kreiswirth, eds. *The Johns Hopkins Guide to Literary Theory & Criticism.* Baltimore: Johns Hopkins University Press, 1994.

Grudem, Wayne. *Systematic Theology: An Introduction to Biblical Doctrine.* Grand Rapids: Zondervan, 1994.

Gunn, David. *The Fate of King Saul: An Interpretation of a Biblical Story.* Journal for the Study of the Old Testament Supplement Series 14. Sheffield, UK: Sheffield Academic Press, 1980.

———. *The Story of King David: Genre and Interpretation.* Journal for the Study of the Old Testament Supplement Series 6. Sheffield: Sheffield Academic Press, 1978.

Gustafson, James M. "Just What Is 'Postliberal' Theology?" *Christian Century* 116.10 (1999) 353–55.

———. "Liberal Questions: A Response to William Placher." *Christian Century* 116.12 (1999) 422–25.

Gutierrez, Gustavo. *Doing Theology in a Revolutionary Situation.* Philadelphia: Fortress, 1975.

———. *A Theology of Liberation: History, Politics, and Salvation.* Maryknoll, NY: Orbis, 1988.

Hagerty, Barbara Bradley "Doomsday Redux: Prophet Says World Will End Friday." *NPR News: Morning Edition.* October 18, 2011. No pages. Online: http://www.npr.org/2011/10/18/141427151/doomsday-redux-prophet-says-world-will-end-friday.

Halverson, Marvin, and Arthur Cohen, eds. *A Handbook of Christian Theology: Essential Information for Every Christian.* London: Fontana, 1958.

Hardy, Barbara "Towards a Poetics of Fiction: An Approach Through Narrative." *Novel* 2.1 (1968) 5–14.

Hauerwas, Stanley. *Hannah's Child: A Theological Memoir.* Grand Rapids: Eerdmans, 2010.

Heim, S. Mark. *The Depth of the Riches: A Trinitarian Theology of Religious Ends.* Grand Rapids: Eerdmans, 2000.

Henderson, Frances M. "The Logic of Belief and the Content of God: Hans Frei's Theological Grammar." PhD diss., University of Edinburgh, 2010.

Henry, Carl. *Confessions of a Theologian.* Waco, TX: Word, 1986.

———. *Frontiers in Modern Theology.* Chicago: Moody, 1964.

———. *God, Revelation and Authority*, vols. 1–6. Waco: TX: Word, 1967–83.
———. *The Protestant Dilemma*. Grand Rapids: Eerdmans, 1949.
———. *Towards a Recovery of Christian Belief*. Wheaton, IL: Crossway, 1990.
———. *The Uneasy Conscience of Modern Fundamentalism*. Grand Rapids: Eerdmans, 1947.
Hick, John. *God Has Many Names*. Philadelphia: Westminster, 1982.
Higton, Mike. Review of *Edward Schillebeeckx and Hans Frei: A Conversation on Method and Christology* in *Modern Theology*, by M. Abdul-Masih. *Modern Theology* 19.4 (2003) 590–92.
Hodgson, Peter C., and Robert H. King, eds. *Readings in Christian Theology*. Minneapolis: Fortress, 1985.
Holcomb, Justin, ed. *Christian Theologies of Scripture: A Comparative Introduction*. New York: New York University Press, 2006.
Hume, David. *An Enquiry Concerning Human Understanding*. New York: Oxford University Press, 1999.
Hymes, Dell. *Language in Education: Ethnolinguistic Essays*. Washington, DC: Center for Applied Linguistics, 1980.
Jenkins, Willis. *Ecologies of Grace: Environmental Ethics and Christian Theology*. New York: Oxford University Press, 2008.
John Paul II, "Apostolic Constitution: Fidei Depositum." In *Catechism of the Catholic Church*. New York: Doubleday, 1995.
———. "On Liberation Theology." No pages. Online: www.bbc.co.uk/religion/religions/christianity/beliefs/liberationtheology.shtml.
Johnson, Elizabeth. *Quest for the Living God: Mapping Frontiers in the Theology of God*. New York: Continuum, 2007.
Johnson, Luke Timothy. *The Creed: What Christians Believe and Why It Matters*. New York: Doubleday, 2003.
Jones, Gareth, ed. *The Blackwell Companion to Modern Theology*. Malden, MA: Blackwell, 2004.
Jones, Serene. *Trauma and Grace: Theology in a Ruptured World*. Louisville: Westminster John Knox, 2009.
Kant, Immanuel. *Prolegomena to Any Future Metaphysics*. Translated by G. Hatfield. Cambridge: Cambridge University Press, 2004.
Kelsey, David H. *Eccentric Existence: A Theological Anthropology*. Louisville: Westminster John Knox, 2009.
———. Warfield Lectures. Delivered at Princeton Theological Seminary, March 2011.
Kierkegaard, Søren. *Journals of Søren Kierkegaard*. Translated by A. Dru. Oxford: Oxford University Press, 1948.
Kim, Donald, ed. *How Karl Barth Changed My Mind*. Grand Rapids: Eerdmans, 1986.
King, Jr., Martin Luther. "Revelation." No pages. Online. www.thekingcenter.org
King, Stephen. *On Writing, 10th Anniversary Edition*. New York: Scribner, 2010.
Kirmse, Ann-Marie, and Michael M. Canaris, eds. *The Legacy of Avery Cardinal Dulles, S.J.: His Words and His Witness*. New York: Fordham University Press, 2011.
Kittredge, Cynthia Briggs, et al., eds. *The Bible in the Public Square: Reading the Signs of the Times*. Minneapolis: Fortress, 2008.
Knitter, Paul. *Introducing Theologies of Religions*. Maryknoll, NY: Orbis, 2002.
Leitch, Vincent B. *Postmodernism—Local Effects, Global Flaws*. Albany, NY: State University of New York Press, 1996.

Lewis, C. S. *The Problem of Pain*. New York: Touchstone, 1996.
———. *The Voyage of the Dawn Treader*. New York: Collier, 1952.
Lindbeck, George, *The Church in a Postliberal Age*. Grand Rapids: Eerdmans, 2002.
———. *Dialogue on the Way: Protestants Report from Rome on the Vatican Council*. Minneapolis: Augsburg, 1965.
———. "The Gospel's Uniqueness: Election and Untranslatability." *Modern Theology* 13.4 (1997) 423–50.
———. *The Nature of Doctrine: Religion and Theology in a Postliberal Age*. Louisville: Westminster John Knox, 1984.
———. "Unbelievers and the '*Sola Christi*.'" *Dialog* 12 (1973) 182–89.
Livingston, James, ed. *Modern Christian Thought: The Twentieth-Century*. Minneapolis: Fortress, 2006.
Locke, John. *An Essay Concerning Human Understanding*. Edited by P. Nidditch. Oxford: Oxford University Press, 1975.
Lohse, Bernhard. *Martin Luther: An Introduction to his Life and Work*. Minneapolis: Augsburg Fortress, 2000.
Longfellow, Henry Wadsworth. *The Poetical Works of Henry Wadsworth Longfellow: With Numerous Illustrations*. New York: Houghton, Mifflin and Company, 1885.
Lopez, Antonio. "Eternal Happening: God as an Event of Love." *Communio* 32 (2005) 214–45.
Lopez, S., ed. *The Encyclopedia of Positive Psychology*. Malden, MA.: Blackwell, 2009.
MacAskill, Ewen. "George Bush: 'God told me to end the tyranny in Iraq.'" *The Guardian* Oct 7, 2005. No pages. Online: http://www.theguardian.com/world/2005/oct/07/iraq.usa.
MacIntyre, Alasdair. *After Virtue: A Study in Moral Theory*. Notre Dame, IN: University of Notre Dame Press, 1981.
Macquarrie, John. *Paths in Spirituality*. London: SCM, 1972.
Mangina, Joseph. *Karl Barth: Theologian of Church Witness*. Burlington, VT: Ashgate, 2004.
Mansini, Guy. "Balthasar and the Theodramatic Enrichment of the Trinity." *The Thomist* 64 (2000) 499–519.
Marmion, Declan, and Mary E. Hines, eds. *The Cambridge Companion to Karl Rahner*. Cambridge: Cambridge University Press, 2005.
Marshall, Bruce, ed. *Theology and Dialogue: Essays in Conversation with George Lindbeck*. South Bend, IN: University of Notre Dame Press, 1990.
McBrien, Richard P. *Catholicism: Study Edition*. Minneapolis: Winston, 1981.
McGrath, Alister, ed. *The Blackwell Companion to Modern Theology*. Malden MA: Blackwell, 1993.
———. *The Christian Theology Reader*. Malden, MA: Blackwell, 2005.
Meier, John P. *A Marginal Jew: Rethinking the Historical Jesus*, vols. 1–4. New Haven, CT: Yale University Press, 2001–9.
Merriam Webster Dictionary. No pages. Online: www.merriam-webster.com/dictionary
Metz, Johann Baptist. *A Passion for God: The Mystical-Political Dimension of Christianity*. New York: Paulist, 1997.
Milbank, John. *Theology and Social Theory: Beyond Secular Reason*. Oxford: Blackwell, 1990.

Min, Anselm, *Dialectics of Salvation: Issues in the Theology of Liberation*. New York: SUNY, 1989.
Mitchell, Nathan. "Symbols Are Actions, Not Objects." *Living Worship* 13.2 (1977) 1–4.
Moltmann, Jürgen. *A Broad Place: An Autobiography*. Translated by M. Kohl. Minneapolis: Fortress, 2009.
———. *Anfange der dialektischen Theologie*. Munich: Kaiser, 1966.
Morson, Gary Saul. *Narrative and Freedom: The Shadows of Time*. New Haven, CT: Yale University Press, 1994.
Murphy, Francesca Aran. *God is Not a Story: Realism Revisited*. New York: Oxford University Press, 2007.
Neusner, Jacob, ed. *World Religions in America*. Louisville: Westminster John Knox, 2010.
Nicholson, William. *Shadowlands*. London: Samuel French, 1989.
Niebuhr, H. Richard. *Christ and Culture*. New York: Harper Colophon, 1975.
———. *The Kingdom of God in America*. New York: Harper and Row, 1937.
———. *The Meaning of Revelation*. New York: Macmillan, 1946.
Niebuhr, Reinhold. *Man's Nature and His Communities: Essays on the Dynamics and Enigmas of Man's Personal and Social Existence*. New York: Scribner's sons, 1965.
Noll, Mark, et al., eds. *Evangelicalism*. New York: Oxford University Press, 1994.
O'Hanlon, Gerard F., S.J., *The Immutability of God in the Theology of Hans Urs von Balthasar*. Cambridge: Cambridge University Press, 1990.
O'Meara, T. F. "Toward a Subjective Theology of Revelation." *Theological Studies* 26 (1975) 401–27.
O'Neill, Onora. "The Power of Example." *Philosophy* 61 (1986) 5–29.
Oden, Thomas, ed. *Ancient Christian Commentary on Scripture*. Downers Grove, IL: IVP, 1998.
Okholm, Dennis, and T. Phillips, eds. *Four Views of Salvation in a Pluralistic World*. Grand Rapids: Zondervan, 1995.
———. *The Nature of Confession: Evangelicals and Postliberals in Conversation*. Downers Grove, IL: Intervarsity, 1996.
Olson, Roger. *How to Be Evangelical without Being Conservative*. Grand Rapids: Zondervan, 2008.
———. *Reformed and Always Reforming: The Postconservative Approach to Evangelical Theology*. Grand Rapids: Baker Academic, 2007.
Ormerod, Neil. *Introducing Contemporary Theologies: The What and the Who of Theology Today*. Maryknoll, NY: Orbis, 1997.
Packer, J. I. *The Evangelical Anglican Identity Problem: An Analysis*. Oxford: Latimer House, 1978.
Padgett, A., and P. Keifert, eds. *But Is It All True? The Bible and the Question of Truth*. Grand Rapids: Eerdmans, 2006.
Panikkar, Raimon. *The Experience of God: Icons of the Mystery*. Minneapolis: Fortress, 2006.
Pannenberg, Wolfhart. *Faith and Reality*. Philadelphia: Westminster, 1977.
———. *Revelation as History*. New York: Macmillan, 1969.
———. *What Is Man?* Philadelphia: Fortress, 1970.
Parker, Trey, et al. *The Book of Mormon: The Complete Book and Lyrics of the Broadway Musical*. New York: New Market, 2011.

Perrin, Nicholas. *Jesus and the Language of the Kingdom.* Philadelphia: Westminster, 1976.
Pesch, Christian. *Praelectiones dogmaticae,* vol. 1. Freiburg: Herder, 1915.
Peterson, Christopher "The Values in Action (VIA) Classification of Strengths." In *Life Worth Living: Contributions to Positive Psychology,* edited by Mihaly Csikscentmihalyi and Isabella Selega Csikszentmihalyi, 29–48 New York: Oxford University Press, 2006.
Pickstock, Catherine, and Graham Ward, eds. *Radical Orthodoxy: A New Theology.* London: Routledge, 1999.
Pitstick, Alyssa Lyra. *Light in Darkness: Hans Urs von Balthasar and the Catholic Doctrine of Christ's Descent into Hell.* Grand Rapids: Eerdmans, 2007.
Placher, William C. "Being Postliberal: A Response to James Gustafson." *Christian Century* 116.11 (1999) 390–92.
———. *Essentials of Christian Theology.* Louisville: Westminster John Knox, 2003.
———. *Unapologetic Theology: A Christian Voice in a Pluralistic Conversation.* Louisville: Westminster John Knox, 1989.
Plato, *Symposium.* No pages. Online: http://classics.mit.edu/Plato/symposium.html
Pojman, Louis, ed., *Philosophy of Religion: An Anthology.* Belmont, CA: Wadsworth/Thomson Learning; 2003.
Prince, Gerald. *Dictionary of Narratology.* Omaha, NE: University of Nebraska Press, 2003.
Propp, Vladimir. *Morphology of the Folktale.* Translated by Lawrence Scott. Austin, TX: University of Texas Press, 1968.
Punday, Daniel. *Narrative After Deconstruction.* Albany, NY: State University of New York Press, 2003.
Rae, Michael, and Oliver Crisp, eds. *Analytic Theology: New Essays in the Philosophy of Theology.* New York: Oxford University Press, 2009.
Rahner, Karl, and Joseph Ratzinger, *Revelation and Tradition.* New York: Herder and Herder, 1966.
Rahner, Karl, ed. *Encyclopedia of Theology: The Concise Sacramentum Mundi.* New York: Seabury, 1975.
———. *Foundations of the Christian Faith: An Introduction to the Idea of Christianity.* Translated by W. Dych. New York: Crossroad, 2005.
———. *Hearers of the Word: Laying the Foundation for a Philosophy of Religion.* Translated by J. Danceel. New York: Crossroad, 2005.
———. *Inspiration in the Bible.* Translated by C. Henkey. Edinburgh: Nelson, 1961.
———. *Our Christian Faith: Answers for the Future.* Translated by Karl-Heinz Weger. New York: Crossroad, 1981.
———. *The Trinity.* Translated by J. Donceel. New York: Crossroad, 2005.
———. *Theological Investigations.* 23 vols. London: Darton, Longman and Todd, 1961–84.
Rambo, Shelly. *Spirit and Trauma: A Theology of Remaining.* Louisville: Westminster John Knox, 2010.
Ramm, Bernard. *After Fundamentalism: The Future of Evangelical Theology.* San Francisco: Harper & Row, 1983.
———. *The Christian View of Science and Scripture.* Grand Rapids: Eerdmans, 1955.
———. *The Evangelical Heritage: A Study in Historical Theology.* Waco, TX: Word, 1973.

———. *The Evangelical Heritage: A Study in Historical Theology*. 2nd ed. Grand Rapids: Baker, 2000.

———. *The God Who Makes a Difference: A Christian Appeal to Reason*. Waco, TX: Word, 1972.

———. *His Way Out*. Glendale, CA: Regal, 1974.

———. *Protestant Christian Evidences: A Textbook of the Evidences of the Truthfulness of the Christian Faith for Conservative Protestants*. Chicago: Moody, 1953.

———. *Special Revelation and the Word of God*. Grand Rapids: Eerdmans, 1961.

———. *The Witness of the Spirit: An Essay on the Contemporary Relevance of the Internal Witness of the Holy Spirit*. Grand Rapids: Eerdmans, 1959.

Ratzinger, Joseph. *God's Word: Scripture—Tradition—Office*. San Francisco: Ignatius, 2008.

———. *Introduction to Christianity*. Translated by J. R. Foster. San Francisco: Communio, 1969.

———. *Principles of Catholic Theology*. San Francisco: Ignatius, 1987.

Richardson, A. *History Sacred and Profane*. Philadelphia: Westminster, 1964.

Riches, John. *The Analogy of Beauty: The Theology of Hans Urs von Balthasar*. Edinburgh: T. & T. Clark, 1986.

Riley, Gregory. *One Jesus, Many Christs: How Jesus Inspired Not One True Christianity, but Many*. Minneapolis: Fortress, 2000.

Ritschl, Albrecht. *The Christian Doctrine of Justification and Reconciliation*. Translated by H. R. Mackintosh and A. B. Macaulay. Edinburgh: T. & T. Clark, 1900.

Roberts, J. Deotis. *Africentric Christianity: A Theological Appraisal for Ministry*. Valley Forge, PA: Judson, 2000.

Roberts, Kathleen Glenister "Texturing the Narrative Paradigm: Folklore and Communication." *Communication Quarterly* 52.2 (2004) 129–42.

Roberts, Robert C., ed. *Limning the Psyche: Explorations in Christian Psychology*. Grand Rapids: Eerdmans, 1998.

Ruether, Rosemary Radford. *Catholic Does Not Equal the Vatican: A Vision for Progressive Catholicism*. New York: New Press, 2008.

———. *Sexism and God-Talk: Toward a Feminist Theology*. Boston: Beacon, 1983.

Saatkamp, H., ed. *Rorty and Pragmatism: The Philosopher Responds to His Critics*. Nashville: Vanderbilt University Press, 1995.

Sabatier, A. *Outlines of a Philosophy of Religion Based on Psychology and History*. London: Hodder & Stoughton, 1897.

Sasson, Jack. *Ruth: A New Translation with a Philological Commentary and a Formalist-Folklorist Interpretation*. Baltimore: Johns Hopkins University Press, 1979.

Schleiermacher, Friedrich. *On Religion: Speeches to Its Cultured Despisers*. Translated by J. Oman; Louisville: Westminster John Knox, 1994.

Scola, Angelo. *Hans Urs von Balthasar: A Theological Style*. Grand Rapids: Eerdmans, 1995.

Segal, Robert. *Myth: A Very Short Introduction*. New York: Oxford University Press, 2004.

Seligman, Martin. *Authentic Happiness: Using the New Positive Psychology to Realize Your Potential for Lasting Fulfillment*. New York: Free, 2002.

Shermer, Michael. *The Believing Brain: From Ghosts and Gods to Politics and Conspiracies*. New York: Times, 2011.

———. *Why People Believe Weird Things: Pseudoscience, Superstition, and Other Confusions of Our Time*. New York: Freeman, 1997.
Shults, F. LeRon. *Reforming the Doctrine of God*. Grand Rapids: Eerdmans, 2005.
Smith, Christian. *The Bible Made Impossible: Why Biblicism is Not a Truly Evangelical Reading of Scripture*. Grand Rapids: Brazos, 2011.
Smith, Huston. *The World's Religions*. San Francisco: HarperOne, 2009.
Smith, K., J. Lalitha, and D. Hawk, eds. *Evangelical Postcolonial Conversations: Global Awakenings in Theology and Praxis*. Downers Grove: IVP Academic, 2014.
Spiegel, James, and Steven Cowan. *The Love of Wisdom: A Christian Introduction to Philosophy*. Nashville: B. & H. , 2009.
Spiegel, James. *The Benefits of Providence: A New Look at Divine Sovereignty*. Wheaton, IL: Crossway, 2005.
Spretnak, Charlene. *States of Grace: The Recovery of Meaning in the Postmodern Age*. San Francisco: Harper Collins, 1991.
Stibbe, Mark. *John as Storyteller*. Cambridge: Cambridge University Press, 1992.
Stone, Jerome. *Religious Naturalism Today: The Rebirth of a Forgotten Alternative*. New York: State University of New York Press, 2009.
Stott, J. R. W. *Fundamentalism and Evangelicalism*. London: For the Evangelical Alliance by Crusade, 1956.
Stout, Jeffrey. *Ethics After Babel: The Language of Morals and Their Discontents*. Boston: Beacon, 1988.
Strange, J. J., and C. C. Leung. "How Anecdotal Accounts in News and in Fiction Can Influence Judgments of a Social Problem's Urgency, Causes, and Cures." *Personality and Social Psychology Bulletin* 25.4 (1999) 436–49.
Stump, Eleonore. *Wandering in Darkness: Narrative and the Problem of Suffering*. Oxford: Clarendon, 2010.
Sykes, S. W., ed. *Sacrifice and Redemption: Durham Essays in Theology*. Cambridge: Cambridge University Press, 1991.
Tanner, K., and C. Hall, eds. *Ancient and Postmodern Christianity: Paleo-Orthodoxy in the 21st Century*. Downers Grove, IL: IVP, 2002.
Tanner, Kathryn. *Christ the Key*. Cambridge: Cambridge University Press, 2010.
———. *Economy of Grace*. Minneapolis: Fortress, 2005.
———. *God and Creation in Christian Theology*. Minneapolis: Fortress, 1988.
———. "How My Mind has Changed." *Christian Century* 127.4 (2010) 40–45.
———. "Incarnation, Cross, and Sacrifice: A Feminist-Inspired Re-appraisal." *Anglican Theological Review* 86.1 (2004) 35–56.
———. *Jesus, Humanity and the Trinity: A Brief Systematic Theology*. Minneapolis: Fortress, 2001.
———. *The Politics of God: Christian Theologies and Social Justice*. Minneapolis: Fortress, 1992.
———. "Shifts in Theology over the Last Quarter Century." *Modern Theology* 26.1 (2010) 39–44.
———. Warfield Lectures. Delivered at Princeton Theological Seminary, March 2011.
Teresa, Mother. *Come Be My Light: The Private Writings of the "Saint of Calcutta."* New York: Crown, 2007.
Thiele, Leslie Paul. *The Heart of Judgment: Practical Wisdom, Neuroscience, and Narrative*. Cambridge: Cambridge University Press, 2006.

Thiemann, Ronald. "Response to George Lindbeck." *Theology Today* 43.3 (1986) 377–82.

———. *Revelation and Theology: The Gospel as Narrated Promise*. Notre Dame, IN: University of Notre Dame Press, 1985.

Tillich, Paul. *Dynamics of Faith*. New York: Harper, 1957.

———. *Systematic Theology*. Chicago: University of Chicago Press, 1951.

Tolmie, D. F., *Narratology and Biblical Narratives: A Practical Guide*. San Francisco: International Scholars, 1999.

Topping, Richard R. *Revelation, and Scripture, Church: Theological Hermeneutic Thought of James Barr, Paul Ricoeur and Hans Frei*. Farnham, UK: Ashgate, 2007.

Torres, S., and V. Fabella, eds. *The Emergent Gospel*. Maryknoll, NY: Orbis, 1976.

Treier, Daniel. *Introducing Theological Interpretation of Scripture: Recovering a Christian Practice*. Grand Rapids: Baker Academic, 2008.

Trembath, Kern Robert. *Divine Revelation: Our Moral Relation with God*. New York: Oxford University Press, 1991.

Troeltsch, Ernst. *The Social Teachings of the Christian Churches, vols. 1–2*. Translated by O. Wyon. New York: Harper & Row, 1960.

Turner, Victor. "Social Dramas and Stories about Them." *Critical Inquiry* 7.1 (1980) 141–68.

Vacote, V., L. Miguelez, and D. Okholm, eds. *Evangelicals and Scripture: Tradition, Authority, and Hermeneutics*. Downers Grove, IL: IVP, 2004.

Vanhoozer, Kevin, ed. *The Cambridge Companion to Postmodern Theology*. Cambridge: Cambridge University Press, 2003.

Volf, Miroslav. *Captive to the Word of God: Engaging the Scriptures for Contemporary Theological Reflection*. Grand Rapids: Eerdmans, 2010.

———. *Exclusion and Embrace: A Theological Exploration of Identity, Otherness, and Reconciliation*. Nashville: Abingdon, 1996.

Wainwright, William, ed. *The Oxford Handbook to Philosophy of Religion*. New York: Oxford University Press, 2005.

Wallner, Karl J. "Ein trinitarisches Strukurprinzip in der Trilogie Hans Urs von Balthasars?" *Theologie und Philosophie* 71 (1996) 532–46.

Warren, Max. *What is An Evangelical? An Enquiry*. London: Church Book Room, 1944.

Webster, John, et al., eds. *The Oxford Handbook of Systematic Theology*. New York: Oxford University Press, 2007.

Werpehowski, William. "Ad Hoc Apologetics." *Journal of Religion* 66.3 (1986) 282–301.

Westphal, Merold. *God, Guilt, and Death: An Existential Phenomenology of Religion*. Bloomington, IN: Indiana University Press, 1984.

White, Hayden. "The Value of Narrativity in the Representation of Reality." *Critical Inquiry* 7 (1980) 5–27.

White, Victor. *God and the Unconscious*. Cleveland, OH: Meridian, 1952.

Whitehead, Alfred North. *Adventures in Ideas*. New York: Free, 1967.

———. *Religion in the Making*. Bronx, NY: Fordham University Press, 1996.

Williams, Clifford. *Existential Reasons for Belief in God: A Defense of Desires and Emotions for Faith*. Downers Grove, IL: IVP, 2011.

Wolterstorff, Nicholas. *Divine Discourse: Philosophical Reflections on the Claim that God Speaks*. New York: Cambridge University Press, 1995.

Work, Telford. "Don't Call Me Postconservative." Review of *Reformed and Always Reforming* by Roger E. Olson. *Christianity Today* 52.2 (2008) 79.

Wright, N. T. *Small Faith, Great God: Biblical Faith for Today's Christians.* Downers Grove, IL: IVP, 2010.
Zimmerman, Jens. *Recovering Theological Hermeneutics: An Incarnational-Trinitarian Theory of Inspiration.* Grand Rapids: Baker Academic, 2004.
Zizioulas, John. *Being as Communion: Studies in Personhood and the Church.* Crestwood, NY: St. Vladimir's Seminary Press, 1985.

www.ingramcontent.com/pod-product-compliance
Lightning Source LLC
Chambersburg PA
CBHW051054230426
43667CB00013B/2291